ETHICS FOR AN INDUSTRIAL AGE

Ethics for
an Industrial Age

A CHRISTIAN INQUIRY

By Victor Obenhaus

AFTERWORD BY F. ERNEST JOHNSON

HARPER & ROW, PUBLISHERS

NEW YORK

FIRST EDITION

LIBRARY OF CONGRESS CATALOG CARD NUMBER: 65-21020

K-P

Contents

Foreword, by Charles P. Taft   vii

Preface   xi

1. Roots of Religious Concern for Economic Life   1
2. Industrialism as Our Culture   24
3. Issues Challenging Industrialism   40
4. Automation—Cybernation   56
5. Welfare and Our Industrial Economy   68
6. U. S. Agriculture in Domestic and World Economy   82
7. The Consumer—Power or Pushover?   101
8. Organized Labor's Role   117
9. Disarmament and the Economy   137
10. International Trade and Aid   151
11. Government Power and the Economy   169
12. The New Meaning of Leisure and Work   189
13. Status and Stratification in Industrial Society   207
14. Ethics and Business   221
15. The Role of the Church   239
16. Spiritual Foundations   255

Afterword: Reflections on Ethics and Economics, by F. Ernest Johnson   273

Notes   319

Index   331

Foreword

BY CHARLES P. TAFT

Chairman of the Commission on the Church and Economic Life

This book is the final volume in a larger study of Christian Ethics and Economic Life which was begun in 1949 by the Department of the Church and Economic Life of the Federal Council of the Churches of Christ in America. At the beginning of 1951 the Federal Council was merged with other interdenominational agencies to form the National Council of the Churches of Christ in the United States of America, made up of thirty-four Protestant and Orthodox church bodies within the United States.

In recent years religious leaders have recognized that the ethical problems of economic life have become increasingly urgent. The ethics of everyday decisions and practices in economic life, both private and public, are matters of wide concern. We need to go behind individual acts and group pressures for a deeper understanding of the motives underlying what people do in their economic activities, of how the system fits together, of how close our preconceived ideas are to reality.

Change is dominant in our national life and perhaps nowhere so much so as in its economic aspects. During the past half-century our ways of life and work have undergone a vast alteration. The change has been accomplished without violence, but with increasing if not always obvious upset, and the tempo of its pace is revolutionary. Certainly if people whose span of life was in the nineteenth century could see what we see in everyday life, they would hardly accept any word but revolution for the process that has brought it about.

This accelerated change demands that all thoughtful people understand its effects upon ethics and human values. How shall we deal with the dynamism in our economic life so as to preserve and extend the dignity of the individual, respect for the rights of minorities, sensitivity to the public welfare, and free discussion and peaceful persuasion? We cannot rely upon business statistics to measure these intangibles. Judgments of even the best qualified individuals about actual or impending changes, affected as opinions are by individual temperament, vested interests, or political partisanship, are also inadequate if considered separately. The fullest use of all our resources for information and face-to-face discussion is required for sound progress toward solution of our complex problems.

There is no vital threat to our inherited and cherished values either in the status quo as such or in change as such. We cannot separate ethics from practical economic concerns. What is needed is a better understanding both of economic facts and of those ethical convictions and values which have special significance in the meaning and direction they should give to economic activity.

In many parts of the world we find a fanatic cynicism or a false philosophy in opposition to the foundations upon which Western society is based. What earlier generations took for granted, such as the value and integrity of the individual, the character of government as a means for service of the people, the capacity of human life for essential decency and justice—these are now challenged by conflicting assumptions also claimed to be moral or at least essential for an efficient society.

Here lies the real crisis of the second half of the present century. We must meet this challenge, in so far as it is evil, and clarify in relation to our own institutions the basic ethical affirmations which we support.

The Federal Council of Churches conducted for many years, and the National Council of Churches has continued, an educational program on the ethical issues involved in economic life. Many denominational bodies have likewise been active in this field. It became clear, however, that we needed a more careful and realistic investigation of economic life and its relation to spiritual and moral values in a Christian frame of reference. We needed to make use of the capacities of social scientists and theologians, in close association with other persons drawn from many occupations.

Accordingly, a study was begun in 1949 under a grant from the Rockefeller Foundation and continued under further grants from the same source in 1952 and 1959. The Foundation has not sought to exercise any supervisory control over the study and does not assume responsibility for any of the findings. The results of the study so far are presented in ten volumes: *Goals of Economic Life, The Organizational Revolution, Social Responsibilities of the Businessman, American Income and Its Use, The American Economy—Attitudes and Opinions, Christian Values and Economic Life, Social Responsibility in Farm Leadership, Social Responsibilities of Organized Labor, Responsibility in Mass Communication,* and *The Church as Employer, Money-Raiser, and Investor.*

This final volume in the series subjects to further analysis and interpretation some of the major economic issues of the study as a whole in their relation to the concern of the churches in social education and action.

Gratitude is due to the several authors in the entire series for their devotion and creativity in the writing of these books. In all the volumes of the series the authors have been free to write as they wished and to accept or reject suggestions or criticisms; each book is the responsibility of the individual writer.

Others have made valuable contributions to the total study effort of which this volume is an important part. The Reverend Cameron P. Hall, executive director of the Department (now Commission) of the Church and Economic Life, has given the project his unfailing and effective administrative support. Dr. Howard R. Bowen, former economic consultant to the study, made an invaluable contribution in the formulation of the project and aided also in criticism of manuscripts. The Reverend A. Dudley Ward served as director of studies from the beginning in 1949 unitl the fall of 1953. He carried out his responsibilities as organizer and coordinator with imagination and efficiency, and also gave help after he had left for other important work. Since September 1953 Dr. F. Ernest Johnson has been in charge of the studies. His long experience in research and education, with the Federal Council and in other connections, has made him exceptionally qualified for this service.

A study committee of the department, including both lay and

clerical members and representing a variety of occupations, has reviewed the program of the study at various stages. Dr. Roy Blough, professor of international economics at Columbia University, has chaired the study committee since 1958 and given close supervision to its work. The late Charles H. Seaver served as editorial consultant and secretary of the study committee and carefully edited most of the manuscripts.

The National Council of Churches has taken no official position and assumes no responsibility regarding the content of any of the volumes. In no sense, therefore, can or should any statement in the series be regarded as an official declaration of the National Council of Churches or any of its units.

Preface

It is taken for granted that religion and culture are closely intertwined in American life. This is not different from other types of
society since religion in most areas of the world is an integral part
of the culture which prevails. Economic life is also an integral part
of culture.

In many areas of the world primitive economic life and religion
have been closely related. In the Middle Ages they were indistinguishable. In some parts of Colonial America and some immigrant and utopian communities they were intimately connected.
With expanding industrialism, the relationship has become increasingly ill-defined. Attempts have been made, both in Europe and
the United States, to indicate the desirable correlation of these two
facets of culture necessary to the health of each. America's most
impressive contribution to this correlation was the Social Gospel.
Regardless of one's theological persuasion the problem remains
inseparable and the viability of any religious emphasis is tied to
the manner in which it relates our means of livelihood and our
faith.

Despite the pluralistic nature of our present society a marked
homogenization has been occurring. "Americanization" has blurred
many hitherto observable differentiations. What is "American"
has superseded what is "Christian" or "Jewish" and what is American has come to mean what is identified with business or economic
life. By this process the role of religion in economic life has been
diminshed or obscured.

A fundamental thesis of this volume, and of the entire Series
on The Ethics and Economics of Society, is that economics and

religion cannot be divorced without peril to society. That they have been separated in the minds and actions of very large numbers is painfully obvious. The indifference of nominally religious people to the economic activities which may be undermining their faith represents a defaulting of their whole religious heritage. This is why the volume begins with a chapter on "Roots of Religious Concern for Economic Life." It is a further hypothesis of this volume that only as the relation between religion and the various forms of economic expression is realized can there be genuine health in either religion or economics. At present there is much in industrial life to impair that relationship.

Each of the areas dealt with in this volume involves profound ethical issues. Obviously there are no simple solutions. One's religion and his faith cannot provide formulas for the quick resolution of these issues. Nevertheless, there are criteria in the religious heritages of each of us which raise fundamental questions concerning the values which are served or sabotaged by current practices. I have, therefore, attempted to lift up a few of the major economic issues of our times and present them as areas for consideration in the light of the values and standards inherent in our faith. No doubt readers will feel some very important ones have been omitted. It was necessary to be selective. In each of the issues chosen it is possible for religiously motivated people to engage in constructive action. In many instances action in concert with sympathetic-minded people is essential; in others, independent action is possible.

This volume is intended for those who are or might become seriously concerned with the relation between religious faith and economic issues. In other volumes of this series fuller theological and philosophical treatment of ethics and economics has been provided. My purpose here has been to portray some of the problems in both their historic development and their present-day implications. Many of the changes which have occurred are coincident with the development of industrial life. This does not sanctify them or make them inevitable despite a widely held assumption that economic practices are validated only in a world of their own. Inherent in the entire presentation is the conviction that not only are religiously-sensitive people not helpless before these changes but that in their heritage is a mandate to alter what stands in violation of faith's demands. Thus, though this volume is not intended as a technically comprehensive resource for the expert in the areas discussed, it is hoped that religio-ethical implications would be apparent. For the greater body of nonexperts it is hoped that the documentation of the issues would serve to illustrate and clarify what is for religiously-sensitive people an inescapable relation between religion and economics.

As is always the case, an author is indebted to far too many people to be able to mention them all and give proper credit. In this instance the author is indebted above all others to Dr. F. Ernest Johnson, editor of most of the volumes which comprise the Series on the Ethics and Economics of Society. He patiently and painstakingly reviewed and helped in the development of the entire volume. Out of a rich wisdom and long experience in the total area of ethics and economics he gave sage counsel. It is fitting he should provide the "Afterword" which concludes both this volume and the entire series. To Professor Roy Blough, chairman of the Study Committee, is owed a profound debt of gratitude. He has not only read the contents but has made invaluable suggestions out of his own extensive professional skill in the areas he knows best and has given counsel in organization of other materials. Dr. Cameron Hall, director of the Commission on Church and Economic Life, after aiding in the initiation of the volume has followed each step of its development and has given helpful implementation at many points. Miss Elma Greenwood, associate director of the Commission, in her quiet and efficient way has similarly facilitated the progress of the volume. A committee of specialists representing some of the areas dealt with in the volume, each a member of the Commission on Church and Economic Life, gave much help along the way. However, the author alone must assume responsibility both for the form and content of the pages which follow. Complete authority was given to the author to develop what he thought would be the needed treatment of the over-all theme. John Loeschen, a student at the Chicago Theological Seminary, was most helpful in the gathering of materials and in making useful suggestions. To Mrs. Frances Ritsch is owed a special debt of gratitude for serving as typist for each of the many editions. Finally, as is so often the case, an author's debt to his family is unlimited. They listened to or read many sections and suffered numerous inconveniences during the writing.

V. O.

Chicago, Illinois
July 1965

1

Roots of Religious Concern
for Economic Life

To separate the spiritual aspects of Hebrew-Christian religion from the economic is impossible, for all of life is one piece. It is summed up in the affirmation, "Hear, O Israel, the Lord thy God is one God; thou shalt love the Lord thy God with all thy heart, and soul and mind, and thy neighbor as thyself." This declaration is the basis of a most profound and at the same time ever-continuing revolution. The earliest Hebrews understood this, and they knew that whenever they had departed from it, their personal and national life had lost something of its purpose and true dimension. Embedded deeply in the individual and collective life of this people was a conviction that religion could be expressed fully only when it incorporated responsibility to both God and man. The love of God and the love of neighbor inescapably involved man in economic relations.

The seminomadic people delivered from Egypt by God through Moses lived in an economy of grain cultivation and sheep herding. The social structure which held that order together was a patriarchal society with each local unit dominated by the head of the family and the larger clan governed by a cluster of heads of families. Responsibility for members of the families resided with the leadership. Such a pattern was not confined to the Hebrew tribes and their families; any difference from other nomadic tribes derives from the manner in which the family and the clan regarded themselves in relation to their God. Economics, worship, family ties, and communal relationships were woven together into a common fabric; but the unifying factor was a conviction that their ultimate obligation was to a God who had a special concern for the well-being of His people. Only out of such a communal conviction can the powerful affirmations of the Hebrew prophets be understood.

Moving into a new land following the departure from Egypt, the Israelites found it necessary to establish property regulations in which dividing lines had to be established and the inheritance of land made integral to the national and communal life. Land was conceived not as being owned outright but as being held under a stewardship, a conception of property which has never been disavowed by those who inherit the Hebrew-Christian tradition. The combination of the Israelitic conviction that the land belonged to God, the subsequent corruption of this belief in personal and family life, the conflict with other cultures which maintained no such ideas of property, occasioned protests and indictments on the part of sensitive religious leaders. This line of judgment and the theological-economic insight run from the middle of the eighth century B.C. to the middle of the twentieth century A.D.

To say that the Hebrew prophets were primarily interested in the economic question is of course a distortion, for the simple reason that the economic question is fundamentally a part of the larger issue of the nature of man and his obligation to the God, who is both Creator and Redeemer. It was the Hebrew prophets who confronted men with the fact that the distortion of their relation to God often came at the point of communal irresponsibility and the blindness fostered by pride. They recognized that perversions which led to individual arrogance and acquisition constituted a form of false worship. Other neighboring religions found no difficulty with property arrangements which provided for individual appropriation. Therefore, the struggle against false gods was focused, in part at least, on the problems of land ownership. The issue at stake is God's sovereignty as seen in the acts of His creation and the subsequent stewardship of creation by those who held it in trust. Stewardship is corroded by pride, and the Hebrew prophets understood this.

So axiomatic is the corrosion of ownership through pride that wealth was suspect and often regarded as synonymous with failure to abide by God's commands. The rich are identified with the wicked, while the poor are more nearly capable of qualifying as God's children. "And they made his grave with the wicked and with a rich man in his death . . ." (Isaiah 53 : 9).

The messages of the prophets bear down on the pride of possession as well as express the conviction that all property belongs to God, the Sovereign. "Take heed . . . lest when you have eaten and are full, and have built goodly houses and live in them, and when your herds and flocks multiply, and your silver and gold is multiplied, and all that you have is multiplied, then your heart be lifted up, and you forget the Lord your God. . . . You say in your heart, 'My power and the might of my hand have gotten me this wealth.' You shall remember the Lord your God, for it is He who gives you power to get wealth . . ." (Deut. 8 : 11–18).

Despite the belief that virtue is materially rewarded, the delicate balance of possession and stewardship created the dilemma in which disobedience is punished through property loss. The resolution of this dilemma lay in the recognition that wealth belonged not to an individual but to a whole family or community, which in turn derived its possession from God, the Sovereign.

Man's defection from his true heritage is seen in his disregard of the rightful claims of God upon him, especially as they are manifested in his communal and personal relations. Amos points the finger of judgment at those who take advantage of others: "You who trample upon the needy, and bring the poor of the land to an end, saying, 'When will the new moon be over, that we may sell grain?'" (Amos 8 : 4).

The corrosion of justice has gone so far that Amos complains, "The end is come upon my people Israel" (Amos 8 : 2). And Jeremiah asks, "Can the Ethopian change his skin or the leopard his spots? Then also you can do good who are accustomed to do evil" (Jer. 13 : 23). Isaiah condemns those "who join house to house, who add field to field, until there is no more room, and you are made to dwell alone in the midst of the land" (Isaiah 5 : 8).

Standing in judgment against all such injustice and the selfish use of economic power, the Hebrew prophets saw a Sovereign God whose will for His people included justice in economic arrangements and the proper subordination of human pride. Willful exploitation and manifestations of personal aggrandizement could be nothing but an affront to this true Sovereign of the nation. Such willfulness could only be regarded as sacrilegious. Not even by a king of Israel could the deeply rooted and elemental rights be abrogated. Property a man needed to provide for his family was guaranteed to him against the personal desires and acquisitiveness of even the most powerful force in the land. When Ahab, unable to secure Naboth's vineyard by persuasion, secured it through trumped-up charges and murder, he was indicted by Elijah, and an ignominious fate is foretold. The king and his greedy queen, Jezebel, sought the land to satisfy pride. For Naboth it was an extension of himself, satisfying his need for existence. In its truest sense the earth belonged to the Lord, but within that ultimate ownership individuals held rights of use which were subject to criteria of need. Property might be privately held, but ownership was not absolute or without judgment from a higher source.

The idea of land held in trust or under stewardship was embodied in the institutions of the sabbatical year and the year of jubilee. It was expected that by lying fallow in the seventh year, the land would benefit the poor. Similarly, in the seventh year a slave was freed from bond service (Ex. 21 : 2) and debt was to be forgiven (Deut. 15 : 1). The year of jubilee brought recovery of liberty throughout the land for everyone at intervals of fifty years. At this time land reverted to its original owner. "The land shall not be sold in perpetuity, for the land is mine; for you are strangers and sojourners with me" (Lev. 25 : 23).

When Nathan charged the great and popular King David with the usurpation of property rights in the stealing of another man's wife, he knew he had behind him the full force of a just God. Ostensibly he presented his case in the form of a tale involving the stealing of one little lamb (II Sam. 12 : 1–14). Revealed in this tale is the deep conviction that not even temporal leaders may violate the more basic rights and human justice granted by a Sovereign God.

The Old Testament principles concerning property, says Charles

L. Taylor, "can be summarized as, (1) the ownership of God; (2) the goodness of God's gifts by which He shares Himself; (3) the community of rights and responsibilities in which there must be justice; (4) the unremitting condemnation of the use of property for selfish advantage; and (5) an awakening appreciation of service and sacrifice."[1]

The Hebrew people sense realistically that economic relations constitute one of the means by which spiritual values find expression. Any spirituality devoid of fruitage in human relations was truncated and false. Man's inclination to self-justification in the acquisition of possessions stood constantly under the judgment of a God whose worship included economic justice to one's fellow men.

THE NEW TESTAMENT AND PROPERTY

There is no major emphasis on the economic theme as such in the gospel message, certainly not in primary focus as in the case of the prophets. Nevertheless the Gospels are saturated with implications for economic life. Jesus' life and message, though concerned primarily with the kingdom of God, have economic implications largely for the same reasons that actuated the prophets. Primary preoccupation with goods and things can serve to dilute, if not actually obliterate, the awareness of man's ultimate obligations and commitment; for example, ". . . take heed, and beware of all covetousness; for a man's life does not consist in the abundance of his possessions" (Luke 12 : 15), or "for where your treasure is, there will your heart be also" (Matt. 6: :21).

The purity of heart which enables one to seek the pearl of great price can be destroyed by preoccupation with possessions. The parable of the servants and the talents, like almost all of Jesus' parables, makes use of an economic framework understood by listeners to illustrate a more profound insight than the economic facts narrated. Scarcely any phase of Jesus' ministry is without reference to common experience and ordinary human need. From the parables and the accounts of His association with those about Him it is apparent that He was concerned with these

ɔ   ɔds by which life was sustained. A hungry multitude
        before they could hear and understand His message.
        solicitude for the poor, whose lives were not yet dis-
        ssessions, attests sensitiveness to economic differences.
        d poverty must be alleviated, but unless their alleviation
        with something more than a mere change in physical
condition they have missed the purpose of life itself. Finally, in
one of His last acts together with His associates, Jesus had ar-
ranged for a common meal. There He used the most common
components of a meal, bread and wine, to symbolize the reality
of His own relation to all men. They were not ends in themselves,
but rather, as was and is true of all economic realities, they pointed
to and were a part of life's more profound meaning.

Possessions are intended to be instruments for the service of
God, but instead they can become man's master. Jesus' life served
as the best example of the command "Do not lay up for yourselves
treasures on earth . . . but lay up for yourselves treasures in heaven
. . ." (Matt. 6 : 19–20). Or again, "No servant can serve two
masters. . . . You cannot serve God and mammon" (Luke 16 : 13).
Jesus confronts men with the hard fact that money can become
their god or it can be utilized in the service of God. A large part
of Jesus' teaching dealt with wealth and possessions, not because
they were significant in themselves but because of their consequences to persons. Of prime importance was the intent behind
the acquisition of wealth. Its disposition revealed what the
temporary owner regarded as first in importance.

The kingdom of which Jesus spoke so frequently and which
constituted so all-penetrating a part of His message was both "at
hand" and was "coming" in the not distant future. Concern with
physical arrangements, legal actions, and specifications were of
secondary importance in the face of the demands of the God who
was establishing the present and coming kingdom. Presumably,
economic arrangements would be consummated in the light of the
all-consuming purpose claiming the attention of Jesus' followers.
In spite of this great concern with the kingdom there could be no
mistaking Jesus' intention that personal relationships, including
economic activities, must be subjected to the supreme demands

of the One whose kingdom it is to be.

In the centuries following the life, death, and resurrection of Jesus Christ, innumerable groups have sought to incorporate the principles and admonitions of the Gospels into their common life. Many have done this on the assumption that they are recapturing the spirit of the first-century Christians, those who knew the disciples or who were influenced by the Apostle Paul. We are told that some members of the early church liquidated their possessions in expectation of the early return of Christ. Both because of the expected return and because of the close relationship among those who held this expectation, there was disposition to sacrifice for each other and to share their worldly possessions; ". . . and no one said that any of the things which he possessed was his own, but they had everything in common" (Acts 4 : 32).

This desire to share with others who are bound together in common ties of devotion to one God and one Lord has had numerous manifestations throughout the generations. But no small part of the inspiration and authority of such ventures derives from the biblical narrative describing the life of Jesus and the experience of first-century Christians. The primary citizenship of the members of these colonies is in Heaven, according to the Apostle Paul, and his letters contain frequent admonitions concerning the conduct of the members while they wait to take up their full membership in the new life. Paul's concern with property and economic matters is therefore not spelled out in detail. There are general suggestions for individual and social conduct; "Each one must do as he had made up his mind, not reluctantly or under compulsion, for God loves a cheerful giver" (II Cor. 9 : 7). The political conditions of the time were hardly such as to warrant specific suggestions for economic reorganization.

Property and ownership were not a concern of the Apostle Paul for the simple reason that the ultimate concerns of man were for him always dominant. The latter could be seen in their proper relationship only when the primary concern of the individual was understood; that primary concern was Christ. "For me to live is Christ . . ." (Philip. 1 : 21). "The colonies of Heaven" which Paul visited and to which he wrote, were thus bound together by a common hope and a conviction of one common ultimate purpose. An act of sharing worldly goods among fellow believers was not an act of religious communism so much as an act of common faith inspired by mutual devotion. St. John could write, "But if anyone has the world's goods and sees his brother in need, yet closes his heart against him, how does God's love abide in him? Little children, let us not love in word or speech but in deed and in truth" (I John 3 : 17–18). Since the church was but an "earnest" of the final age, there was little point in challenging the present age.

With the passing of the disciples and the Apostle Paul from the active life of the early church congregations, the spiritual direction of these small but growing clusters of devotees of the new religion came from a group of individuals widely scattered geographically but united in the fellowship of the church and contributing to its emerging tradition. This group would include such figures as Clement of Alexandria, Origen, Cyprian, Ambrose, and Chrysostom. To this list of church fathers must be added the name of the one who influenced the life of the church most pronouncedly for a thousand years—Augustine, bishop of Hippo. With the emergence of the church as an institution there came a marked separation in the roles of church and state, particularly as they are reflected in relation to property. The world of the church and the world at large developed their own spheres of influence. The distinctiveness of the church required a separation in areas of authority but gave encouragement to the conviction that economic activity on behalf of the church merited a special place in the decisions and aspirations of its members. Clement of Alexandria argued, "What we are called on to surrender is not necessarily property as such, but excessive attachment to it; this is the danger of the wealthy but also of the poor—in fact, the anxious desire for what one lacks may be as soul-destroying as undue interest in what one has."[2] One outcome of the early church's attempt to find a solution to the difficult problem of economic life was the monastery. Here, under the aegis of the church, it was possible to govern all economic activities and to direct them toward the ends which were not as attainable in the world outside the church.

This partial answer served the church for more than a millennium. With numerous variations and deviations the principle behind the monastic society has found expression up to the present day.

THE MIDDLE AGES

There are many people in our own time who long for the reputed harmony and seemingly well-structured society which characterized the Middle Ages. It is believed that in the preindustrial era when life was administered by the church, the kinds of infraction which later came to disrupt society were unknown. If only we could get back, they say, to that well-ordered era, many of the tensions and competitive aspects of an industrial-technological society could be eliminated.

What were the distinctive features of economic life in the Middle Ages? The establishment of the church as integral and official in the life of the state by Emperor Constantine placed it in an ambiguous position. It was official and therefore had to represent the state, but at the same time it inherited the traditions and affirmations of the prophets, of Jesus, the first-century Christians, and the early church fathers. Augustine had provided a partial resolution of the church-state dilemma by confronting the church with its sacred objective to make the world into the City of God. Such an ideal could be held persistently only by a small group or a monastic order. The two levels of society had to be maintained side by side. A. T. Mollegen says: "Augustine achieved a catholic synthesis of sect and church outlooks by posting a higher order, the kingdom-life on earth, which has its highest expression in monastic asceticism where the counsels of perfection were obeyed; and a lower order of kingdom-life in general human society, that is, in the family, the city, the state and the world, expressed in the Christianization of natural life where the *precepts* were obeyed."[3] It was held that all of life had been created by God, but its purity had been corrupted by human sin. Since men, because of their sin, could not be counted on to conduct their relations in a manner consistent with the pure order God had intended, regulations had to be imposed. Private property, for example, though its protection is a responsibility of the state, is not sacrosanct, and its possession is dependent upon the use to which the property is put. "It is clear that St. Augustine regarded private property as being normally a creation, not of the divine, but of the positive law and as subject to the determination of the state, and limited by the degree of its utility."[4] All of this becomes more comprehensible when we recognize that possession did not have the same meaning in the Middle Ages as the modern use of the term implies. Personal and household goods could be regarded as property, but land was held under a tenure arrangement with the justification for its use dependent upon the degree of social obligation accepted by the manorial lord or overseer of the land.[5]

By the thirteenth century, Thomas Aquinas had introduced some refinements in the concept of ownership. For him there is a moral difference between the acquisition of property and its use. Under this theory an individual is justified in taking another man's possessions if he himself is starving, but it may not be designated as theft.[6] Such a theory of property finds expression even down to recent years, in the encyclicals of the late nineteenth- and early twentieth-century popes. They derive from an Aristotelian affirmation that "things should be held privately but should be public in their use."

When we refer to the economic life of the Middle Ages, we are not looking at a well-ordered system, even though it is operated under the combined aegis of a church and a state. As Tawney says, "All that we call the economic system was not a system but a mass of individual trades and individual dealings."[7] What gives uniqueness and distinction to the economic life of the Middle Ages, however, is the fact that "economic interests are subordinate to the real business of life which is salvation and that economic conduct is one aspect of personal conduct upon which, as on other parts of it, the rules of morality are binding."[8]

Lacking formal rules for determining the size of one's income or the ethics of his relationship to those with whom he had commerce, the individual could but be reminded of the consequences resulting from the sin of avarice and therefore was subject to condemnation by ecclesiastical authorities. Charging interest for the loan of money created a problem which taxed self-restraint, but ecclesiastical·needs rendered less severe the condemnation of those who were actually or potentially benefactors of the church. Usury, i.e., taking money for the "use" of money, was prohibited, but the line between usury and interest donated to the church was difficult to establish. This remains one of the unresolved and contentious issues in the church's attempt to cope with emerging economic practices.

From the combined church-state domination of all life, wherever that relationship prevailed, there emerged another concept correspondingly difficult to define but representing an attempt to avoid the harshness and injustice of an unregulated economy—the "just price." Where this was exceeded, restitution must be made to society in the form of almsgiving. To guide the seller in the establishment of his price, public agencies were given authority to establish rates which would restrain the negotiator and conform more nearly to the social ideal. Where private conscience was an inadequate control, a collective appraisal was more effectual.

Through the monastic order the Middle Ages sought to build a church impelled to the creation of a city of God, the elimination of avarice, the sensitizing of conscience to care for the needy, and the establishment of regulations for commerce, and also the endowment of posterity with incentives for the application of religious norms in economic life. Though inadequate for the new type of life which was emerging, they were valuable as reminders of the ultimate ends toward which all life, including its economic aspects, is directed.

The Reformation

Great new forces were being unleased in the land, and such cohesiveness as the feudal system and the church could give was not sufficient to withstand them. The resultant of these forces is well known by all—expanding commerce, a money economy, discovery of new sources and markets, a rising merchant class with its allies, the bankers, and new colonial empires—all of these and many more elements rendered obsolete the economic structures which had prevailed in the Middle Ages. Concomitant with the economic changes and contributing to them was the intellectual reconstruction identified with the Renaissance. John Herman Randall, Jr. has commented that "if the roots of the new world of the Renaissance are to be sought in economic conditions, its justification and its means are to be found in the new spirit and knowledge that destroyed monasticism and Aristotelian science as capitalism was destroying feudalism and the guilds."[9] It was within this atmosphere that the Protestant Reformation emerged.

Max Weber, Ernst Troeltsch, Richard Tawney, and many others have made twentieth-century Christians sensitive to the fact that Protestantism was powerfully influential in reshaping medieval attitudes toward property and economics in general—in addition to the fact that the intellectual and economic forces were also contributing to the shaping of Protestantism. The two figures who have left their imprint on Protestant economic thought with such forcefulness that their interpretations still shape the convictions of contemporary Christians and non-Christians, are, of course, Martin Luther and John Calvin.

It is understandable that Luther, steeped in the experience of the medieval church, thought in terms of a church which encompassed the whole of society. Though he departed from the one all-inclusive church of his own experience, he did not disavow the authority of the church in areas of its rightful supremacy. Yet it was just on the issue of the rightful areas of the church's supremacy that he defied the church in whose service he had been a devoted monk. From the New Testament he learned the distinction between the church as a spiritual reality where men love each other because they are loved by God, and the requirements of the church as an institution. Yet love finds expression in all of life and is not divided between the life of the individual and the life of the church. The church, therefore, was not the final arbiter of the way in which man's love shall find expression; it, too, stood under the judgment of God. And when faith fails, it is God alone who grants forgiveness to a repentant individual and a repentant church.

Dependence of the individual conscience upon the church and

its claims being replaced by personal loyalty to God does not, however, make the individual autonomous and independent in his political life as well. The state has its own existence, and it is the duty of the Christian to serve as a Christian within its confines and under its obligations. He may defy that state only when it commands him to contravene the will of God as he discerns it. In his personal relationships and in the life of his church he thus acts from the motive of love and assumes that others do likewise. The state, being composed of fellow citizens similarly motivated, may be trusted.

All of this has profound implications for economic life. Both Calvin and Luther evolved a doctrine of vocation recognizing that the way a person engaged in his labors and disposed of his earnings constituted an index of the ultimate authority for his life. In Luther's view, man served in his work to give evidence of his faithfulness; for Calvin, man worked as an earnest of his conviction that the work he performed and the society of which he was a part reflected as best he knew how the intended order of God's creation. In the instances of both the reformers, man stood in a relationship of need for justification and under judgment in the totality of his life. Since man's economic life constituted so large a part of his existence, it was inescapable that its correlation with the divine purpose be examined.

These two systems led for centuries to varying interpretations of man's obligations to the economic order. Now with the fuller implications of the trends which were first observable in the destruction of feudalism becoming clear, the fundamental question to which the reformers sought an answer confronts us with new clarity. It has become increasingly apparent that the problems of property, of earning, of disposition of earnings, have implications for the totality of society and can no longer be regarded solely on an individual basis.

Love for one's neighbor and love for God are given expression in Luther's concept of vocation, *Beruf*. A man's calling, then, is the means whereby he participates in economic life and in response to God's claims upon him works in faithful obedience. The kind of work one does in his calling is not the primary consideration.

Formerly there prevailed a hierarchy of importance by which the spiritual quality of work was rated; now, presumably, any work one does as an obedient Christian is sanctified.

With the state freed from ecclesiastical control, it could proceed to set up its own ethical and economic norms. This created for the Christian a new set of complexities whose validity the church's demands did not clarify. Since the state had become the ultimate arbiter of economic life, the Christian was at a loss to know what God required of him. For the followers of Luther the resolution of the dilemma would lie primarily in the performance of their tasks as Christians, the decisions of the economic order being left to the state. Thus Lutheranism offered its adherents insufficient guidance for adapting to the type of economy coming into existence through the trade, manufacturing, and financing innovations which swept over the lands where the religious impact of Luther had been dominant.

Men turned to Calvin more than to any other theologian for an explanation of the release of the feudal mind from the restrictions of an ecclesiastically dictated economy. Calvin also stressed the ultimacy of a calling, but with marked differences from Luther's position. Calvin believed that man served God through his calling rather than simply in it, as Luther had contended. Serving God through one's calling makes it necessary for the individual to raise fundamental questions about the thing he is doing. A man's calling, for Calvin, was accepted and pursued with diligence as a means of qualifying for his "election" to salvation. He had no way of knowing whether he was one of the elect, but at least by vigorous pursuit of his calling he would be ready if it turned out that he were one of the elect. Such a condition impelled man to labor within society, but inevitably he was forced to raise the question whether his activity could truly be thought consistent with God's requirements for man and society. This was less of a problem for Luther, because men were saved individually by God's love even though the world around them remained evil. For the Calvinist the rectification of the evils of the world itself became an integral part of the fulfillment of his calling. As Paul Lehmann expresses it, "Vocational faithfulness was for Calvin a matter of working *against* (i.e., in anticipation of) the day of deliverance rather than working *until* the day of deliverance. When you are working *against* the day of deliverance you are more likely to work so hard as to find the material well-being the mark of piety; whereas if you are working *until* the day of deliverance you are more likely to find contentment with whatever favors have fallen to your lot as the surest clue to pious duty."[10]

All of this inspired the followers of Calvin to labor with vigor to create the kind of society which God had intended for man and which would in turn glorify God. Calvin sought to subject all forms of human activity to God's sovereignty and thus to reestablish a life world reflecting the society described in the Old Testament.

The new dynamic in this situation, the subjection of all forms of life to the sovereignty of God, lent itself to the new types of political and economic life which were beginning to find expression in the breakup of the feudal order. The norm by which the Christian is regulated, then, is not some dictate of an ecclesiastical organization but is rather his personal responsibility to the sovereign Lord of man and history. Individual obligation and self-examination, plus the counsel of one's peers, serve to keep in check the inordinate striving for wealth which might destroy the zeal to labor against the day of deliverance. The time was not far off, however, when the acquisition of goods could be regarded as one symbol of God's favorable attitude toward one who labored so zealously.

Unimpeded by restrictions imposed by church authorities, the seeker for deliverance could look with openness on the new patterns of economic life which were becoming available: the acceptance of profit, justification for interest on money loaned, the increased opportunities for private property, etc. This does not assume that Calvin approved high rates on loans, for in fact he laid it upon the heart of the lender to keep his demands within modest limits and according to conscience.

Along with the obligation to work diligently in a manner acceptable to a sovereign God, another key to Calvin's interpretation of Christian life in the economic realm is the idea of stewardship.

"We are not our own . . . we are God's: toward Him, therefore, as our only legitimate end, let every part of our lives be directed. There cannot be imagined a more certain rule or a more powerful exhortation to the observance of it than when we are taught that all blessings we enjoy are divine deposits committed to our trust on this condition that they should be dispensed for the benefit of our neighbors. Whatever God has conferred on us which enables us to assist our neighbors we are stewards of it and must one day render an account of our stewardship."[11] The very fact of possession is an indication of the Creator's benevolence. If one accepts all that is temporarily his as held in trust, he acts toward it in a different way than he would if he assumed it all to be solely his own. Here is the check on man's egoism and on his temptation to arrogance through the exploitation and exhibition of possessions. Likewise, if all possessions are held in stewardship, his neighbor has a partial claim upon them, and his act of generosity or consideration toward his neighbor becomes another evidence of his comprehension of the meaning of stewardship. In its political application, this could make possible regulatory activities causing the possessions held in the name of the state or under private stewardship to be allocated to the needs of others. By the same token the temptations to arrogance would be restricted in the name of the body politic and because of the mandate of stewardship.

Both Calvin and Luther maintained the conviction of the rightfulness of private property. Their difference from a more strictly interpreted capitalism would be: ". . . according to the Reformation, the right to use determines the right to possess; whereas the capitalist doctrine is that the right to possess determines the right to use. Rightly understood possession is an order to use and is not an order to possess."[12]

The full import of the Reformation is not embodied in the life and thought of Luther and Calvin. They do, however, represent the principal lines of conviction and the emerging trends. Economic life is thus held under judgment of a sovereign God who seeks that men shall love each other and live in harmonious community because they are children of one father. Earthly possessions are held not as solely private but under stewardship wherewith man serves his fellow men since all that he possesses has been entrusted to him; and through or in his vocation he attests his acknowledgment of God's benefactions to him, and he labors to be worthy if salvation should be granted to him. For those in the Lutheran tradition the political and economic orders of the state are presumably under the direction of men who love God, and therefore their actions will reflect this devotion. The inheritors of the Calvinist tradition are less trusting of man's propensity or capacity to live in loving relationship with his fellow men, and so they assume a greater responsibility for shaping the nature of the society in which man must live out his days.

ENGLAND: ECONOMICS AND THE REFORMATION

The scientific discoveries of Newton along with the writings of Locke and Hume released a flood of scientific and intellectual curiosity in the seventeenth century which prepared the mind of the educated Englishman for the acceptance of innovations in economics, government, and religion. "Men saw in the world no more chaos, no more confusion, but an essentially rational and harmonious machine. This was an intoxicating discovery."[13] The Reformation and the Renaissance on the continent were bearing fruit in the lessening of limitations formerly placed by institutionalized religion on the human spirit. As individuals were released from the requirements based upon supernatural obligations, it became possible to develop the implications of scientific discoveries in the form of industrial life and the kind of economy which best accompanied it. Thus came about the industrialization which transformed a rural England into the foremost processing and manufacturing center of the world.

Three hundred years after the Protestant Reformation, with the Industrial Revolution in full force in England and increasingly in evidence on the continent, it became apparent to religious leaders that the benefactions of the new order were not wholly constructive. Under a combination of Lutheran, Calvinistic, and Arminian influences John Wesley brought to a disintegrating social life his passion for man's redemption. Industrial society had taken its toll of the spiritual vitality of the English people, and forces of violence were gathering. Wesley brought to this situation a reawakening to man's spiritual heritage and destiny, and set them over against the forces of secularization which in his judgment and that of many others were corrupting church and nation. Within the framework of his spiritual message he uttered the famous mandate "Gain all you can, save all you can, give all you can." It was a reaffirmation of the stewardship principle, plus an exhortation to the diligence by which acquisition and integrity could be used as witness to faith. This was no solution of the economic problem, but it fostered a new sense of responsibility within the then existing economic order.

CHRISTIAN SOCIALISM

Still another manifestation of protest against economic ills came almost a century later, with the Industrial Revolution now in full swing, in the development of Christian socialism. Since the beginning of the nineteenth century there has been a small but steady stream of activity on the part of persons who identified themselves as Christian socialists. Their purpose was to bring the Christian witness to bear upon and reform economic practices in general and upon the activities and programs of socialism in particular. Among the earliest of the religious leaders to adopt a Christian approach to socialist activity was a French Catholic priest, de Lamennais. For him a function of the church, in addition to its traditional religious role, was to be the heart and soul of economic life as well. In his primary concern for the workingman, he pleaded with the Roman hierarchy, including Popes Leo XII and Gregory XVI, to share his opposition to the stratified and crystalized economic system supported by the temporal leaders.

Best known of the Christian socialists in the Protestant tradition, however, were Frederick Denison Maurice, John M. Ludlow, and Charles Kingsley. Maurice and Kingsley were clergymen, Ludlow a lawyer. They all agreed that all of life derived from God's creation and beneficence, but that it had been distorted and partially defeated by human selfishness.[14] It is more than mere coincidence that the thinking of these men found expression at the same time that Marx and Engels wrote the *Communist Manifesto*. There were forces giving rise to many different kinds and degrees of socialism untempered by the restraining qualities which these three leaders and others associated with them felt were the contributions a Christian society should exhibit; only in this way could socialism be rescued from its tendency to reduce man to his lower instincts. Maurice wrote: "We are teaching true socialism, true liberty, brotherhood and equality—not the carnal dead-level equality of the Communist, but the spiritual equality of the church idea, which gives every man an equal chance of developing and rewards every man according to his work."[15] In their journal, *The Christian Socialist*, under Ludlow's editorship, it was contended that "socialism without Christianity on the one hand is lifeless as the feathers without the bird, however skillfully the stuffer may dress them up into an artificial semblance of life."[16]

The period of prominence for the Christian socialist movement as such, in England at least, was a brief one; it had come to an end by 1855. But in the meantime it had strongly influenced both clergy and laity, for whom the idea of a Christian society expressing itself in the economy of the times was substantially novel. Though the life of the movement was brief, a seed had been sown which produced innumerable outcroppings of the same purposes throughout the following century. Christian socialism was not restricted to England; similar expressions were formed in Germany, Austria, France, Belgium, and other countries.

The interest in Christian socialism in England found later expression in the Christian Socialist League, which incorporated participation by representatives from other denominations as well as from the Church of England. As part of its goal it states: "The League will work in close connection with the labor and socialist movements. It believes that the necessary transformation of our social order requires a change of heart and mind and will and a corresponding change of political and industrial arrangements; substituting mutual service for exploitation and a social democracy for the struggle of individuals and classes."[17]

Though there are few definite recorded consequences of the interest in Christian socialism in England, it is generally felt that it gave substantial impetus to the cooperative movement as an economic expression of Christian concern. Toyohiko Kagawa could insist, on one of his visits to the United States, that the cooperative movement was the kingdom of God in action and must therefore merit the full-fledged support of Christians. Christian socialism sensitized the Christian conscience of the community, especially of those who were not themselves members of the underprivileged class. This characteristic may in some measure be responsible for the brevity of the movement's life. It was never able to come to grips with the deeper problems of those constituting the "lower" class. Its closest approximation to the working economics of the latter was its support of the cooperative movement to which many of them had turned.

For reasons worth exploring, there has never been a strong Christian socialist movement in the United States. Though there have been organizations incorporating the name "Christian" and "socialist" and containing some powerful intellectual and religious leaders, they have been few and for the most part without great influence. Possibly the closest approximation in America to the Christian socialist movement in England has been what is commonly designated the Social Gospel movement, a few of whose leaders eagerly welcomed the designation "Christian socialist" while others carefully avoided that title.

The Social Gospel

America's most distinctive contribution to the relation of religion to economics comes from what has been very broadly designated as "the Social Gospel." The Social Gospel involves no clear-cut theological or belief system. It takes its name from the conviction that an individualistic religion preoccupied with personal salvation to the neglect of any implications for society was leaving untouched the forces which were shaping the lives of people in an industrializing culture. As America changed from a rural to an urban nation, from agriculture to industry as the dominant element in the economy, it became apparent that the concentration of power in financial and industrial centers and the concentration of people in the cities created problems of justice, equitable distribution of goods, and other problems resulting from people's living in greater propinquity and dependence upon regularity of employment and an adequate living base. Irregular and inadequate income brought deprivations for which charity resources were inadequate, and suffering was widespread. The result for many was disintegration of life and a measure of hardship destructive of both health and morale.

A great host of religious leaders, representing many denominations and many sections of the nation, were convinced that these conditions were inconsistent with the ideals of Jesus' life and message and were making difficult the presentation of the Christian gospel. There followed an intensive study of the Hebrew prophets, the life and teachings of Jesus, and of current social conditions. The latter study sent many ministers into the field of sociology. Another factor intensifying the social concern on the part of ministers was the development of a scientific study of biblical sources and of the conditions prevailing at the time when biblical materials were in preparation. A correlation between the social concerns of the Hebrew prophets and of Jesus served to deepen the sense of responsibility for the then current situation in the United States. One of the consequences of this interest was the staffing with clergymen of several newly formed departments of sociology in colleges and universities. In addition the new sociological concern and the new-found relation between the life and teachings of Jesus and the prophets on one hand and the current economic situation on the other stirred a number of economists to bring their talents and skills to bear upon the situation. The result of this total combination was an impetus to the social sciences and an attempt to use these new disciplines for the alleviation of suffering and maladjustment in society at large.

Prominent among the leaders of the Social Gospel movement were George F. Peabody, Washington Gladden, George D. Herron, and—best known as the intellectual and spiritual leader of the entire movement—Walter Rauschenbusch. The writings of the latter are by far the most widely known among the clergy and theological students of that period and of a generation thereafter. It is likely that he influenced more ministers in his time than any other contemporary theologian. Many of the major seminaries affiliated with universities became strongly committed to the underlying purposes of the Social Gospel movement. Close association with departments of economics, sociology, and related social sciences stimulated the intellectual pursuit of the causes and conditions of social degradation and deprivation.

Few of the adherents of this undefined but nevertheless evident movement identified themselves with political socialism or even with an American version of English Christian socialism. The same reasons that deterred Walter Rauschenbusch from identifying himself with political socialism served as a deterrent to many others. He believed that political and economic socialism failed to take account of the spiritual factors which ultimately must shape human purposes and directions, and he himself never lost sight of the fact that man's ultimate end was not economic but spiritual.

What is said to be the most widely published book in history with the exception of the Bible is a product of Christian concern with economic issues, emerging in the era of the Social Gospel's greatest strength. It is Charles M. Sheldon's *In His Steps*, which is based upon a set of imaginary responses to the command to live like Jesus in our time. The story is a series of incidents relating to the way in which people—a newspaper man, a railroad man, a singer, and others—fulfilled their understanding of this commandment in their respective types of work. Whether they would designate this self-consciously as their Christian vocation is doubtful; neither the theology of Luther nor that of Calvin, at least in its vocational emphasis, was widely familiar at the time. Nevertheless, consciously or unconsciously this was a manifestation of the Christian doctrine of vocation. That the book had a profound effect is attested by the widespread attempt to live in this same fashion by thousands of others who undertook similar experiments.

Much more significant as a product of the Social Gospel is the development of support for the labor movement and for attempts to secure justice for agriculture and to alleviate misery through social service activities and political action. Not least among its accomplishments was the incentive to collective activity on the part of certain denominations when it became apparent that the economic forces determining many of the conditions in American life were too powerful to be met by single denominations. An indirect consequence was the formation of the Federal Council of Churches, and a direct consequence was the establishment of a working relationship between religion and labor within the Federal Council of Churches. This movement led to the Department of Church and Economic Life of the present National Council of Churches, and coincidentally to the series on Ethics and Economic Life of which this volume is a part. More will be said of the activities of this department in later chapters.

By the time of the first World War it was becoming apparent that the broad and multifarious concerns and points of view incorporated in the Social Gospel were inadequate to offset the forces which were shaping and disturbing the life of the time. The roots of change lay much deeper, and the Social Gospel was unable to cope with so profound and far-reaching a debacle as the Great Depression. Some of its leaders may have been naïve enough to expect that devotion to Jesus and his principles would suffice to rectify economic injustice; others were not so sanguine. They realized also that the root of the economic problem lay much deeper than anything which could be remedied by good will and the application of the love ethic as it was currently understood. Instead, the great contribution of the Social Gospel was its quickening of human sensitivity to injustice and its use of new resources both from sociology and theology in the attempt to understand the social and especially the economic life of the nation in which the Social Gospel found its warmest reception. Prominent in its concerns was the question of war and its hostility to all that war involved. For some of its adherents this meant fostering the development of a militant pacifism. The assumption was that war was a force which could be dealt with by itself. The infinitely more complex aspects of war—its psychological, theological, as well as economic components—had not been sufficiently explicated or comprehended. These factors will be considered in further discussions in this volume.

2

Industrialism as Our Culture

Many of the members were left with the impression as voiced by one of them, that modern industrial society is radically reshaping human personality and life in directions opposite to that transformation intended by the Gospel, and that consequently most of our mission program ad methods appear to be utterly theoretical and irrelevant. This realization makes us humble and penitent and it moves us to a searching re-valuation of the aims and methods of the mission now employed in the ministry of reconciliation in Jesus Christ which God has committed unto us.[1]

The bewilderment and anxiety thus expressed in a world missions seminar reveals the apprehension and confusion on the part of many others besides world mission exponents over the extension of the industrializing process. For good or ill, industrialization is the dominant phenomenon of our era, as it has been for more than a century.

In the preceding chapter Christian socialism and the Social Gospel were portrayed as attempts of religiously sensitive people to provide remedies for the hardships and inequities caused by the emerging industrial society. It was not apparent to most of those seeking resolution of the social disharmonies and injuries to human life created by its emergence that the real problem lay in the industrialization process itself. As was described in that chapter, economists, sociologists, and clergymen sought to remedy the evil consequences through pressure for humanitarian measures and an appeal to religious sanctions for a more just consideration for one's neighbor. It had not yet become apparent that growing technological competence and the very expansion of education, both technical and humanistic, were themselves giving an impetus to an industrializing phenomenon from which there was apparently no retreat. It is no wonder that entire religious organizations and diversely stationed individuals looked longingly to the "holistic" society which was reputed to have existed under the medieval synthesis. In fact, however, it became increasingly apparent that the gains in education and science and the transformation in ways of living, enjoyed by beneficiaries of the technological-industrial era, were not going to be relinquished but instead increased and accelerated. Efforts of humanitarian leaders to rectify the abuses of the all-engulfing industrial system were directed toward the evils causing blighted lives and loss of personal freedom. Many of the specific evils could be remedied, and were, through the formation of the labor movement, whose historic trilogy, "wages, hours, and working conditions," became the battle cry for the war to eliminate the sordid and injurious conditions under which many persons were required to work. Interestingly, a century later the same objectives exist, but with varying emphasis, as will be indicated subsequently. With the sweat shop and the other labor conditions leading to human disintegration all but eliminated in modern industrial life, however, the industrializing process itself continues with increasing acceleration. Many of its injurious aspects have been eliminated, at least in the more advanced nations, but new and unforeseen consequences have take their place.

Under industrialization and its economy we have moved almost overnight from a condition of scarcity to one of abundance and surplus in the advanced nations. All of this has placed us in a climate for which previous economic systems, philosophies, and religious formulations have not been prepared. We have not been without seers and prophets, but a world which has lived in an economy of scarcity cannot quickly adjust its thinking to a basis so radically new. It is therefore not surprising that religious institutions and their leaders could not visualize the type of society which industrialization has created. In the total span of the life of mankind only the last few minutes, figuratively speaking, represent the industrial era as contrasted with the agricultural era.

INDUSTRIALISM'S NATURE AND REQUIREMENTS

Possibly industrialism began with the use of the lever and the wheel, but this is an historical question we need not debate. Suffice it to say that wherever the benefits resulting from labor saving and new forms of energy have been appropriated, industrialism has been fostered. Industrialization involves the full utilization of the resources of science to make any products which people can or will use. It means the willingness to explore every possibility for production and then in turn to find or create a market for acceptance of its products. Science inevitably leads those engaged in industry to find all possible means for the utilization of new and potentially less expensive forms of energy to replace manpower and outmoded mechanical devices. Industrialism makes use of manpower, of course, but only to the extent that machines cannot perform the functions now or at any time undertaken. It means capital for the development of new instruments and for the marketing of the products and research for the finding of new means of creating and distributing. More will be said later of its characteristics and consequences. In short, it means the use of every available means for creating products and meeting needs in so far as available scientific resources make this possible. The manipulation and direction of human energy is integral to industrialization. Management of those who are responsible for the oversight and operation of machines is indispenable to the total system; the respective and interrelated roles of management and labor result.

Ramifications of this phenomenon lead into the problems of urbanization and larger collectivities of people within reach of the place of work.

The evolution of the various means of production from the lever and the wheel to nuclear fission has been too well documented to need amplification here. What have not been so well portrayed are the consequent beliefs and attitudes resulting from this transition. For modern man the most significant development in the use of new energies is the industrial system itself with its organization of production and distribution, the social life emerging around that process, and the cities and even small communities whose life and thought have been shaped by all that underlies and finds expression in industrialism. If there is one phenomenon that stands out more clearly than any other in modern times, it is the fact that personal, national, and international life are being dominated by the concept of industrialism, and are in a large measure the achievement of industrialization. Some have called this urbanization, and we are witnessing a major attack on the consequences of urban living. But behind urbanization lies the development of technology and the industrial-economic thought pattern which creates it.

Though Karl Marx understood the fact that a revolution in thought processes and the organization of society was taking place because of the growth of industrialism, he erred in assuming that freedom could somehow be channeled to support a set of values for the kind of society which was being produced. He did not understand that if the resources of technology were to be fully utilized, they must be permitted development and application wherever, whenever, and in whatever way their discoverers performed their tasks. Now after forty years of experimentation with a system which, if it is to be effective, cannot be thus curtailed, the USSR has had to grant permission for collaboration and cooperation in free research with those who represent a diametrically opposite type of political system. Freedom in scientific research cannot be hampered without destruction or deterioration of the industrial process, and the success of the Soviet experiment hinges on its superiority in the development of technology and industry.

The enterprise-capitalism system, which evolved with industrialism and was founded on the premises of freedom and the rights of individuals to explore and express themselves as they wish, finds itself in a similar dilemma. In addition to realizing that the research of its scientists must go on in cooperation with those of a rival political system which it disavows, the capitalistic system has had to face the fact that the range and scope of scientific discovery and technological development is greater than can be contained in the backroom laboratories of individual scientists. The day of making scientific observations from the falling apple or a set of test tubes and beakers may not be wholly past, but the vast network of interrelated team research, 85 per cent supported by the Federal government, attests what has occurred. If the process of industrialization is to expand—and it is—it is dependent upon research so vast in scope that only the taxpayers' money and unified authorization by a national government can make it possible, objectors notwithstanding. The result of all this is that in the forty years since the Russian Revolution of 1918 the inexorable forward movement of industrialization has forced a modification of some of the fundamental tenets of that revolution, and on the capitalistic side has forced a corresponding modification in a direction contrary to some of its fundamental tenets. "In our times it is no longer the specter of communism which is haunting Europe, but rather, emerging industrialization in many forms that is confronting the whole world. The giant of industrialization is stalking the earth, transforming almost all the features of older and traditional societies."[2]

Marx saw capitalism as the demon restraining man's attainment of his full potential, and so he insisted that the class struggle was responsible for the impairment of human opportunities. The problem was one of property ownership and the control of one life by another or many lives by one. What he could not foresee was that under a system of free access to ideas, including the ideas by which technology is advanced, human beings may not be enslaved but may actually be made freer of drudgery and have freer access to the products of industrial technology. He was not sufficiently aware of human psychology or of the nature of man, as it is understood in the West at least, to believe that human rights would ever transcend property rights. The irony of all this, of course, is that the system which Marx espoused, though it has given impetus to the most rapid industrial development in any country in history, has, in contrast to the system he denounced, precluded opportunities for the expression of freedom and the achievement of fuller human potential. Even with the rapid increase in communication in our time it may be another generation before both sides of this ideological argument can be freed sufficiently from the pseudo fears and the false convictions built up by each system, and both recognize that if industrialism is to be maintained, it will be only after both ideologies have given up the luxury of their obsessions.

Psychologists and sociologists long ago discovered that the transition from a rural to an urban society involves more than adopting technology and its skills. It involves a traumatic experience and a major revolution in cultural outlook. A family accustomed to cooperative work arrangements and a common schedule with a recognized hierarchical structure can no longer be maintained. The family in urban society, as we have now come to recognize painfully, is a very different social unit from that which prevailed in the rural setting. But almost as profound is the change in outlook on life for those who remain in agriculture, at least in the highly commercialized type of agricultural life. Primary attention is focused on the markets and the use of laborsaving, cost-cutting machinery. In industrialized nations the rapid decline in the numbers engaged in agriculture indicates the measure of that nation's industrialization.

While this volume was in preparation, large-scale campaigns were being waged to convince both young and old that new skills will be required to meet with the ever-changing needs of industrial society; this means education of a type and to a degree not heretofore attained. High premium is increasingly being placed upon ability to read instructions and to make calculations. All of this requires more education.

Free public education has become the great leveler and the instrument for upward mobility. Without universal education the industrialization process is hamstrung; separate industries are imperiled, and the total life of the industrialized nation is restrained. National policy cannot permit these restrictions on its development; and so government enters the picture with increasing vigor to force a wider availability of education and an intensification of training in industrial skills. In the process traditional class structures are undermined. So irresistible is the demand for industrialization that even traditional societies, steeped in religiously dictated class structures, eventually yield. The alternative is extinction.

"The industrial society," Clark Kerr and his co-authors contend, "is an open community, encouraging occupational and geographical mobility and social mobility. In this sense, industrialism must be flexible and competitive; it is against tradition and status based upon family, class, religion, race or caste."[3] If the society is to remain competitive and if the individual is to be mobile, he must possess the facility to adapt himself to varieties of situations. The new complex of forces, with the realignment of labor-management relations, necessitates the entrance of government into the field as the initiator and the preserver of actions designed to protect "the public" as well as to guarantee justice for the participants in industrial conflicts. Special attention will be given to the increasing role of government in industrial society. Suffice it for the moment to suggest that all the changes indicated above involve a measure of governmental participation, far greater than anything at least some parts of the free society have heretofore known.

SOME CONSEQUENCES OF INDUSTRIALIZATION

In another inaccurate projection into the future Marx, unable to foresee the fuller consequences of industrialization, misjudged the future role of classes. Not only did he fail to credit the elements of human equality and justice which would reduce the crystalization of the classes, but he could not foresee the heightened demands for skilled workers and the education which would support the possibilities for their development. Widespread general education and technical competence would increase the importance of the worker and render him indispensable to the processes of production, where the line between owners and workers would become less distinct as each became increasingly dependent upon the other.

The result is that religious sanctions go by the board. This is the meaning of India's eagerness to press for new steel mills, electronics factories, and all the other symbols of an industrializing nation. Under this pressure there is no place for caste and class systems, whose justification is the traditional religious life and whose stronghold is the small rural communities which have harbored the traditional systems. "Similarily, the Muslim religion has not interfered with the industrial development of banking, trading, or commercial and industrial institutions in Egypt. Traditionalist religious values do not seem to have been as serious an obstacle to economic thought in the long run as some anthropologists have thought."[4]

The obliteration of class sanctions is not the only result of the industrialization process. Community government, the type of education required, physical factors such as highways and shopping centers, the concomitant shift in purchasing times which keeps stores open nights and Sundays—all these things have wrought changes in the thinking of people who occupied the same communities in what were less revolutionary times. Small and seemingly quiet rural communities have become, in many instances in less than five years, booming industrial towns with the advent of one or more new factories. In days prior to the availability of rapid transportation the advent of industrialization in a single community brought a concentration of people in types of residence throwing together large numbers heretofore unacquainted with and unprepared for communal living. Practically every great metropolitan center has been the victim of this process, most notably in England and in the older cities of the United States. There are very few large communities which have come into existence since the achievement of rapid transit and the automobile; Los Angeles, of course, is the major exception. Its problem, however, is compounded by the desirability of establishing new industries, both because of seemingly felicitous climatic conditions and because of a market prepared by those who had moved into that area in such large numbers for purposes of retirement, recreation, or some specialized form of productivity.

The new conditions of living which confronted migrants from more stable and established backgrounds, whether in the rural or urban life of Europe or from the rural hinterlands of the United States, have been expressed in the discomfiture and anguish of those whose roots had been torn up before new ones could be established. Families which moved to a new and industrializing country did so with their own roots deep in the "stem-type" family, the great family where care was assured and where age was respected. For many who moved to the United States in the period of its greatest influx of immigrants the stem-type family could still be held in esteem and respect, so long as the family, whether with all generations or a single generation, worked on the land. It was not until a later period, when the land could no longer support the diverse generations, that the ones who were forced to move to the city found themselves creating a nuclear family in which individual effort counted rather than the teamwork of the agricultural background. Meanwhile, the immigrant to the city, though attempting to maintain roots in the stem-type family, found even more quickly that the nuclear family was the only type which could maintain itself in urban and industrial life. In each case, the religious backgrounds represented were based on the life of the family and that of the total community, often with major emphasis on the life of a single parish. A common background of work made possible a genuine community of interests, but unless all the members of the now nuclear family were related to a single plant to which their destinies were tied, there was little sense of community. Added to this is the fact that the type of work done in plant and the new social arrangements based upon skill rather than familial or hierarchical status further served to fracture the homogeneity of social life. Religious sanctions based upon the class structure and the family system of a rural or common community background in the Old World could no longer be maintained. The work ethic and its production demand have created new alignments of class, and the controls once so commonly accepted no longer have meaning. Recreation, long tied to the rural pattern of life and the sanctity of the seventh day of rest observed in rural society, placed its stamp temporarily on the industrial portion of the nation's life. Finally, however, either pressures of work made laboring on the Sabbath necessary, or the longer weekend and a means of faster travel gave incentive to foresake the familiar places of worship on the traditional day. Industrialization has thus brought about a large-scale revolution in the traditional observances of religion and in the instruments which have historically served to reinforce religious objectives.

A dilemma fraught with both philosophical and economic factors in the advancement of industrialization is the problem of labor surpluses. Through all human history until recent times the production of food and the cultivation of land have taken all the available manpower. Few facts are better known in the leading industrial nations than those which contrast the numbers employed in agriculture and required to feed persons not specifically engaged in work on the land with the small number now required to feed a much larger population occupied in industrial activities. At present no viable large-scale options for utilizing the mounting surplus of labor have appeared, except in programs of public works and the increase of service activities. The problem for our times is high-lighted by the widespread concern for the high school dropout, for those released from the trades or skills by which they formerly earned a living and which have been since eliminated, and for those adults and young adults for whom unskilled manual labor is simply unavailable. All of this is further complicated by the failure of birth rates to decline appreciably in industrialized nations and the actual increase in population through improved health and the decline of infant mortality in the nations now anxiously seeking to industrialize. These are the nations which W. W. Rostow describes as being in the traditional or take-off stages.[5]

WELFARE'S NEW IMPORTANCE

Industrialization and welfare economics are coordinate phenomena. Partly for reasons indicated above and partly for reasons inherent in the industrializing process itself the welfare aspects of industrial society have to match the progress of industrialization. A fuller treatment of this theme will appear later, but here it must be indicated as an integral aspect of industrial society. The growth of the profession of social worker parallels the growth of the professions of scientist, technologist, and industrial manager. In turn the political scientist and the politician are called upon to convince the individuals and forces fostering industrialization that a substantial portion of their earnings must be used to provide for the temporarily unusable member of the labor force or those who are rejected because of the advances in technology. The politician may not understand the reasons for the close relation between industrialization and welfare, but he is caught between the managers and those responsible for the financial welfare of industry, and the ever-increasing numbers for whom at least a minimum living standard must be provided and who in addition possess voting strength.

Debate as to whether people are assuming sufficient responsibility for their own well-being or are taking advantage of the welfare programs as a form of escape from the exercise of initiative, will go on endlessly so long as individuals are differently constituted. The number of the dishonest or the shiftless may in the aggregate appear large, but the evidence points to the fact that there are many more who would like to take responsibility for their own well-being, particularly at the point of finding work.

From the standpoint of health services still another factor enters. It is the provision of health resources, which Peter Drucker has discussed in various writings.[6] The organization of these resources —the modern hospital in particular—has adopted the techniques and philosophy of the industrializing process. Though techniques for diagnosis and restoration of health have been inexpressibly improved, they have also involved commensurate costs. These in turn have made maintenance and restoration of health beyond the personal financial resources of a great many people. One consequence has been the burgeoning of insurance plans, such as Blue Cross and Blue Shield, to spread the costs more equitably. Industries have protected themselves against losses in time and costs by providing as a "fringe benefit" various types of health insurance. To all this are added, of course, welfare benefits provided through taxes, especially in terms of medical services made available at minimal cost for the indigent. But topping all others and symbolic of the welfare requirements both created and made possible by industrialization, has been the vast social security enterprise of national governments. We have come to take for granted, though not without a struggle, that a society which rests on an industrial basis must include in its costs the casualties which are incident to it. Transition from dependence upon the great family to dependence upon the great society with its great government and the great semipublic agencies for health and economic undergirding is a phenomenon less than a century old.

SPECIALIZATION OF SKILLS 1372719

Running like a thread through all the manifestations of the advance of industrialism is the role of the innovator and the expert. Mass movements cannot decide the direction of industrialism, hence the decline of ideologies. The internal rationale of industrialism lies in the advancement of technical knowledge and the means for adapting it to the needs and capacities of the individuals affected. Mass movements may call attention to inequities and violations of human well-being, but they cannot formulate the technical structures required to produce the devices for reducing labor or increasing production. These are the products of individuals or groups technically competent to foster such developments. Here is a dilemma in which the labor movement has increasingly found itself. Its more astute leaders have equipped themselves to meet the technical competence of industrial managers or have provided a philosophical counterbalance to the objectives and directions which management has pursued. In the industrializing process it has been necessary for labor organizations to develop persons competent to cope with the technological advances of their respective industries. Mere protest is obviously no longer sufficient, and significantly in the major industrialized nations labor groups, recognizing the futility of opposing scientific developments, have become increasingly cooperative with the advances of the industry itself.

Another way of saying all this is to recognize that the role of the technically qualified manager has become the primary role in industrialization. This does not mean that he is solely concerned with the sciences of physics, chemistry, and mathematics, etc. A science of adapting individuals to suitable work or changes in work and the investigation of work qualification has been evolving. All of this is of a piece with the total managerial role. This has meant specialization, with the highest rank going to those who know how to appropriate the talents of other specialists and coordinate clusters of specialists toward the advancement of the industry or organization. Related to the specialization within industries and between industries is the task of evaluating the total potential of a department or a product and making the allocation or withdrawal of financial support. Specialization in the management of money relative to the industrial development is a coordinate function of industrialization.

Included in the general catalog of consequences of industrialization are also suggestions of the continuing requirements made mandatory in an industrializing economy. Among them is the new type of leadership, which Kerr et al. designate as the elites, the individuals who singly and collectively foster the advancement of industrialization, who are thus both a consequence and an ever-expanding requirement of the process. As Kerr points out, however, the problem is not whether elites will emerge; that is a foregone conclusion. The real question is which one will come to dominate the life of a given nation. Different types of societies will be dominated by different types of elites. They are designated as (1) the dynastic elite, (2) the middle class, (3) the revolutionary intellectuals, (4) the colonial administrators, (5) the nationalistic leaders.[7] From these vividly descriptive titles one can readily surmise the roles they perform and the sources from which they emerge.

Still another consequence and requirement is the type of personality at home in the industrialized culture. Max Weber has been vigorously attacked but possibly even more vigorously supported in his thesis that Protestantism rendered its adherents more comfortable than Catholicism in the capitalist-industrial evolution. The fact that industrialization has proceeded furthest in the nations which departed earliest from the strictures and controls of a hierarchically dominated religion has been viewed by some as the justification for Weber's contention. Others have attributed the disposition toward industrialization and the economy which accompanied it to climate, diet, and other correlated factors. Yet one social analyst, Gerhard Lenski, has contended that even now the residual influences of an authoritarian religion serve to restrict the ambitions of its people to a greater degree than is the case with those who are inheritors of the Protestant tradition.[8] Whether the findings of his study can be universally applied is open to question, but at least the data he acquired in Detroit, one of the most industrial of all cities, seem to bear out the Weber thesis. Another study conducted in an industrializing rural area reveals the fact that among those who have lived a generation or more in this region there remain no appreciable differences in ideologies or social attitudes relative to issues which have been markedly affected by industrialization, e.g., welfare, approval of labor organizations, and international relations, etc.[9] A common technology and its concomitant patterns of living make for uniformity of ideas, whatever the variation in work incentives.

EMOTIONAL ADAPTATIONS

We are not adequately fortified with records of mental ailments during the medieval period, and thus we cannot assume that the high incidence of mental breakdown characteristic of the industrial society is actually any greater than that which prevailed in a simpler and more cohesive economic and social existence. We do know that as the profession of the social worker has mounted in importance with the increase of industrialization, so has the importance of the psychologist and psychiatrist. It would seem that psychological security and a sense of what is of ultimate importance have declined with the advance of technology and the independence of man from the religious cohesiveness he knew in another era. The result is a new type of person, more insistent upon experiencing the full limits of existence within the type of life which unlimited productivity and its satisfaction of wants is attempting to provide.

Opponents of industrialism and those who long for the simpler society have pointed to its evil consequences and gloried in the more wholesome order of an earlier day. In answer to this a United Nations study suggests that industrialism may appear to breed wretched working conditions, starvation wages, child labor, broken families, overcrowding, filth and sordidness in slums, delinquency and corruption of youth. But these agonies are not a necessary consequence of industrialization; they may simply represent evils of poverty and overcrowding that are independent of industrial growth; they represent a rapid transfer of rural misery to an urban setting where it is more conspicuous. What is needed in such cases, the UN study observes, is not less but more industrialization.[10]

The patterns of living required by industrialization have exacted their toll in the readjustment of human relationships, but they have also brought a measure of freedom from drudgery which modern man prefers to the reputedly well-ordered life of another era with all of its discomforts. The disruption of his security, his being cut loose from long-established mores and customs, have created a new frontier for religion.

There is strong agreement concerning one consequence of industrialization and the culture which it has created. This is that disintegration of the homogeneous community, the almost complete elimination of the stem type family and corresponding threat to the nuclear family, and the disappearance of unchallenged religious authority, have caused participants to ask fundamental questions about themselves: What is my ultimate destiny? By what regulations, if any, shall my existence be governed? Is the objective of my work deserving of the full expenditure of my energy? These are modern versions of the question which emerged in the Reformation, asked by Luther, Calvin, and many others: What is my calling? Thus to enable people to find meaning for their lives in a type of society which is increasingly able to provide their physical comforts, the proponent of religion has asked more fundamental questions than he as industrialized man has thus far been able to answer. Many of these questions have to do with the quality of interpersonal life which is possible in the new era, the obligation one may have to work in the interest of his neighbor, whether he be in the same production plant or in another hemisphere. In the same vein he is forced to ask whether the destitution and deteriorated lives of even a small percentage of people in industrialized nations, in addition to the very large percentage of those in lands undeveloped industrially, can be justified.

Industrialization and the economy which accompanies it are as much a part of twentieth-century man as breathing. The changes they have produced in cultural patterns of work and leisure and the life style of those dependent on them have effected profound modifications in attitudes, beliefs, and aspirations. It is in industrialized society where religious attitudes, beliefs, and aspirations must also find expression. If they are relevant, there results a harmony of man and his world; if not, either the beliefs or the economic practices must be relinquished. The fundamental issue is thus the relevance of faith to the economic life of industrial man.

3

Issues Challenging Industrialism

It is a basic assumption of this capstone volume in the Series on Ethics and Economics of Society that industrialism shapes our culture but that it now confronts some profound problems. There are those who contend that automation, instead of freeing society from wide discrepancies in income, for example, will actually accentuate these differences and begin a return to the type of differences in wealth prevailing in the Middle Ages. Despite fears that increasing concentration of ownership and control may lead to a reversal of the trend of the past century which gave the widespread benefits from increasing technology, this reversal seems unlikely. Nevertheless, in the processes of humanization fostered by our almost universal education, a free press, and rational control of communication instruments, many in our society have become convinced that unless the economy which undergirds our industrial and business order can provide adequately for people, it must be modified.

Until now the increase of real income for workers has proved Marx wrong, i.e., that their position would deteriorate. There are some who believe that the accelerated use of laborsaving devices and the necessary concentration of ownership of these instruments may well reverse the trend. Hitherto it has been beneficial to both owner-manager and worker to make certain that the fruits of industrialism be widespread. It is no foregone conclusion today, however, either that the benefits of automation will or that they will not be widely spread; neither is it inevitable that the humanitarian concern of the Hebrew-Christian tradition, that all human systems allow man to fulfill his ultimate destiny as a creature of God, will be realized.

The suggestion that some other pattern of socioeconomic arrangement might come into being is not made with intention to disturb, but rather to take account of the fact that there is no guarantee that the present formulas and generally accepted philosophy of economic structures will prevail. Nor should there be. To insist upon such a guarantee would involve us in the establishment of a legal framework and a set of regulations too complex to administer.

Our economic system is undergoing constant modification. At stake is the issue of the direction being taken and the objectives of those most responsible for that direction. Obviously lines of least resistance or short-term goals cannot provide adequate justification. Inherent in this volume and all the others in the series is a conviction that the purposes and goals delineated for man in the Hebrew-Christian heritage constitute the desired objective of our economy. We think it imperative, therefore, that modern man come to know the essentials of that heritage.

Industrialism will always have unfinished business if it is allowed to develop. It cannot be rigidly structured, for its very essence is unrestricted recourse to change in whatever direction new developments and discoveries may dictate. As vast programs of research go forward, however, there are warning signs pointing to immediate, unfinished business, neglect of which could injure if not kill the advances of industrial life.

UNEMPLOYMENT

One sign suggested in the preceding chapter is the increasing ratio of the unemployed and the (under present conditions) unemployable to the number actually employed. A volume of unemployment in excess of 5 per cent of the available working population may not be statistically alarming to some people, but in those numbers are persons who cannot be readily retrained for other kinds of work and who are potentially permanent relief recipients.* There are school dropouts who fall steadily behind the procession (we shall discuss them in greater detail below), and the aged, of course, for whom little or no employment is likely, and the large number, both white- and blue-collar, for whom some kind of adequate retraining program has not been found. And compounding all these issues is the fact that despite the increase of educational opportunities for the rest of the nation, a group that comprises more than 10 per cent of the total population, the nonwhite, is steadily falling further behind in the ability to make a useful contribution to the total economy. Here the principal handicap is not inherent in the persons concerned; it is simply the handicap of color. Though the civil rights law of 1964 will hopefully go a long way toward making job opportunities accessible to this large segment of the population, the necessity for beginning at such low levels due to heavy educational limitations and correspondingly limited accomplishment places a majority of those included in this 10 per cent of the population under an oppressive and frightening handicap.

The Dropout

The term "dropout" (from school) has become a symbol of our unemployment dilemma. Though it is not an economic problem by itself, it is integral to the ability of our industrial economy to provide employment or to make provision for all who need it. The dropout is so distinctive a type that special comment concerning him is in order. One-fourth of all the unemployed in America are teen agers. In 1962 the number of jobless teen-age boys averaged 472,000, and the number increased in 1963 and again in 1964 by more than 100,000. The tragedy lies not simply in their present state of unemployment but in the fact that the dropout is making a move that will affect all the years of his active life. Of youth 14 to 24 years of age (1962) out of 14,772,000 not in school, 1,212,000 were both out of school and out of work; and

* In this number, too, are those unemployed for short periods and the "hard core" of unemployables, i.e., those physically or mentally incapable of employment.

of these, 338,000 were described as "not even looking." In every category the per cent for nonwhites is higher than for whites. And as might be inferred from previous figures, the dropouts constitute a steadily decreasing percentage of the work force. In 1940 the number of dropouts was 68 per cent, in 1962 only 46 per cent of the active work force. Every indication points to a continuing decline in the percentages. As is true for the economy as a whole, low-skilled jobs are drying up.[1]

There are no simple solutions or easy adjustments which would accommodate these young people in the work force. Some see this problem as "structural." Basically it is a question of how the nation's resources available for production are allocated. For example, it has been pointed out that 2.7 billion dollars spent in producing the TFX airplane would finance the creation of something like three hundred thousand jobs; the same amount spent on urban renewal would create three million jobs.[2] Behind the decision to allocate is the question whether a concern with defense shall have priority over the elemental needs of the population. This is more than an economic question in the strictly technical sense, since it involves us in a problem of human values.

POVERTY

On March 16, 1964 President Johnson said in a message to Congress:

We are citizens of the richest and most fortunate nation in the history of the world . . . the path forward has not been an easy one. There are millions of Americans . . . one-fifth of our people . . . who have not shared in the abundance which has been granted to most of us and on whom the gates of opportunity have been closed. . . . The war on poverty is not a struggle simply to support people, to make them dependent on the generosity of others. It is a struggle to give people a chance. . . . Our fight against poverty will be an investment and the most valuable of our resources . . . the skills and strength of our people. . . . If we can raise the annual earnings of ten million among the poor by only $1,000 we will have added fourteen billion dollars a year to our national output. . . . Because it is right, because it is wise and because for the first time in our history it is possible to conquer poverty, I submit for the consideration of the Congress and the country, the Economic Opportunity Act of 1964.

The President then went on to indicate what he believed the measure would do and some of the activities that would necessarily be undertaken by the government to provide those opportunities.

It is safe to say that never before has the attention of this nation been as heavily concentrated on the subject of poverty. (A possible exception is the period giving rise to Franklin D. Roosevelt's oft-quoted description "one-third of a nation ill-fed, ill-clothed and ill-housed." The circumstances however were substantially different at that time. The entire nation was in the depths of a depression and was concerned not primarily with poverty as a social phenomenon nor with the ability of the economy itself to meet the needs of an industrial society. The chief concern was with the relief of suffering.) The very fact that the President of the United States is free to talk about poverty and to expose it as vigorously as does his message, indicates more than merely a concern with poverty itself; it reveals the belief that poverty need not exist to the degree that his announcements indicate, and that it is not a political liability to acknowledge so great a weakness existing in the nation's life. That poverty can be eliminated with the resources of our economy and that it shall be eliminated because it is a drag upon the rest of the nation as well as because it is injurious to persons affected reveal the dual emphasis underlying the reasons for attempting to cope with it.

As President Johnson spoke, four-fifths of the nation were enjoying the highest measure of prosperity the world has ever known. There was little doubt that the economy through which this prosperity had been achieved was basically sound. Thirty-five years of watching an alternative system in the Soviet Union had disillusioned many who had entertained the notion that a totalitarian society under a Marxist-Leninist economy could provide both goods and freedom. Thus the deliverances of Presidents Roosevelt and Johnson came under vastly different circumstances in the nation's life and the life of the world.

Poverty is a relative thing. A movie portraying the poverty of

Appalachia makes an ex-coal miner and his family the central figures. They are poor because there is no more opportunity for mining coal. Other forms of energy have supplanted the "black gold" under the hills of Appalachia. But the family still had an automobile and was making payments on some very modern electric appliances.[3] However only a small fraction of the 20 per cent of Americans classified as poor are as well off as this ex-mining family. Only two out of every five nonwhite families live in sound structures with running water and a flush toilet. The figures are even worse in the South, where 60 per cent of the nonwhites still live.

Some may say, "What's all the excitement about? Things are getting better all the time, aren't they? We have moved from one-third of a nation in poverty to one-fifth in a single generation. At this rate it will be down to an infinitesimal percentage in a comparatively few years." The National Policy Committee on Pockets of Poverty answers that "unless remedial steps are undertaken, there will be considerably more poor even with a more affluent America." The circumstances which made possible the remedy of some of the conditions deplored by President Roosevelt can no longer be relied upon. The acceleration of automation has injected a virtually new feature into the economic scene. It is very doubtful that a stepped-up economy can of itself absorb the numbers of people who are being displaced economically by advancing technologies.* What the National Policy Committee says in reference to people in the Appalachians could equally apply to others who are being divorced from the benefits of our economy. It will not do to argue, as most policy makers and economists do, "that poverty will be done away with by policies aimed at bringing about full employment."[4]

A special assistant in the President's program against poverty, Daniel P. Moynihan, contends:

The central fact about poverty in America is that it is a political problem. This is a fact we must face. . . . Consider that in the last three

* And considerations of regional poverty must of course take into account the fact that there are always those who will not leave a familiar locus, even preferring deprivation to the difficulties and uncertainties of departure.

years, 1961, 1962, 1963, our gross national product grew by one hundred billion dollars. This is considerably greater than the entire GNP of Great Britain. Yet nowhere in the United Kingdom will you find the extensive areas of massive poverty such as you find here in our urban slums and rural wastelands. Having reached the point of something very much like mass affluence we remain one of the few great industrial nations of the world to retain within its borders mass poverty. Half as many people live here in poverty as live in all the United Kingdom. . . . Everyone says we have the opportunity to be the first nation in the history of mankind to eradicate the scourge of poverty from our borders. That is no longer true. It is too late for us to be the first to do this; other great nations have in effect done so. . . . To a great extent it is our size, our diversity and our lack of homogeneity that have produced our situation. To a great degree poverty in America is the aftermath of a hard-driving exploitation of men and materials which has also been one of the causes of today's economic affluence. The poor are left-over miners; the used-up coal and iron rangers; the small-skill southern white farmers eking out livings on used-up land; Negroes living in the aftermath of three centuries of the utmost exploitation; the Indians driven off the best land.[5]

Michael Harrington in *The Other America* has focused the attention of an entire nation on a comparatively recent aspect of the problem of poverty. Though there are still large areas such as Appalachia where the poor may be seen (as they were by John F. Kennedy when he went to West Virginia to campaign for his nomination), the fact remains that much of current poverty is what Harrington designates as invisible. It includes those who have been provided for in a minimal way by public housing and relief checks, the rapidly increasing number of persons over sixty-five who are living on one of several forms of government assistance,* and the minorities who because of prejudice are being afflicted with increasing handicaps. It includes people who follow the crops and who for a fraction of the year appear to be adequately employed but who for the remainder of the year live in abject poverty and out of the mainstreams of society.

Poverty's consequences have been so vividly and voluminously described that it is hardly necessary to amplify them here. Harring-

---

* At the time of this writing 9 per cent of the American population is over 65 and the Department of Health, Education, and Welfare estimates that in 1975 nearly 10 per cent will have reached that age.

ton, in his moving documentation of the fact of poverty and its consequences, conforms with many other conscientious students of society who have confronted us with the incontrovertible facts. Collectively they have pointed in prophetic fashion to the consequences for American life in particular when poverty becomes accepted as all but inevitable. Among such consequences is the mental and emotional distortion which racks the bodies and minds of individuals and exacts a terrifying price from the community at large. Commenting on one study of this factor, Harrington writes: "The stress factors listed by the Cornell Study are the very stuff of the life of the poor: physical illness, broken homes, worries about work, money and all the rest. The slum with its vibrant dense life hammers away at the individual. And because of the sheer grinding, dirty experience of being poor, the personality— the spirit—is impaired. It is as if human beings dilapidate along with the tenements in which they live."[6]

A conference on the Churches and Persistent Pockets of Poverty in the U.S.A., sponsored by the Division of Christian Life and Work and the Division of Home Missions of the National Council of Churches of Christ in the U.S.A., concluded:

Today for the first time in human history the great productive potential of our economy and the creative imagination of our citizenry provide the means to eradicate poverty and alleviate its evil consequences. In view of the rapidly increasing economic interdependence of our world, America's plans for the elimination of poverty can no longer be nationalistic or isolated. They must take account of the tragic depths of poverty which characterize wide stretches of the globe.[7]

The conference report suggested as the consequences of poverty:

There can be no question that material want, not voluntarily chosen but externally imposed, places severe pressures upon individuals, families, communities, the nation and the church.

Among the injurious effects of poverty upon *individuals* are: physical dangers in terms of poor health, inadequate medical care, malnutrition, poor housing, severe crowding; sometimes forced intimacy with its moral dangers; cultural deprivations in terms of interrupted schooling and underdeveloped capacities, restricted opportunities; psychological damage, resulting in frustration and resignation or resentment and rebellion, possibility of antisocial attitudes leading to crime and delinquency, mental breakdown, the undermining of initiative, and a sense of isolation or rejection. . . . Poverty puts severe strain upon the family, already threatened by rapid changes of modern life.

Poverty means deprivation for the community; poor schools and high dropout rates, the social costs of bad health and crime, the thwarting of human capabilities and the loss of their potential contribution. . . . Poverty means trouble for the entire *nation;* class divisions lead to class conflict; attenuation of educational and cultural services; the weakening of economic growth, national security, democratic processes and political stability. . . . Poverty also has serious consequences for the *church.* Its outreach is seriously restricted in depressed areas. Some churches and church programs, while rendering important service, often tend to reinforce separation of rich and poor, white and non-white, both in the community and in the household of faith. . . .[8]

Though we are profoundly concerned with and disturbed about the consequences of poverty, the principal focus of concern lies in its economic and social causes. The conference cited above suggested that though physical and mental handicaps, chronic ill health, and false value orientations uncongenial to economic advancement are significant as causes—

Far more influential factors, especially for explaining pockets of poverty, are to be found in the structure of our society and in the lags in adjustments to far-reaching and fast-moving technological, economic and social changes. Illustrations include: (1) lack of opportunity for general education and/or vocational training; (2) discrimination in employment on grounds of age, race, nationality or sex; (3) lack of employment opportunities due to cyclical or structural factors; (4) part-time employment and under-employment in industry and other occupations; (5) employment in traditionally low-wage jobs; (6) under-employment in agriculture due to a lack of adequate land, tools or capital; (7) exploitation of seasonally employed farm labor under chaotic systems of farm labor utilization; (8) exhaustion of resources in an area; (9) population pressure on resources in an area; (10) relative immobility of people and resistance to change; (11) inadequate rate of economic growth; (12) absence of collective bargaining power through lack of organization.[9]

Professor Oscar Ornati in a panel as a part of the same conference stated: "The American economy is now so productive as to have passed the cross-over point. It is clear that while in the recent past this was not so, now the Ameican economy is producing enough to do away with poverty."[10]

He went on to comment on the absence of precise data even though the phenomena are very evident. Precise data are of inestimable value and an absolute requirement for facing the problem fully. However, many facts concerning the extent and nature of the phenomenon of poverty are readily at hand.

It is not possible to charge poverty against industrialization or technical change. The phenomenon of poverty existed long before these aspects of society were prominent. Neither is it justifiable to contend that poverty in its continuing form is a product of inadequate economic growth. What Professor Ornati and his colleagues are contending is that the problem runs deeper than mere tinkering with present economic and industrial schemes can affect.

ECONOMIC GROWTH

If we have assumed that natural growth in our economic welfare will automatically take care of these conditions, some hard facts are in order. Fifteen years ago 20 per cent of the population with the lowest income received 5 per cent of our national income. Fifteen years later the 20 per cent with the lowest income still receive 5 per cent. The problem is simply not being solved.

Roy Blough is pointing to the same facts from another statistical perspective when he comments that the average annual rate of economic growth between 1909 and 1960 was 2.9 per cent in real terms; this was also the average rate for the periods 1909–1929 and 1929–1960. Technological progress has resulted in rapid economic growth with rising employment, civilian employment increasing from approximately twenty-seven million in 1900 to sixty-six million in 1960. From the standpoint of personal consumption expenditure per capita there was an increase between 1939 and 1962, based on 1962 prices, from $1,072.00 to $1,912.00, 2¼ per cent a year in real terms. Despite all this, as Professor Blough points out, there were many who did not share in the increases of income or shared so little that their condition can still only be described as very severe or even desperate poverty.

"Clearly economic growth in the past has not eliminated hard-core poverty and there is no reason to expect it to do so by itself in the future."[11]

UNDERDEVELOPED NATIONS

However significant the gap between the rich and poor, the privileged and the underprivileged in the United States, it is less significant for the world at large than the gap between the rich and the poor nations. America's poor are much better off in physical comforts and diet than the great majority of people in the under-developed nations of Africa, Asia, and South America; not much sympathy from the latter can be expected for their counterpart in the United States. It is the poor of the underdeveloped nations who present to industrialism and its economy its greatest challenge. The contrast in relative per capita output, which in 1960 was $2,800.00 for the United States and $75.00 for South Asia, $135.00 for Africa and $250.00 for Latin America, tells the story.[12]

People in developed nations may wonder why the underde-veloped countries cannot grasp the fact that economic develop-ment is not something to be achieved quickly. For the latter, political freedom was reached in a comparatively short time after momentum in that direction was initiated. The ideals of liberty, equality, and brotherhood are slogans of political emergency which fire the imagination and instill hope. But here is one of the paradoxes of the technological revolution: in the widespread knowledge of possibilities of enhancing human freedom resulting from technological advances in communications, the psychological and philosophical, or in other words, the intellectual resources for freedom become available; but the educational disciplines and the educational system required to provide the benefits of tech-nology quickly dampen the hope burgeoning in the hearts of those who still live in what is termed traditional society. And with the experience of the new freedom it becomes apparent that the mate-rial resources for freedom, the foundation of industrialism, remain almost a mirage. Describing millions of those involved in such a situation, Gunnar Myrdal says: "Above all they are poor, mostly illiterate and backward, and they are being made conscious of it. The important thing is that they are not satisfied with liberty but demand equality of opportunity and common brotherhood as well. They describe themselves as underdeveloped with the clear implication that they should have economic development and a fuller share of the good things of life."[13]

Underdeveloped nations and their people are given encouragement when they look upon the accomplishments of the Soviet Union, and they cannot but be receptive when the latter offers them technical assistance and material resources for quick industrialization. It is understandable that they do not question immediately the obligations and commitments in which they become enmeshed. Sugar-coated promises of industrial expansion have to be matched with a frank appraisal of what is to be expected. "Financial aid the Soviet Union can supply, she can also supply technicians. But she cannot supply an example of a free and functioning industrial society. Russian communism denies that such a society is possible, that its problems exist and are real. It must deny this or else give up the beliefs in its own tenets and especially in the dogma that all social and economic problems are automatically solved by the mere establishment of the dictatorship of the proletariat."[14] Honest protagonists of industrialism thus become the true servants of the only viable option for giving freedom from misery as well as enslavement to the people of emerging nations.

POPULATION

Inseparable from any discussion of underdeveloped nations is the ominous problem of population. Underdeveloped countries have historically maintained a balance between birth rates and death rates (35–40 per 1,000), but improved technology has sorely disrupted this balance. Its first consequence is the reduction of the death rate, particularly infant mortality; then follows a sudden population increase. With the incidence of disease no longer as high and with insufficient means of communicating to illiterate people the necessity for reducing birth rates, the peril mounts.

Not until sufficient numbers have been drawn into industrial communities where the implications of high birth rate become apparent is there a noticeable tendency to curtail family size.

India, for example, as a national policy has sought to find means of acquainting its millions of small village people with the fact that if it is to be a nation capable of holding its own in the world of nations, it cannot have its strength vitiated by a population which it cannot feed and which in turn lacks the strength to provide for itself through industrial production. Egypt, in attempting desperately to industrialize, finds it similarly difficult if not impossible to restrict its population increase so that it will not become such a drain upon the productive capacities of the nation. Even with all the assistance from many other nations, Egypt faces disaster unless through its rapid industrialization it can reduce the force which is undermining its national expectations. What is true of India and Egypt is similarly true of China in its powerful drive toward industrialization. Now new African nations eagerly striving to come into the main stream of human history are beginning to face the same issue. However, "if raising the standard of living is a prerequisite for reducing the birth-rate, therefore, the problem of surplus population and surplus labor is likely to persist for many years in most of the under-developed countries."[15] With two-thirds of the world's population now in the process of industrialization or eagerly anxious to participate in it, any rationale for industrialism must carry with it the capacity to indicate to underdeveloped nations and their peoples the imperativeness of population control.

EDUCATION

Among the most obvious and oft-repeated facts coincident with the rise of industrialism is the necessity for an educational system commensurate with, but also creating, the advancing requirements of an industrialized society. In one major segment of the world's population, the U.S.S.R., education has been vigorously supported because it contributes to the industrializing process itself. In what is generally designated as the free world the function of education is to develop the whole being with full consideration of the individual's needs in relation to his fellow man. This philosophy places demands upon the industrial system and determines the economy which shall prevail within it. Thus industrialism and its economy are not regarded as autonomous forces, but are subject to the requirements and objectives of man.

Rightfully, much is being made of the disparity of opportunity for advancement between whites and nonwhites. In the southern segment of the United States, for example, agriculture has provided the economic base from the nation's beginning until the middle of the twentieth century. Unskilled labor could provide in the form of "field hands" all that was necesesary for that economy. Besides the few skilled artisans needed for the plantation houses of the Old South, training for advanced skills or education beyond minimum requirements for communication was unnecessary. Mechanization of agriculture and increasing industrialization of southern cities, however, made new requirements. The availability of communication resources—television, radio, the press—placed an increasing premium on literacy, and excited interest in and demand for the products so glamourously presented by the advertising specialists. The demand for education increased in geometric ratio. Gunnar Myrdal relates that when he was conducting his now famous study *An American Dilemma,* he asked Southerners what whites were going to do when the education being provided for Negroes caused them to insist upon the same rights and opportunities as whites. He attests that the question produced animated response, to the effect that the "mores" would be unaffected.

An industrial society cannot have widespread discrepancies in educational opportunities, or its potential markets are curtailed and the progress which is mandatory on a technological society is reduced in its rate of acceleration. In 1961 President Kennedy's Council of Economic Advisors estimated that if the education and training of the Negro population were utilized, it would increase the income of the nation by thirteen billion dollars a year.

Education of the nonwhites, however, is but one part of the

total problem. The real issue is whether an industrial society can take from its earnings or create sufficient earnings to provide the kind of education required by everyone who would live adequately in that kind of a society. This means minimal competence in reading instructions, of course, but even more it means capacity to comprehend the very nature of the social system, the government, and the type of demands a free society places upon individuals. Thomas Jefferson saw this even before an industrial society had shaped the life of this nation. Industrialism in a free and democratic society must run the risk of its people making demands on the economic system, which demands may even go counter to certain concepts of property fostered by that system. Though this could be detrimental to the ownership patterns and economic concepts held by some people, it has the salutary consequence of making it possible for free citizens to understand the nature of the economy of which they are a part and from which they derive their livelihood. It could enable them to assume responsibility for directing that economy. The alternative is a system where responsibility has been abdicated and is conducted by those who through power, however achieved, essay to govern the lives of others according to their own personal desires. This is the paradox of unrestricted education in and for a free industrial society. Some would contend, of course, that so few are capable of grasping the importance of assuming responsibility for the life and work in our economy, that it is necessary for an elite to exercise the paternal or dominant role. This is obviously the risk which the Soviet Union is unwilling to take and yet which a free society, if it is to be fully free, must assume.

We are discussing here not simply the formal educational institutions of all levels, public and private, but the manifold variety of other educational instruments through which one discovers his role in relation to the rest of society and the necessity for responsible action in it. Countervailing forces are present in every form of social organization, but there are special reasons for their vitality in a free society committed to the use of all instruments and resources for its enhancement. Too great conservatism in economics may serve to restrict the forward movement of technology and the industrialism which utilizes it. If it is restrained, for example, by the suppression of new inventions, this may cause special advantages to accrue to those who benefit from monopoly of idea or ownership, to the detriment of the majority. On the other hand, widespread availability of discoveries and innovations can bring benefit to the population at large. Our patent laws have provided protection for the innovator, and they have benefited the rest of society as well by limiting the length of time a person's discovery or creation may be controlled, whether by an individual or a corporation. Behind this governmental action lies a theory that a government representing its people has the wisdom to decide whether and how long a needed instrument shall be preserved for limited benefit. At the other extreme is the disposition to share the discoveries relative to nuclear fission with any others who indicate willingness to accept responsibility and to use the discovery in accordance with mutually agreed regulations. The widespread mutual sharing of information relative to the most basic scientific discoveries attests both their universally valid nature and the mutual trust of those who are engaging in fundamental research. There is no private ownership of the profoundest wisdom of the universe.

The discovery of nuclear energy and the sharing of basic scientific knowledge parallel and symbolize the role of education at all levels in society. If industrial society is to advance in keeping with the essence of its own life, it is axiomatic that its fundamental tenets, its organization, and its regulations become a part of the common wisdom of as large a percentage of its beneficiaries as are capable of appropriating them. This means both unlimited access to all the facets of industrial society and a willingness to use an adequate portion of its benefits to encourage all who will do so to extend their general education.

4

Automation—Cybernation

The editor of the *Saturday Review*, Norman Cousins, has contended that two fears are stalking America: automation and peace. The first fear stems from the fact that automation could take over the tasks of more than half our labor force. The second from the fact that peace could bring economic disaster to an economy heavily dependent upon military preparation. That the two fears are related becomes obvious. We have become dependent on the national defense program for maintaining present levels of employment; but at the same time we are insistent upon the use of every means available for increasing efficiency and cutting costs. For our economy this has come to mean automation.

Our concern with the burgeoning phenomenon of automation derives from its implications for the kind of life it will make possible or necessary rather than from its contribution to industrial efficiency, important as the latter may be; it is with its significance for society and the individual who, theoretically at least, is intended to benefit from the automation process.

Whether automation is a new phenomenon or merely a continuation of other forms of mechanization is not important, despite the heat engendered by the discussion of the question. What is important is whether our competence in dealing with the products and instruments of industrial revolution as we have known it, has equipped us to cope adequately with what has been frequently termed "the second industrial revolution." In automation we are confronted with machines which are very much like the human brain, and thus we are faced with a revolu-

56

tion not only in economics but in philosophy as well.

The situation and conditions created by automation present philosophical and theological problems. Automation is a technological problem, of course, and its processes are beyond the range of theological concern; nevertheless the extent of its use and the rapidity of its adoption as a process, having run far ahead of our capacities to adapt to its consequences, have profound theological implications.

What Are Automation and Cybernation?

The general facts concerning automation stagger the imagination of those reared in a less complicated industrial society, and these facts have become widely known. Data relating to computers, transfer systems, the uncanny skills coincident with cybernation, the numbers disemployed in various types of plants, etc., are all subjects of everyday conversation. Many popular journals and weekend magazine sections have carried articles describing the consequences of this rapidly spreading phenomenon. A few of them have attempted to be reassuring and suggest that despite temporary discomfort things are going to be much better in the future.

Definitions of automation are almost as numerous as their authors, but basically they incorporate similar underlying components. They range from Peter Drucker's "the use of machines to run machines" to A. H. Raskin's "automation is the harnessing of the electronic brains to mechanical muscles" to those which incorporate the manifold processes involved in the broad gamut covered by the theme. Such definitions would include the integration of automatic machinery with automatic materials-handling equipment, the development of electronic computing machines capable of storing, counting, recording, surveying and selecting data, and the capacity to perform simple and highly complex mathematical operations with great rapidity. These capabilities all involve the use of "feed-back" control devices to supervise and control the process flow. Because it incorporates this feed-back process, automation is more than mechanization.

The U. S. Department of Labor defines automation as "the partial or full replacement of workers as a source of energy and/or control by machines." Automation is a way of thinking as much as a way of doing; it has become a way of organizing and analyzing production, and has heightened concern with the production processes as a system.

Cybernation involves attaching a computer to the automated machine, thus making possible the storing and evaluation of data and a corresponding expansion of the automated machine's function.

IMPLICATIONS AND BENEFITS

So much has been written about the dire consequences of automation that its benefits have tended to be obscured. High on the list of beneficial consequences is the potential for dignifying human life. The human machine is much too valuable to be wasted on some of the processes to which it has been applied. Human dignity, which in theological terms is the product of God's creation and can be expressed in the poetic biblical affirmation "Thou hast made him little less than God" (Ps. 8 : 5), can be greatly enhanced by the much-feared phenomenon of automation. Surely anything which assists man in achieving the fuller dimensions of which he is capable must be in keeping with the Creator's purpose. Can it be anything but destructive to have a potentially active mind dulled into inactivity by a routine action involving no decisions or judgments?

One finds abundant basis for identification with either camp, both with those fearful of large scale unemployment and economic slump and with those who regard with optimism the increasing adoption of automated methods. If there is one aspect which can be beneficial to both sides of the argument, however, it is the assurance that whatever direction the economy takes, there is going to be information available at a rapid rate, which will better enable us to plan policies and thus mitigate the danger of a slump. Capacity to amass the necessary data can give direction to whatever course is needed, and thus constitutes one of the plus factors in the emergence of the whole phenomenon of automation.

Another implication of the growing acceptance of automation is the impetus accorded the development of increased accuracy and clarity of both thought and action. We are referring here not only to the consequences for the advanced nations but also to those for the less developed nations as they attempt to leap over centuries of experience of industrialized nations. For both, however, the hit-or-miss, trial-and-error process which has been accepted as a part of the earlier industrializing experience is no longer a viable option where more reliable resources are available. Accuracy in machine operations and computations is indispensable in a technical society. This means the ability to read and make mathematical calculations. Hence for the less developed nations, already handicapped through inadequate educational programs, the need accelerates and the pressure mounts. If they are to compete in a world increasingly technological, traits and values evolved through centuries must quickly be replaced or modified. Thus automation, the newest symbol of the technological society, forces the reorganization of national life.

A concomitant benefit may be the fact that workers will be encouraged to think of the plant as a whole, to see the correlation of their participation more readily than has been possible heretofore. Social gain could be the result. Teamwork assumes increased importance, and the results of coordinated activity supplant those of individuals. In many industries teamwork is already indispensable under present arrangements, but automation promises to increase the practice. What the long-term consequences of this trend may be cannot be fully foreseen, but it seems likely that attitudes of both management and labor toward the whole production process will be altered. "A new work morality may arise in place of a morality based on unit worth concept. . . . Worth will be judged on the basis of organization and planning and the continuously smooth functioning of the operation. As the individual worker loses his importance and is replaced by the team greater value is placed on the operating unit as a whole. The traditional individualism of American society may soon be replaced."[1] One man's contribution is still important, but it is submerged in the cooperative action of the larger producing unit. Thus whether the worker philosophizes or not over the meaning of his new relationships, he is compelled to know something of the meaning of mutual dependence and responsible coordination.

The father of the term "automation," John Diebold, in taking account of the fact that heretofore machines had to be designed within the limits of the operator's potential skills, says: "With the introduction of the new concept in technology of self-regulating systems it is no longer necessary to design the production process around the limitations of human skills."[2] The undulating curve of human capacities, fatigue or freshness, no longer need determine the planning for production, and the factor in labor thus diminishes in importance. The fact that productive processes can be maintained continuously with predictable regularity has other significance besides the easing of human strain. It means that the shift system, with occasional breaks in the operation where one or more shifts are "down," becomes even less economical due to the heightened expense of the machinery and the necessity for deriving maximum performance from it.

SOCIAL COSTS

What is being said here is that it is easier, perhaps, to extrapolate the benefits than the social costs of automation. Much of the anxiety about automation is based upon the scale of threatened unemployment. Many economists believe that we actually have nothing to fear "in the long run."[3] Ultimately, they say, more jobs will be created, as has been the case with other innovations in the industrial revolution preceding the present one. This optimistic expectation seems to overlook the fact that the kinds of jobs being created require on the part of a very large percentage of our work force a level of skill necessary to earn a living in an automated society which they will not be able to achieve in the forseeable future. No one can predict how many people are going to be needed for the work force in twenty years, but all present statistics indicate that jobs are being eliminated faster than people can be trained for new work and faster than the economy can accommodate the numbers of young people coming into the labor market. It is this piling up of excess labor, both from those "disemployed" and those who are unemployable because of age or insufficient training, which creates for an industrial nation a philosophical, moral, and ethical problem.

While it is recognized that any figures relating to employment are liable to quick change and may subject the written record to the charge of being outdated, it is nevertheless estimated that during the 1960s twenty-six million new young workers will need to be absorbed into the employment rolls.[4] A drop of 10 to 15 per cent in the wage force in steel, autos, transportation, and of course even more than that in coal, has not been offset by increased employment in the automated industries which are expanding most rapidly. It is this "short-run" situation which is the special concern of organized labor and which constitutes a serious dilemma for all who are concerned with opportunities for work. And who isn't? At this writing (1965) about 5 per cent of the labor force is unemployed, and something approximating this figure has been the unemployment rate for an extended period.

One of the basic differences of the present period from the past is the rate at which human effort is being displaced. Earlier forms of mechanical progress downgraded the job and created a large number of semiskilled functions to which existing human capacities were readily adapted. Automation eliminates manipulative tasks and transfers the direct human control functions to an intermediate and higher order. Machine operators are displaced by the technician and the engineer, making it difficult for a large number of workers to adapt to the new job situation. The result will be a serious downgrading of those workers into residual low-order jobs. Some individuals can be retrained for the more complex types of manipulation. For many in our society, however, a new set of values will have to emerge. We say "many" because there are some who have long contended that human need and the provision of humane services are primary concerns of society itself. In another era, as an earlier industrial revolution was in sight, John Stuart Mill, one of the most perceptive political economists in the western tradition, commented: "There cannot be a more legitimate object of the legislator's care than the interest of those who are thus sacrificed to the gain of their fellow citizens and posterity—those displaced by changing methods of production."[5]

GROUNDS OF CONCERN

Some would contend that whatever the consequences, the victims of any down-turn need not be as badly damaged as were the victims of the earlier industrial revolution. The existence of supplemental unemployment benefits, the thirty-hour week, retraining programs, minimizing of accidents, better health resources, etc., have cushioned the shock of the industrial revolution in our period. Equally beneficial supports will presumably be made available as automation expands. The combination of humanitarianism, efficiency, and the need for stability will serve beneficially. They may provide poor consolation for those already suffering the ill effects of automation, but the extent of suffering may not be as great as that which characterized other innovations.

Organized labor has been profoundly exercised and anxious concerning the extension of automation in industries now substantially organized and also in those not yet organized. Management contends that the introduction of automated processes is required for efficiency and is the only means of remaining competitive. Organized labor naturally looks at the issue from the viewpoint of the numbers disemployed. The bargaining which ensues does not deal with the question of increased efficiency but with that of the human consequences. In the dispute over dismissal of firemen on diesel locomotives, for example, there was little disposition to deny the disposability of the fireman's role except as a safety factor. Major attention was focused on what would happen to the thousands of men then employed who in many instances could not be trained for other kinds of work. The railroad dispute also brought into focus other issues in addition to the problem of income maintenance for dismissed firemen. It caused the industry and the nation at large to look at the entire industrial complex and to ask where responsibility lay for the major changes required by the introduction of laborsaving machinery. The introduction of the diesel engine may not be exactly described as a part of the automation process, but it symbolizes the direction taken and decisions required where large scale disemployment has occurred. It has become possible and necessary for labor and management to look at the consequences of the production process of which they are both a part. This new labor-management relationship will be discussed in a later chapter.

Erich Fromm is but one of many who fear that automation tends to isolate man psychologically from his colleagues. He contends that there is loss of companionship and camaraderie on the job, which affects those workers who are reduced to a "push-button" existence. Another analyst of automation, James Bright, says: "I do not find that the upgrading effect has occurred to anywhere near the extent that it is often assumed. On the contrary I find that automation has reduced the skilled requirements of the operating force and occasionally the entire factory force including the maintenance organization."[6] To this we may add Bruno Bettelheim's comment that the modern workman in a rapidly changing technological social order is very much like a prisoner in a concentration camp who is told daily that he may be thrown at any moment into the yawning mouth of the giant rock crusher he is required to feed with the labor of his bare hands.[7]

It is not without significance that one of the most optimistic advocates of automation, Paul Einzig, concludes his glowing praise of its possibilities with these words: "It will be perhaps the most difficult of all the difficult problems arising from automation to insure that mankind in its impatient drive for material betterment does not lose its soul."[8]

CONSEQUENCES TO VALUE AND BELIEF STRUCTURE

As suggested earlier, some of the most pronounced effects of automation will be on the values and beliefs currently held in much of our society. An individualistic religion is confronted with the fact that only a corporate solution is possible for attaining the well-being which a healthy society requires. The processes of automation require an integration of manufacturing organizations, of community life, of buying practices and of many current patterns of life. These forces cannot be allowed to proceed unguided and independent of the common good. Government action becomes an increasingly necessary consequence. Undoubtedly the charge of socialism will be leveled, but the very term itself becomes irrelevant and inconsequential in the face of the fact that an ever-increasing centralization in industry makes necessary a corresponding action on the part of government to deal with the consequences of centralization. The implications of increased concentration of government power for providing balance and giving a direction to the integration of the total economy increase proportionately the necessity for participation in government on an intelligent basis; the alternative is abdication to the world of George Orwell's 1984. Whether a heightening of educational reorganization and redirection can occur in time is a speculative question. We are thus faced with moral and educational issues involving society in a reorientation of its traditional values.

This is not a matter of concern to any one nation alone. Automation merely reflects what is occurring on a worldwide scale and gives accelerated impetus to the process of world unification. Of this process Gustave Weigel says: "As Teilhard de Chardin supposed, our evolution at the present time is to an ever greater solidarity of mankind. We are moving to become a single species-subject of action. Individuals can no longer consider themselves in isolation in the stage of evolution which we have entered. All individuals become closer in action and —belong to all other individuals."[9] It would appear that the technology of automation is proving to be one of the major factors in fostering the solidarity which Teilhard de Chardin predicted.

The problem of leisure will be dealt with more inclusively in chapter 12, but since the processes of automation contribute increasingly both to the opportunities and to the problem of leisure, we take note of that fact here. Whether automation provides opportunities for increasing dignity and fulfillment of man's creative purpose constitutes one of the major philosophical and ethical issues of our time. The biblically oriented culture under which most of us have been reared and which has been (correctly or incorrectly) designated by Max Weber "the Protestant ethic" insists that work is an essential part of human existence. Traditionally, we have been taught that the pain of work brings the pleasure of rest and accomplishment. We have become imbued with the conviction that our reward is to come as the result of the sweat of our brow. Only if one works hard may he enjoy rest, leisure, and pleasure. Now we have a society in which extended hard manual or clerical labor will be unlikely for an increasing number. It becomes apparent that many will have to be rewarded for not working hard or for working in ways which are not traditionally regarded as work.

What this possibility would seem to suggest is that work may not be identified with earning, but that there are other forms of reward, for example, the earning of time to do the things one much wants to do. The increase in wisdom, the capacity for creativity, will increasingly have to be developed for their own sakes because the very nature of the human psyche requires development to prevent disintegration. Those who are responsible for the increase of automation or are caught in its seemingly inevitable extension are thus rediscovering a fundamentally spiritual problem with which the writers of the creation story in the Garden of Eden dealt.

Earlier it was stated that we are finding ourselves plunged into the necessity of devising or discerning a new set of living standards. We have become able to produce enough food, shelter, clothing, and medicine for all, even though we have

not achieved an acceptable standard for distribution. But automation is pressing us at the distribution level as well. It is true
that at the moment we have some thirty to forty million people
living below what is a commonly accepted standard of decency,
but this deficiency has now been lifted to the level of a national concern. Either the needs of all will be met, or the automation process itself will be challenged. The facts that the
process of automation is capable of providing those minimal
requirements and that the other four-fifths who are living above
the minimal standard and profiting from the contributions of
automation will probably not seek to curtail it place the total
society in a new frame.

The compounded effect of this greatly improved capacity for
production may be the complete triumph of the enterprise and
may at the same time contain the disavowal of some of the
very values which created it. This, it seems to some, is ironically
the era into which we are moving. A *Reader's Digest* article on the
consequences of automation says: "The new automation of
the intelligent machine is a benefactor that will help us grow
and help our way of life to survive."[10] If the writer means by
"our way of life" an adequacy of goods, he may be right; but
the structure of society under which those goods are produced
will be greatly changed, and marked by sharp deviations from
what we think of as our way of life.

Religious and ethical pioneers have long wrestled with the problem of distributive justice. The industrial revolution made necessary the breakup of a feudal society which placed a premium on
class and disparity of income. Industrialization, with its concomitant necessity for spreading buying power, and the emergence of
democracy fostered a measure of egalitarianism, partly in self-
defense and partly as a result of an awareness of the biblical
commands for sharing, mutual aid, etc.

With automation the concept of buying power takes on substantial new importance. Not only will some people probably have to
be paid though not "working," but the gains from automation will
have to be spread much more widely as a means of guaranteeing
the continuing use of machines which cannot be laid off without

serious harm of the economic structure itself.

Frictional unemployment will have to be reduced through a series of regulatory actions by central decision-making agencies. It seems inevitable that an automated economy will increasingly approximate one integrated output plant. Centralization of decision-making is one of its concomitants; and thereby comes the correlative expansion of bureaucracy. This is affirmed on the hypothesis that the efficiency required by automation—the continuous flow of raw materials and finished product—cannot be assured in any other way.

In rethinking the values for our society as influenced by automation, an allocation of resources to service industries, to health, education, highways, and many other components would seem to be called for. There is no surplus of workers in the areas of social service, where the remedies of society's ills are most required. Whatever our apprehensions about machines taking care of machines, etc., automation cannot take care of children and those who are sick, for example; it may, however, help diagnose their ailments and reduce the incidence of disease.

Presumably no extensive apologia is needed for including the theme of religion and automation in a discussion of ethics and economics. Whatever affects human life is included in the concern of religion. We have not attempted to formalize the theological implications of automation but rather to indicate some of its consequences to persons and to society. Justice, freedom, and order have been central concerns of the more thoughtful and religious-minded persons in our day. The attainment of these ends has been both accelerated and jeopardized in industrial society. Freedom to learn has enabled men to discern societal structures which enhance concern for justice and order. If automation releases man still further with freedom from drudgery and enables him to create an order which is equitable and just, it will have helped provide him with a new dignity. Within this dignity he may better realize the potential given him by his Creator.

Welfare and Our Industrial Economy

The evolution of welfare* is an index of our industrial economy, each stage of it emerging as an outgrowth of industrial development. Poverty and calamity to individual and group life were at least as severe in preindustrial periods, but not until the advent in industry of advanced technology was welfare organized in a systematic way. Whereas in an agrarian society poverty and calamity were met by the family or the community, from the resources of the soil and out of a bond of mutual obligation, industrialism altered and in a large measure removed both the resource and the bond.

Poverty is not the only cause for welfare activities, but the two are so inseparable that it is mandatory for a consideration of the change in welfare to follow a chapter contending that reduction of poverty tests the validity of our industrial economy.

Every modern nation has become a welfare state. Despite the attempt of some people to blame this upon socialism or communism, the fact remains that it is impossible to have a modern industrial state without its becoming at the same time a welfare state. Communist welfare had its inception in the theory of society which underlay the Marxist-Leninist experiment in the Soviet Union. The state from the beginning was the guarantor of minimal decency, even though in the process it was necessary to deprive the beneficiary of the opportunity to express his convictions to the rest of the body politic in the form of a voting

* As used here the term connotes the meeting of needs for which individuals and groups cannot of themselves make adequate provision. This would include concerns related to mental and physical health, income maintenance, family, employment, care of children and the aged, etc.

franchise. For those nations whose economy is designated as capitalist, on the other hand, the provisions for the well-being of its citizens derive from the very individualism which is at the heart of the capitalist theory. For generations it was assumed that a person in need had only himself to blame; but the humanitarianism stemming from Hebrew-Christian origins still extended compassion toward the injured or deprived. Eventually it became clear that many thus affected were the victims of circumstances over which they had no control. This is presumably the meaning of that major watershed in American life known as the Great Depression. We finally awakened to the fact that industrious, hard-working, aspiring, virtuous people could be trapped and mangled in economic circumstances not of their own making; capitalist welfare thereby came into being.

ORIGINS OF PRESENT WELFARE SITUATION

A seemingly endless and inexhaustible new continent afforded the American people the luxury of Darwinian and Spencerian presuppositions about man's ability to survive. This thesis did not go unchallenged through the series of depressions which periodically deflated the buoyancy of America's industrial economy, but not until the greatest depression of them all, beginning with the stock market crash of 1929 and running through most of the decade of the 1930s, were Americans convinced that the very system which was providing for them so abundantly could not, unchanged, guarantee its working population the ability to purchase the abundant products of its fields and factories. It is more than coincidence that the most comprehensive welfare act in American history, the Social Security Act of 1935, and the National Labor Relations Act became law in the same year. The enactment of these two pieces of legislation was a recognition of the fact that only some form of income maintenance provided by the federal government could stabilize the economy, and that labor should be guaranteed the right to bargain collectively on behalf of income maintenance for its members. Both of these actions were designed to stabilize incomes and to reduce the vagaries of factors which disturbed the regularity of income; and although both enactments were the products of industrialism and its economy, they became the foundation stones of a national welfare program.

The process by which an agricultural nation became industrial is too well known to require repetition here. Almost equally well known are the adaptations made necessary for first-generation immigrants coming from Europe directly to industrial plants, or second-generation immigrants coming off the farms into industrial employment. The history of welfare in the United States parallels the evolution of the city as an industrial center, at least until the decade of the 1930s made it finally apparent even to rural America that its surpluses were no longer temporary and that it could no longer accommodate the population then hoping to make its living from the land. The farm produce and population surplus became acute following the mighty efforts to increase production for World War I; the agricultural depression thus antedated the industrial by almost a decade. For a short period during World War II there was again prosperity in agriculture; thereafter the long decline continued, interrupted briefly by the Korean War. Local aid had long since been exhausted, and the federal government by means of the Social Security Act and a long series of agricultural stabilization programs has maintained minimum adequacy of income for a high percentage of persons living on the land.

The immigrant settling in the cities faced a different but related problem. The factory, unlike his rural European family, offered no guarantees of protection, and his community security was undermined. Other factors were similarly important, however, in changing his way of life: regimentation and discipline created a stress; the tools which he used were not his own, and he became subject to the direction and control of others, including the very machine to which he was tied; and finally, his very place of residence became uncertain because of variation in the need for workers. Such elements combined to cause traumatic experiences for those who had come out of a totally different type of existence. Both at the time and in retrospect it seemed the newcomers were subjected to excessive hardships. In reality this was true, but when compared with their former state, for many at least the contrast was not unfavorable. "When we think of the transition from European peasant to American industrial worker, we are often comparing a run-down rural economy with an expanding industrial economy. It is surprising that life in the urban industrial setting did not seem wonderful by contrast."[1]

A good deal of anguish has been expressed over the physical and psychological consequences of this transition from a rural "mind-set" to that of urban existence. The pain of adjustment was real, and undoubtedly much more could have been done to ease the transition had we comprehended its nature and causes. At the same time it must be recognized that the experiences were a part of the metamorphosis of our industrial economy itself. Philosopher Charles Frankel says: "A great many of the problems that face our welfare programs arise as the result of the migration of rural people to the cities. . . . Successive waves of immigrants, almost all of them with rural backgrounds, have made the history of our cities. Now it is the Latin American and the Negro; a generation ago it was the Italian. Only the Jew on the whole has brought an urban background with him. Most of the problems of urban welfare programs arise in that context. This fact is not a fault in our system. It is the sign, the symptom, and the consequence of the industrial growth of our system and of its creation of increasing opportunity. Adjustment to urban life is a problem, in other words, like the problem of education, not like the problem of crime."[2]

NEW CIRCUMSTANCES BRING ADAPTATIONS

Income insecurity and psychological adjustments to new types of work were only two problems confronting the industrial worker, whether a recent immigrant or a native reared in the industrial milieu, between World Wars I and II when we shifted from an agricultural to a predominantly industrial economy. Among the other experiences tending to strain, confuse, disturb, or warp the new urban worker was the uncertainty about the type of work to be expected of him regardless of whatever he may have done before. No longer did his position in the community depend upon his skills, for these may be only temporarily demanded; tradition became of little significance, while change has become omni-present; family stability has become uncertain and the nuclear family—parents and children—increased the ease of mobility. Being less and less in demand for industrial productivity, youth are increasingly rejected and are finding it more difficult to earn even supplemental income for recreation; marriage for many is thus necessarily postponed. In an aging population in which the number of those over 65 has quadrupled since 1900, the people who must be taken out of the work force to make room for younger workers but who yet have substantial productive capacity constitute one of the most pressing problems. Another is the broken family which cannot be supported by the parent in whose custody the children remain. Here the problem is obviously not simply the custody and support of children, enormous though this problem be, but the accessibility of divorce where cohesive-ness of family life is not a requisite as in agricultural living. Still another is the exhausting pressure of the assembly line, the pace of the machine and the herding effect on multitudes of others regimented by the demands of production schedules. And the list could be greatly amplified. The most important thing is that counterinfluences were set in motion, and welfare programs designed to offset each deleterious phase were instituted.

Wilensky and Lebeaux contend that "the central theme running through our picture of urban industrial America is this: we can perhaps view most of the targets of complaint as transitional, passing results of industrialization under 19th century conditions. Coercive recruitment and painful transformation of peasant im-migrants into urban industrial workers; the insecurities of the factory system; the uncushioned impact of the dilution and obso-lescence of skills; the de-humanization of work (whether through back-breaking labor or machine-paced repetitive routine); class polarization; community disintegration—these decline as eco-nomic growth continues. A new welfare bureaucratic society emerges —more stable than its early form suggests, richer and more varied than men had dreamed when they observed the harsh, initial de-velopment period."[3]

It is popular in some circles to bemoan the suffering and agony accompanying the readjustments which technology forces upon individuals, families, and communities. Because society has not traveled this way before, there are few built-in protective devices; they have to be constructed after the ailments, agonies, and misfortunes occur. The very existence of such problems often induces effective and constructive social change, since activities on behalf of their improvement become integral parts of the system which caused them. This has apparently not been the attitude either of those most basically involved in developing a technological society or, sad to note, not always the attitude of those engaged in ameliorating the consequences of industrialism.

As Charles Frankel suggested, our inability to see the larger process of welfare as a sign of the success of the industrial system rather than as an evidence of its failures, is one of the obtacles to the advancement of human welfare.[4] This is not to condone its ills, but to accept them as a part of the price to be paid for innovations. The tragedy appears when people refuse to face the fact that the disorganizing and destructive elements can be remedied within the framework of the same society which created them, and *mirabile dictu* the same forces of technological progress are capable of providing an economy within which its casualties can be rescued.

We might use as illustrations of our capacity to adapt constructively to a problem created by our society the development of treatment for the aged, or the broken home, or of the rising incidence of mental disease resulting from the individual's inability to find his place in a fast-shifting culture. Juvenile delinquency illustrates the total situation with special aptness. It is a far cry from the day when small children tended spools in cloth mills, providing the cheap labor on which fortunes were made and funds accumulated to invest in enterprises in other lands. Not only were the warped bodies and minds of children the reason for eliminating this condition, but industry required more sophisticated skills, which in turn required training programs and an educational system adequate to provide both technical and managerial direction. Juvenile delinquency and its coordinate condition, the high school dropout, present our generation with a situation paralleling the attack on child labor a century ago. Not only are lives being corroded through inactivity and the lives of still others endangered through the misdirected activity of youth out of school and unemployed, but in addition society as a whole is losing the potentially constructive contribution of these young people. Given the requisite training and the assurance that they can make a useful contribution, they are capable of being responsible producers and consumers in our society. All of this places upon us the obligation to create and conduct the institutions and programs which can foster successful adaptation of teen-age youth into the total economy. As public education became a requirement of a democracy and a great gamut of public services emerged to provide for the needs of people gathered together in new forms of communal life, so is our type of urban society now required to find a solution to the unused talents and potentially destructive forces let loose where human energies are unchanneled. Instead of such a solution being a grudging concession to troublesome youth, it becomes a primary mandate of the modern era.

A corollary of the contention that many forms of casualty attendant upon industrialization are the result of its successes and therefore are remediable, is our acceptance of the fact that such casualties no longer are branded as personal failures. In an era of burgeoning industry, of at least periodically unlimited markets and enough mouths to consume all agricultural products, there were jobs enough to go around. Adjustments to a new country and irregularity of employment created only temporary casualties. Meanwhile, there was a growing disposition to express in formal institutions a belief inherent in the American ideal that individuals were entitled to a minimal standard of living as a part of their citizenship. What Locke and John Stuart Mill had affirmed in the eighteenth and nineteenth centuries, and what Augustine and Aquinas had contended centuries earlier, had now become a reality because for the first time an industrial economy could make it possible. On this issue Thomas Gladwin comments: "Obviously the right to a decent manner of life remained an academic issue until sufficient goods were available to supply the needs of the bulk of the people. However, a high rate of productivity does not in itself guarantee that those who remain poor will be considered to have a right to expect the help of others not so poor. As we watch the steady rise of a standard of living in the United States it is easy to forget that for many years this rise was not accompanied by an attitude we now take as axiomatic: that anyone who is really willing to work has a right to share in the general affluence."[5]

This extraordinary combination—a common respect for humanity born of the Hebrew-Christian tradition, the Renaissance, the Enlightenment, and the democratic tradition—has helped to bring about and is itself brought to flower by a society capable of providing for that need. Gradually but firmly the realization penetrated Western life and America in particular that the unfortunate things occurring to men, inhibiting their opportunities for the good life, were not necessarily their own fault. The poor had known this but had lacked the organization for demanding and the articulateness for expressing it. Now for the first time the middle class became aware of the fact, and thanks to widepread education and a grounding in the traditions of a democratic society and an ethical religion, they refused to remain inert. The result was the burgeoning of welfare programs, for the most part instituted within the lifetime of those born before World War I.

The evolution of welfare and its history is a rich and wholesome phenomenon in the life of this and other Western nations. Our concern however, is not primarily with its history but with the modifications required as it kept pace with the emergence of our industrial economy.

One consequence of the shift in attitude toward welfare is the confusion centering about the word itself. For many people it connotes relief, the elimination of suffering and the provision of minimal sustenance until such time as the recipient can "get on his feet again." Obviously, this is a carry-over from the era when it was expected that one should by his own efforts transcend temporary mishaps or misfortunes. For others it may connote social security, supplementary unemployment benefits, and the pension funds of corporations which benefit both management and labor.

It is significant that today labor-management controversies center increasingly on the extent of those benefits rather than primarily on wages. The pension factors and the various forms of government assistance designed to provide income maintenance have become so extensive that in a comparatively short time the latter came to be considered less as "welfare" than as a "right" of the citizen.

CHANGING CONCEPTS OF WELFARE

One of the consequences of large-scale support and insurance programs, whether privately or publicly initiated, is the blurring if not elimination of distinctions between what is welfare and what are the standard programs for meeting common needs. In a single generation governmental agencies have not only been initiated but have become accepted as a permanent and normal part of ongoing life. Such has been the rapid evolution in our acceptance of the welfare principle. What was born of an emergency now continues because the emergency itself is permanent. No index of this phenomenon is more striking than the proliferation of schools of social work in most major public universities and many private ones. Almost within a generation a new and highly self-conscious profession has come into being; its standards have been articulated, and its place as an integral part of a technological society has been established.* Although the private agencies, called into existence originally by the phenomenon of immigration and the casualties of individual and family life in an urban society, still remain highly useful and frequently pioneer in special kinds of work, for the most part welfare has become predominantly a public responsibility. The scale of this evolution has greatly contributed to the obsolescence of the old concept of welfare. "It seems likely that distinctions between welfare and other types of social institutions will become more and more blurred. Under continuing industrialization all institutions will be oriented toward and evaluated in terms of social welfare aims. The 'welfare state' will become the 'welfare society' and both will be more reality than epithet."[6]

GOVERNMENT ROLE

Special attention will be given later to the increasing role of government in our economy, but nothing illustrates this trend

* There are 96,696 persons indicated as "Social and Welfare Workers" in the United States. (Source: Statistical abstract of the U. S., 1963, p. 232)

more vividly than increasing governmental involvement in welfare. We are here using the term "government" in its inclusive sense, designating all local, state, and national units concerned with public welfare. Space permits no complete listing of welfare areas in which government is involved, but even a partial list is indicative of the scope: old age and survivors' disability insurance, public assistance, child welfare, vocational rehabilitation, public health, veteran's services, unemployment insurance and employment service, federal court social services and federal correctional system, Indian welfare services, housing programs and income security programs for railroad workers.

Each of these agencies and programs is dependent upon tax support and federal participation. Many of these programs parallel or are conducted in relation to the state governments, which in turn may have their own programs supplemented by federal funds. The compounded effect of governmental participation in welfare at all levels results in an expenditure of approximately 11.5 per cent of our gross national product. "Even where private charity is involved directly with the poor," says Edgar May, "frequently much of the cost of that involvement is paid by the government. For example, I was surprised to learn that in my own state, New York, of 57 million dollars spent in 1961 by private institutions for children and by child-caring agencies, 42 million dollars came from taxpayers. I wonder if most people realize this."[7]*

No small part of the welfare costs of our time result from technological changes. In the long run those changes may be beneficial in the sense that they create new jobs in types of industry perhaps not even envisaged now. Who should bear the transitional costs? Roy Blough says that an "approach to reducing the rate of labor displacement is to place more of the social cost of a technological change on the benefiting employer than is the case when he bears none of the cost of unemployment or the obsolescence of skills. . . . This would encourage the employer to find ways of keeping on the worker, would result in socially more accurate balancing of

* Social Welfare Expenditures 1961–62:
  Total public (federal, state, local)................$62,496.7 mill
  Total private (health, medical care, income
      maintenance and welfare) ....33,418 mill
  (Source: *Social Security Bulletins*, Vol. 26, No. 11, Nov. 1963)

the benefits and costs of technological progress. . . ."[8]

Attempts have been made to estimate the extent of returns from welfare programs. It is not solely a drain on the taxpayer, as some have implied. Consequences in the form of stabilization of the economy and maintenance of the health of present and future workers are obviously incalculable, as is also the reduction in disease and in the costs of crime. That the latter is very great is incontestable, but that it might have been infinitely greater is also a very real likelihood. High on the list of factors justifying the welfare programs now extant are the minimization of public restlessness and the reduction of turmoil and revolt. This was a conscious aim of one of the earliest major welfare programs, that of Germany under Bismarck. It probably forestalled a Marxist revolution; there is good reason to believe that the seething and incipient revolt in the United States during the Great Depression was deterred or deflected by the programs of WPA, PWA, and others initiated during the administration of Franklin Roosevelt and conducted by his trouble-shooting social worker, Harry Hopkins.

Though education is not a part of welfare in the sense in which it is used here, it is appropriate to include a short reference to it because of its implications for welfare. In our society it is almost axiomatic that education is the means for elevating a person and those dependent on him. By this means likelihood of having to depend on others is presumably lessened. In recent years the importance of education as a means of facilitating job adjustments, transfers, and training has mounted greatly. This we have come to accept. Not so well known or understood is the benefit to society at large through reduction of the drain on the public finances where education has been made more widely available. Professor Theodore W. Schultz in his study *The Economic Value of Education* indicates how education provides both psychological values to the individual and serves to reduce "the inequality in the personal distribution of income."[9] A concomitant of active participation in the educative process is the benefit to the economic growth of the nation. Schultz's study and the others upon which it draws conclude that for its own health and welfare the nation cannot skimp its support of public education.

EXPANDED PRIVATE CONCERN

No discussion of welfare in our economy would be complete without taking substantial account of the programs of both management and labor. Whatever the reason for management's introduction of extensive welfare activities, they have provided manifold benefits. Some have been initiated at the instigation and insistence of labor and others—voluntary in many instances—by the companies themselves. The latter's objectives have been: to increase the tenure of the workers, to reduce absenteeism, and to heighten loyalty to the employing organization. And like other programs of welfare emanating from government sources, they have served to stabilize the economy by providing income maintenance.*

Sharp contests have arisen over the administration of these funds, the charge being made by labor that when they are administered by management, they may be used as instruments of pressure to inhibit resistance from the employees in the event that the labor organization decides forceful action against the company to be in order. Unions have preferred that the pension and welfare funds be independent of management.

One of the paradoxical phenomena of our time is the extraordinary financial power developed by unions in the administration of their own pension, strike, and welfare funds. The size of these funds has approached dimensions sufficient to influence the stock or bond market in which they have been invested, and misuse of some of them has created sensational court cases. Management of the funds has contributed to the rapid metamorphosis in union leadership. Obviously labor organizers are rarely if ever qualified to invest and manage these large sums of money themselves, so that financial specialists become indispensable auxiliary aids of the unions. It is not surprising that some unions have become protagonists of a conservative philosophy, since future income of their

* Pensions, sick pay, hospitalization, sabbatical leaves, insurance programs, and many other benefits traditionally identified with welfare have entered the employer-employee relationship, both to stabilize conditions within the organization and to assure continuity of purchasing power. The concept of welfare and purchasing capacity or income maintenance has become one of the newer phenomena whereby industrialism seeks to guarantee the stability of its economy.

retired workers is dependent upon both the rate of investment and their hourly wage.

EMERGING NATIONS AND WELFARE

The distance from the highly developed welfare programs of industrial nations, with their guarantees of minimal existence for all, to the nations emerging from agricultural life or tribal customs is to be reckoned not in income per capita but in the centuries to be hurdled. Emerging leadership in the underdeveloped nations must give promise of greater physical advantages and security.

Instead of waiting for the evolutionary process by which industrially advanced nations developed their welfare programs, they seek to institute them earlier. They have the advantage of perspective and the experimentation of the "developed" nations.[10] The Soviet Union has capitalized on this necessity for providing minimal security, even though by the standards of underdeveloped nations it is among the most advanced. Here, however, a factor has to be reckoned with which is less evident in some developing nations. In conversation with Russian people one hears repeatedly the statement "Though we do not have all that we would like, it is so much more than we formerly had that we are grateful for the gains made." It has also been hypothesized that the Russian people for centuries have lived in an atmosphere of expectation, dominated by an eschatology which assured something good eventually. The great cost in suffering and sacrifice by which the nation carried through its industrialization program could be borne because of the history of suffering which was at long last to be relieved. Nations which have lived adjacent to or under colonial domination by other industrialized nations may have a better idea of the cost to be incurred in their development before the full welfare program can be assured them.

The new nations so recently elevated to self-consciousness may appreciate less well the cost entailed in achieving a level where the state can guarantee freedom from poverty and want. One demand characterizes the populations of nations at either end of the scale, whether the most advanced or the most primitive; it is the insistence that at least minimal opportunities for making a living or maintaining existence shall prevail.

Gunnar Myrdal contends that concern for achieving the welfare society has been a factor in heightening nationalistic awareness and preoccupation.[11] Each nation desires to preserve the levels of individual security achieved by its welfare programs. Citizens suspect that assistance to other nations might (a) reduce the benefits already available at home, (b) impair the nation's economy, and (c) aid a potential competitor. Paradoxically, at the very time when nations are being brought into greater proximity through faster means of communication, they are drawn into greater self-centeredness. Determination to preserve all the advantages accruing from their economy tends to render them increasingly insensitive to the needs of other nations which would like to become welfare societies also. This theme of Myrdal will occupy our attention more extensively in a later section on foreign aid. We cite it here, however, because of this puzzling paradox. Understanding the human propensity toward self-preservation can quickly explain this national phenomenon. Yet the ironical fact is that the ability to maintain the level of welfare experienced by advanced nations hinges in large measure upon their capacity to raise the levels of well-being on the part of aspiring and less developed lands. But a nation is not an individual, and its collective sense rarely coincides with the enlightened understanding of its more sensitive and comprehending constituents. Nations do not voluntarily relinquish the advantage of their advanced welfare stage, partly because the impairment rarely falls equally on the total citizenry. At the same time, nations currently emerging from a stage of tribalism can hardly comprehend the costs and the generations of time required to move into industrial society. Neither can they grasp what is involved in achieving a level of welfare in which such humane provisions as characterize modern "welfare states" have been attained. Nevertheless the harmonization of these divergent understandings and contrasting economies is a mandate upon the industrialized welfare society.

U. S. Agriculture in Domestic and World Economy

Next to defense the largest Congressional appropriations are for agriculture. For more than forty years agriculture has been one of the most consistently aggravating domestic problems confronting those who are responsible for achieving economic stability. The irony is that its magnitude is the result of the success and efficiency of the agricultural enterprise which industriousness, technological advancement, and all the forces we think of as related to progress have accomplished. What gave the stamp of industry to our culture has done the same thing for agriculture, with the result that the two are inseparably interrelated. Compounding the irony is the fact that if the American economy and the related world economy are to remain healthy, agriculture must become even more successful both at home in the United States and abroad.

The fortunate geographic situation of the United States and its combination with a political philosophy which has been consistently favorable to the farmer and agricultural producer have had felicitous results. Because Thomas Jefferson and others associated with him had a profound respect for those who worked on the land and for the consequences to them as a result of their intimate association with the soil, this nation has experienced a long history of friendliness toward the agrarian. Only in recent years has the political center of gravity shifted from the rural areas to urban centers. The most recent evidence is the Supreme Court's decision of 1964 requiring the realignment of voting units for state legislatures. Despite the trend in political power to urban centers, the nation as a whole is deeply sensitive to the welfare of those living on the land and to the even greater number whose economic life is substantially affected by the welfare of those making their living on the land. The ever-increasing integration of agriculture and industry explains some of the reluctance of urban-based legislators to discriminate more vigorously against the claims of rural people who are not their constituents.

THE FARM PROBLEM

There was a time when the slogan "depressions are farm-fed and farm-led" was taken seriously, but that time has passed. There is little temptation, however, to discount the close relationship between the agricultural economy and the economy of the nation as a whole.

The term "agribusiness" has been coined to express the combination of all production work on the farm, the manufacture and distribution of farm supplies, and the processing and distribution of farm commodities and items made from them. Agribusiness employs around 40 per cent of all the people that work in the United States and supplies the commodities which account for about 40 per cent of total consumer expenditures. Agricultural production supplies over 60 per cent of the value of raw materials consumed in the United States.

Of the 65 million people employed in the United States, about 25 million work somewhere in the agricultural industry: 7 million work on farms, 7 million produce for and service farmers, and 11 million process and distribute farm products. In addition, a half million scientists and technicians directly or indirectly serve agriculture.[1]

Though the population now residing on farms represents a very small percentage of the nation's population, they, together with the people whose economic life is tied to agriculture, constitute a portion of the total populace sufficient to influence its total health. It is for this reason that even the most urban of legislators have come to accept the fact that farm price stabilization is a permanent part of our economy.

The fact is that so long as the farmer's capacity to produce far exceeds the demands of his markets, he cannot expect to achieve stability of income and an equitable share of the nation's prosperity unless (1) the producers of the various crops develop bargaining power in the market place as other industries in our free enterprise economy have done . . . or (2) the government by various devices subsidizes farm income to make up the difference between what the farmer receives in the market place and a reasonable income in representing the investment, management, skill and labor he invests in the production of food and other farm commodities.

In the ten years, 1953–62 inclusive, although all of the segments of the economy have been booming, the net income of agriculture was $21 billion less than in the previous ten years, 1943–52 inclusive. Meanwhile the Department of Agriculture spent for all purposes in those ten years, $35 billion more than in the previous ten years. The costs from 1953 through 1962 were almost $20 billion more than all expenditures of the Department in the previous ninety years of its history. However, it must be noted that a great part of the expenditures of the Department of Agriculture in recent years have been primarily for the benefit of consumers and for aid of distressed people in other countries.[2]

Whatever may have been the basis of the general disposition toward agricultural people until now, and however convinced we may be that the economy is so closely integrated that agriculture may not be allowed to suffer impairment, the fact remains that it is not possible to consume in the United States the full production of agriculture's efforts. Meanwhile, surpluses greatly in excess of requirements for drought insurance or even for military exigencies are being accumulated. To complicate matters, there is every assurance that production could be increased from between 50 to 100 per cent through utilization of knowledge and skills already available.

At the very foundation of American agricultural life is a magnificent program of technical education designed to increase the total output of agriculture. Research activities in dozens of land-grant colleges and in government research centers have enabled the American agricultural producer to achieve results which are the admiration of all who know of them. All of this lies behind the steadily mounting surpluses which correspondingly account for the steady decline in agricultural income. Wheat, for example, has increased from 11.2 bushels per acre in 1938 to 26 bushels in 1961. Corn has experienced a comparable increase from 22 bushels per acre in 1933 to 61 bushels in 1961.

Is there no likelihood of these mounting surpluses being utilized in the domestic life of this nation? Undoubtedly improvement in the inadequate diets of an estimated one-fourth of the nation now living at a poverty level could absorb much, but not all, of the available surplus food resources. One might sensibly ask why the farmer does not curtail production when prices go down and his income shrinks. This question has been asked times without end. The plain fact is that the farmer cannot shut down his plant as the manufacturer normally does when his costs exceed his income. The farmer increases his effort and his use of fertilizer and hopes to beat the price decline by increased volume, thus adding still further to the surpluses and price impairment.

We have been presenting the farm problem in terms of surpluses. D. Gale Johnson places it in another context, though with the same implication. "Stated simply, the farm problem is the result of the employment of more labor in agriculture than can earn as large a real income as the same labor could earn elsewhere in the economy. . . . This simple statement of the nature of the farm problem is not universally accepted. Some economists argue that no conceivable reduction in the number of farm workers could result in a significant improvement in the real income position of those remaining in agriculture. . . . Those who argue in this way tend to believe that the solution to the farm problem lies in increasing the bargaining power of farmers, the effective restriction of output and marketing, and, in some cases, the withdrawal of land from agricultural production."[3]

Whether the problem is too many workers—which is undoubtedly an important part of it, or even the major issue as Gale Johnson contends—or whether it is the matter of mounting surpluses which have accompanied increasing efficiency and might even be accelerated with yet greater efficiency, the fact remains that the problem is taxing both the intellectual resources and the patience of all who are concerned with it, and directly and indirectly that means everybody in the country.

AGRICULTURE AND EFFICIENCY

Before turning to some of the proposals for resolving the dilemma, the question must be asked whether agriculture, in spite of its historically privileged position, has now become so patently a part of the industrial complex and culture that it can no longer be regarded as meriting distinction because it is "a way of life," that is, seeing the farmer as a modern version of the traditional yeoman.

Iowa State University has established a Center for Agricultural Adjustment and more recently a Center for Agricultural and Economic Development, and it is noteworthy that so large a percentage of the themes discussed in three major conferences dealt with the philosophical, cultural, and even theological problems created by the new agriculture. The titles of the books containing the addresses and discussions are revealing: *Problems and Policies of American Agriculture* (1959), *Goals and Values in Agricultural Policy* (1961), and *Farm Goals in Conflict* (1963). It is safe to say there are no three contemporaneous books containing a greater wealth of material dealing with the cultural aspects of American agriculture and their consequences for the economy of the rest of the world. There have been many conferences on many continents dealing with the problem of technology in agriculture and its implications for the types of society prevailing on those continents. Nowhere, one suspects, has so much attention been paid to the underlying causes and consequences of technology and the industrialization process for the agricultural and allied economies as are there treated. It is hardly coincidental that there should be such a plethora of profound and penetrating analyses at this particular time. If anything, they are long overdue. In a humorous vein, nevertheless weighted with astute insight, economist Kenneth Boulding suggested in one of the forums that universities such as Iowa State have contributed to the dilemma by their very efficiency. But the universities which have helped so magnificently to increase food production have been primarily commodity-centered and have not given adequate attention to the consequences of their efforts on people. He goes on to suggest abolishing the Department of Agriculture, along with several others, and suggests substituting in a department of science and research a unit on poverty and economics.[4]

For many years in the reports of the Department of Agriculture there appeared charts indicating the mounting use of tractors as against the numbers of horses and mules. These no longer elicit response. We take for granted the mechanization of agriculture. We are now more impressed with the charts on farm mortgages, increase of land values, increase of farm size and corresponding decrease in number of farms, the use of land credit, productivity per capita in agriculture vs. industry, the corporate structure of the agricultural enterprise, etc. The term "agribusiness" is all but universally acceptable and is an accurate description. A few remain who are zealous that agriculture as a way of life be maintained, but if they are farmers themselves, they also have one eye cocked for the market. With the exception of a few pockets, such as the Amish in eastern Pennsylvania, technology has been thoroughly accepted in American agriculture; the findings of research on crops, fertilizers, animal husbandry, and all the rest are being adopted almost as rapidly as their counterpart discoveries in urbanized manufacturing centers. Perhaps all of this is symbolized in a study which reports that 23 per cent of Wisconsin farmers carry union cards. They move with ease between the industrial and the agricultural plant.[5] These part-time workers in agriculture point to another of the increasingly obvious problems in agriculture—the decline in numbers of those required for work on the land. Either they must find part-time work in industry or leave agriculture altogether.

AGRICULTURAL EMPLOYMENT

No statement concerning U. S. agriculture would be comprehensive which failed to include reference to one of the most difficult and trying problems confronting the agricultural economy —the migrant worker. Those who follow the crops, working when harvest time for each arrives and then enduring unemployment between seasons, represent a gross weakness in what is vaunted as an otherwise efficient system. Disruption of family life, low wages, inadequate care of the sick, absence of protection for industrial workers, reduced educational opportunities—these and many other harmful aspects mark the experience of many whose work is necessary for the harvesting of food. Granting of security to those "industrial workers in agriculture" has thus far been successfully resisted. Mervin G. Smith states: "Many farmers find it impossible to make the adjustments required by the continual adoption of new technologies and therefore they have low incomes. Since farm land is limited it is only as some farmers leave farming that others nearby can enlarge their farms for efficient operation. Many farmers do not have this immediate possibility since nearby land is not for sale. Even though they may have changed the combination of their resources by investing in labor-saving new technology, they have not been able to enlarge their farms. This has left them with excess labor (including their own) and sometimes with too much equipment. Some have then obtained another job and become part-time farmers to improve their incomes."[6]

It is estimated that 38 per cent of all Ohio farmers are employed at least one hundred days per year in off-farm work. In other industrialized states the figures would probably not differ greatly. The significant thing here, however, is not simply the number who are occupied part-time in industry but the fact that even with their spending a substantial portion of their working hours away from the farm, agricultural productivity continues to mount. We are facing here the same problem presented in the discussion of industrialism earlier and in the discussion of automation. Technology is creating for agriculture, as in other phases of the total economy, the very efficiency which compounds its dilemma.

Illustrative of the coordination of technology and business in agriculture is "vertical integration." Most notably adopted in the chicken business, it has now spread to other animal production, especially hogs and cattle. Its process is simple: a feed company places its animals in the custody of the farmer who nurtures them from infancy to market, using the company's feeds and finally selling them at the company's direction. The farmer's role is that of custodian and overseer, while technical and financial aspects are directed by the initiating organization.

From its earliest beginnings, in the northern part of this country at least, farming has been centered in the "family farm." Much of the current anxiety over agriculture in the United States stems from the fear that something inherently valuable for our national life will be lost if this historic keystone of agriculture and national stability disappears. Now the entire question of family farming is being reappraised in the light of the new situation. A comment by Emerson Shideler reflects the opinion of many others. "We are now capable of producing sufficient quantities of goods and fiber quite independent of family farming as such. But we are still arguing that in order to preserve stability of the family it is necessary to keep these families in a business that is no longer necessary as a business. We need to re-examine the relationship between these two values."[7]

All these facts together plus a vast complex of statistics related to many other phases of these and other problems combine to create what has been designated as "the farm problem."

Some Proposed Solutions

Belatedly but effectively, agriculture learned the lessons taught it by the expansion of industry. Giant pressure groups emerged in the form of the American Farm Bureau Federation, Farmers Union, the Grange, and more recently, the National Farmers Organization. The latter has taken a leaf out of the notebook of industry in its program for withholding produce and livestock from the market until prices can be brought to an optimum level. Each of these organizations develops its corresponding pressure programs, filling legislative halls with lobbyists seeking to obtain for agriculture what industry long ago learned to secure for itself. The pattern of industry is to be found perhaps even more directly in the development of the farmers cooperative organizations, whether for marketing or for production. Through them the farmer has learned to acquire economic power and to influence, in some measure at least, the price factor. A nation historically kindly

disposed toward agriculture has willingly encouraged the development of such self-help enterprises to the point where they have
become themselves economic giants capable of competing on
finance row, in the research laboratory, and in the legislatures.

The so-called "farm problem" was beginning to make itself
known prior to World War I. Its seriousness was temporarily delayed and then greatly aggravated by that war when American
grain and foodstuff became necessary as a part of the war effort
itself. Large areas of land which we now know should never have
been used for grain production were plowed under; farmers were
encouraged to produce to the fullest of their ability, and they
then found it difficult, if not impossible, to cut back production
when the needs subsided. A result was an agricultural depression
ten years before the world-shaking economic collapse and industrial
depression following the crash in 1929. From that day to the
present each administration has proposed programs designed to
provide income stability for agriculture and a harmonization of
agricultural-industrial-financial situations for the nation and consequently for the rest of the world. At the time of this writing, a
new program is in the offing, but probably such a statement could
be made at the time of any writing in the foreseeable future. A
delineation of those programs makes fascinating study and reveals
much about the political and economic temper of this nation for
the period of their acceptance or rejection. Because a portrayal of
those plans would involve us in too extensive a digression, we will
forego the temptation except for a quick review of the positions of
the major farm organizations. Thus at one time it is possible to
indicate varying programs and something of the pressure groups
behind them. Since the differences become apparent in the areas
of support prices, land use, production payments, the positions for
our purposes are confined to these areas.

The American Farm Bureau Federation states:

A major objective of farm bureau policy is to create conditions whereby
farmers may earn and get a high per family real income in a manner
which will preserve freedom and opportunity. We firmly believe that
this objective can best be accomplished by preserving the market price
system as the principal influence in allocating the use of farm resources
and in distributing farm production.[8]

The Farmer's Union believes: (1) the efficient family farmer should have full parity of income, returns on labor, management and capital invested in comparison with returns to comparable resources invested in nonfarm enterprise; (2) the preservation of the family farm is in the national interest; (3) farmers must acquire more bargaining power in the market place.[9]

The Grange:

The primary goal of Grange farm program policy is the re-alignment of these established and fully accepted government provided protective devices so as to supply equitable income opportunities to farmers. This re-alignment must include programs necessary to give agricultural producers an opportunity to earn and receive for their labor, management, risk and investment a return reasonably comparable to that provided by those same factors in their best nonfarm employments.[10]

The National Farm Organization:

First, farmers must organize, because there is no substitute for organized strength in an organized economy. If farmers want to price their products, they must go to the market place with equal or greater strength than those that buy their products. Therefore, they cannot solve their problems and then organize. They must organize to solve their problems. . . . Secondly, farmers must bring together enough of the total production so that the present marketing system cannot fulfill their needs from other sources. . . . And how do you make your bargaining power felt? By the use of holding actions. There has never been a commodity or a service priced in America on which the holding action has not been used.[11]

Such statements are but small sections of the full policy statements and are included here primarily to give the "flavor" of the organization's position. Nor are these the only organizations which have agricultural programs. They are, however, the major farmers' organizations seeking to influence total agricultural policy formation at the national level.

Agricultural economist Walter Wilcox, reviewing various price stabilization programs, comments:

Government farm price stabilization activities probably have become a permanent part of our economic system. Those who would abolish all these programs are in a distinct minority. Farm leaders find there is widespread disagreement, however, on: (1) the level of supports that should be maintained in relation to long-run normal free market prices; (2) the number of commodities that should be included in the group having mandatory supports; (3) the restrictions that should be placed on the use of diverted acres when marketing quotas and acreage allotments are in effect; (4) the restriction of the conflict between domestic price stabilization and freer international trade; (5) the distribution of benefits among farm families.[12]

There may be disagreement among farm leaders on many parts of the total farm situation, but there is no disagreement on the fact that the farm population is shrinking, that farm technology has made unnecessary a large percentage of those now engaged in farming, that agricultural supplies and production are greatly in excess of what could be consumed in the United States even with a massive reduction in poverty, that there are values inherent in the production of agricultural supplies which contribute to the life of individuals, families, and communities, and that programs must be devised which will preserve the best in agricultural life and at the same time not impair or penalize the rest of the economy.

These areas of common agreement, though they are American in their present setting, have implications for the life of many other nations, both because of the necessity for using American agricultural surpluses for the creation of stable world relationships and because many other nations will face similar problems as they also move from agricultural to industrial predominance. A clue to this latter situation is in the description of European agricultural changes by the Dutch rural sociologist E. W. Hofstee: "What has been said will probably be sufficient to demonstrate that agricultural and rural life in Europe are in a serious crisis which will demonstrate itself in the years to come still far more clearly than it has already. As far as history can tell us, the European countryside faces the most important and the most sudden change of its existence. Even the existence of a class of farmers as a separate group with its own social, cultural and economic characteristics is at stake."[13]

It is the difference between the situation in the United States and that in most of the other countries of the world which not only creates the problem but also may hold a partial key to its solution. "The United States," says agricultural economist Earl O. Hardy, "has a farm problem only because it is wealthy and has progressed far up the path of economic development. In contrast, many other nations have problems of agriculture because they are poor and economic progress has been tardy. Because we are so far advanced in over-all national economic development, we perhaps have 10 to 20 years of slack ahead of us, during which we can adjust toward any more effective use of resources needed in the long-run. It will take longer than this for the other nations with large populations and resource bases to catch up in level of economic development and potentiality in production."[14]

Is there a solution? Not in a great increase of consumption in the United States at least, for demand elasticity is low. Undoubtedly there could be greater food consumption on the part of those at the lower end of the economic scale. Estimates vary greatly as to the amount which could be consumed, were all residents of this nation capable of receiving a balanced and adequate diet. This would, however, be no permanent solution to the problem of agricultural surpluses. Undoubtedly, too, chemistry will find new uses for products of the soil, and further reduction in surpluses will be made during the next decade, providing additions are not made to the surpluses by policies which encourage increased production. The devices we have employed thus far—price supports, soil bank, acreage reserves, conservation reserves, and a variety of income-supporting programs—have served to stablize the income of agricultural producers and have made it possible for many families to remain on the farm when they would otherwise have been pressured off. If the benefits had accrued only to the family-type farm, hostility to the programs on the part of some urban people might have diminished. Well known, however, is the fact that very large farm operators have been the recipients of government benefits, in some instances approximating a million dollars per operator. Sociologist Robin Williams contends: "There is a limit to the subsidization of comparatively well-off commercial farmers that will be politically tolerated in an urbanized democracy. There is a limit to the acceptability to the conscience of the public of the mass misery of migratory farm workers or of the rural slums of stranded populations."[15]

As indicated earlier, a great many people have gotten into the act of making proposals for the resolution of the "farm problem." Another analysis of the situation which has received wide attention because of the competent and distinguished panel producing the proposals is that of the Committee for Economic Development. Their proposal, comprehensive in scope, can be stated in their own words in a single paragraph:

The programs we are suggesting would result in fewer workers in agriculture, working a smaller number of farms of greater average size and receiving substantially higher income per worker. . . . There are two ways to reduce governmental agriculture outlays without great losses to farmers. One is to tighten controls of production and marketing enough to reduce farm output to the point where all output will sell at the higher prices. This will make consumers pay more for farm products and let the government pay less. The other way is to attract and assist enough farmers out of farming so that farm income per farmer will be sustained without rising farm prices despite a decline in government spending on agriculture.[16]

Another popular and widely discussed analysis of the farm problem suggests:

There is no solution which will not hurt some farmer and benefit others. Even to abandon all farm programs would be a boon to some agriculturists and a catastrophe to others. Like everyone else in a dynamic society, farmers are changing as the economy changes around them. . . . Now that farm subsidies run around $5 billion a year instead of .3 billion as they did in 1952, the taxpayer is entitled to believe that the point of diminishing returns has been reached. . . . The end of a process, however, does not mean an end to all evolution. To the contrary, as far as American agriculture is concerned perhaps the end of big government spending will mark the beginning of new and more intensive efforts by farmers to manage their businesses and seek their personal fortunes in more sophisticated ways.[17]

Here the solution, though bound to injure some, is to recognize that farming is itself primarily a business and must henceforth be treated in what the author calls "more sophisticated ways." This does not mean the end of the family farm, but asks that farming as a family occupation accept the criteria of efficiency without demanding of other taxpayers a subsidy for their continued operation disproportionate to any other segment of the economy. It does not

take into account the fact that industry in a very large measure
is dependent upon taxpayers' support in the form of payment for
defense costs, which are approximately ten times greater than the
current outlay for agriculture. Presumably, however, it is reasonable
to expect that an increasing resolution of the world tensions will
make possible a steady diminution in the taxpayers' outlay for
defense purposes. We have no illusions that this will occur without
great hue and cry from those who are now subsidized through
defense outlays, as the response to modest cut-backs in the current
period already presaged.

It becomes increasingly apparent that the defense aspects of the
economy, the projected and hoped-for projects of foreign aid, the
massive attacks on the poverty situation, are all tied together in a
common bundle including the agriculture problem.

Our Surpluses and World Needs

American surpluses in agricultural production have provided a
political and economic headache for the nation as a whole, but
they also present a bright aspect. Our program of storage and
reserve fulfilled its initial purpose in periods of drought and in
times of dire need coincident with World War II and the Korean
conflict. But a succession of highly productive years has again
brought surpluses to a size beyond any immediately foreseeable
domestic needs.

"What we need now," says Byron Johnson, "is an affirmative
program that will bring our domestic agricultural policy into
harmony with our foreign policy. The world needs our food but
the problem domestically is the cost in allocating this food to
places where need exists and the problem of placing the food in
such spots of need without disrupting the economy of the country
receiving it or of other nations which might reasonably expect
to sell their own agricultural products to the needy nations."[18]

It is of this that Charles M. Hardin is speaking when he says:
"We must radically change our Agricultural Trade Development
and Assistance Act and really insure that our overseas disposal
programs make a net addition to consumption and not to a replace-

ment of what would otherwise move in world trade."[19]

The problem is greater than simply that of designating surplus foods for hungry people in other parts of the world. Food, we recognize, can be an instrument for strengthening the bodies of those in recipient nations and thereby can contribute to building up the productive capacities within the receiving nations. Harvard's John D. Black suggests disposal of agricultural products "as an assistance to a backward or undeveloped country in carrying out a program that will increase its ability to feed itself. Such programs and assistance need to be planned carefully because: (1) There is danger that the productivity will not be built up faster than the increased supply of food checks the death rate, so that if the food assistance is cut off at any time, the people of that country will be worse off than before."[20]

Our national policy of food distribution has been characterized by considerable ambivalence. We have not been fully certain that the use of our food resources is primarily intended to strengthen our relationships with other countries and ultimately to contribute to a greater degree of interdependence between nations. We have been inclined to regard the distribution of food and agricultural products as a part of the farm support program, which indeed they were; but to regard them primarily in this fashion is to miss a major opportunity. "On the national and international scene many forces are working together to demand a fresh and bold program. Specifically the U. S. and the UN-FAO have launched a Freedom from Hunger campaign; the U. S. did invite the world and the UN agreed to join in making the 1960's a UN decade of development. In order to deal with the emerging regional economic groupings in Europe and Latin America, the U. S. has strengthened its trade policy through the Trade Expansion Act. Finally, fundamental criticisms of the U. S. farm program at home as well as abroad have underlined our need for a basic revision of the program."[21]

The Food and Agriculture Organization has already designated 100 million dollars to be used for placing foods where most needed. The U. S. has assumed a major role making these funds available and thus participates in an international venture whose long-range outcome will benefit the economy of the whole world.

A program of wise allocation of American surplus foods, in conjunction with other nations similarly blessed, could both strengthen the receiving people and make for a far more comprehensive appreciation of the interrelatedness of the world and its resources. This would not relieve United States agriculture of the necessity for devising programs consistent with the evolution of agriculture's technology, but it would place the total problem in a new context. "We cannot, we must not, turn our backs upon the world. We can, we must, and therefore we will, prepare to cooperate hereafter so that more people are better fed, with fewer workers engaged in agriculture and with better incomes for all. . . . This is our opportunity."[22]

It has become apparent that there are basic differences in the goals of those who seek to improve the overall agricultural situation in the United States. There is no such thing as *the* agricultural position. Even though rural and urban interests may be in conflict in some phases of the political scene, they are very much dependent upon each other in other ways. Willard W. Cochrane, former director of agricultural economics in the U. S. Department of Agriculture, says:

"The only conceivable way of resolving this conflict between our historic commitments to both commutative and distributive justice for farm people is to *limit total farm output* to a level that will bring to agriculture as a whole a fair return and all farm operators of inadequate farms to achieve efficient sized farm units. . . . But this method of resolving the conflict between commutative and distributive justice throws our historic premiums on technological advance and entrepreneurial freedom into opposition and conflict at another conceptual level. This is true because limiting the total output of farm units prevents operators from using new and available technologies in whatever ways they may desire.[23]

This, however, is only a part of the area of conflict and of the difference in goals maintained for agriculture. There are regional differences, differences due to type of agricultural products (e.g., cottonseed oil vs. soybean oil), and fundamental ideological differences over supporting a segment of the total population for the purpose of stabilizing the economy as a whole. Robin Williams contends that entrepreneurial freedom is incompatible with several of the other important goals and values desired by farm people; "because we want several incompatible things, the agricultural programs of the future will continue to represent complex compromises among different values and goals." He adds that "the only hope for an effective agriculture and an enduring rural life is in selective change and adaptation to new conditions. There is no simple panacea."[24]

Conflicting farm interests have also found expression in terms of contradictory national and international political ideologies. Economist T. W. Schultz states:

Farmers in the United States have had a large hand politically in developing our welfare state, long before the New Deal and McNary-Haugenism. The earlier agrarian movements protested strongly against the doctrine of laissez faire not because farm leaders had been schooled in European socialism or in Marxian thought. Their protests were a direct indigenous response to the raw industrialism of the post Civil War decade and to the long decline in the general level of prices. More recently, mainly after the first World War, farmers turned to the Federal government to intervene in their behalf in adjusting agricultural production and in supporting particular farm prices in what John D. Black called "assisted laissez faire." Despite the strong political influence farmers have had in the developing of our welfare state, they have not acquired many of the social services that it renders unto others in society. The puzzle is why? . . .

The combination of the political influence of Southern tradition, the conflict of interest among farm families, the fact that farm leaders are not conversant with the ideas, the philosophical basis and the historical process of which modern agriculture is an integral part and the extraordinary commitment to having the government enact and administer production-price programs, represent a formidable barrier to welfare. It is a high wall against the social services of the welfare state. This wall will not come tumbling down until this combination is undermined. Until then the U. S. welfare state cannot serve the welfare of farm people adequately.[25]

Economist Walter Wilcox contends that the problem is, in part at least, the result of misplaced emphases:

One hears repeatedly that we cannot make progress in adopting more desirable farm policies because of conflicts in goals and values among farm and nonfarm groups. In my opinion, a more accurate statement would be that because of mistaken beliefs about the nature of the economic consequences of alternative policies, groups fail to discover their common interests. Most of the group conflicts as we know them today in the farm policy field are the result of mistaken beliefs regarding the effects of existing policies and expected effects of alternative policies. And we should ask ourselves: Why is this situation so prevalent today?

Why is such a small part of the research and educational resources in agricultural economics devoted to obtaining a better understanding of these policy issues? Why do our brightest graduate students work on the more concrete but less important problems of farm and industry efficiency under static conditions of equilibrium?[26]

Belatedly, perhaps, but nonetheless seriously we have begun to analyze the agricultural dilemma where it is the result of vigorous but noninclusive considerations. We can hope that the kinds of considerations elicited by the Iowa State University Center for Agricultural Economic Adjustment portend further treatment of this vast and complex theme.

As is true of each of the areas dealt with heretofore and of those which follow, differences in policy and their attendant programs cannot be resolved at the level of economic theory, at least in its limited sense. Each of these issues involves fundamental philosophical problems, and many, including myself, would contend that there are theological considerations involved as well.

Since its inception in 1950 the National Council of Churches, as was true of the Federal Council of Churches which preceded this organization, has been deeply concerned with the problem of agricultural policy. This is not by any means solely a Protestant concern. *Mater et Magistra*, an encyclical of Pope John XXIII, has sometimes been referred to as the "agricultural encyclical." The National Council of Churches' statement on "Ethical Goals for Agricultural Policy" was designed with the United States" situation primarily in mind, though it has implications for world agriculture as well. This statement adopted by the General Board of the National Council of Churches comes as close to being an official statement of Protestant position as anything could be, considering the structure of cooperating Protestant organizations. "A Christian ethical approach to agriculture begins with the acknowledgment that 'the earth is the Lord's and the fulness thereof.' God, the Creator, has given man a special position in the world, with specific responsibility for the fruits of the earth and towards all living things. This is the stewardship of the earth's resources for the nourishment and the enrichment of human life. Thus the production of food and fiber—the primary task of farmers—becomes a service to God and man."[27]

Carrying the theme beyond the specifically domestic scene is a resolution approved by the General Assembly of the National Council, titled "Ethical Issues in the International Age of Agriculture." It states: "God's concern for the needs of all His children for nourishment, both of body and soul, is revealed in His act of creation and in the gift of His Son, Jesus Christ. Our Lord made perfectly clear that man's duty to God includes the production and sharing of the material necessities of life. He described the conditions of salvation at the ultimate judgment to include the fact that we did—or did not—'feed the hungry and clothe the naked.' "[28] The implications of such a commission include (a) sharing our food supplies, (b) sharing technological knowledge and experience, (c) sharing economic aid for agriculture and food production, (d) role of religious and other voluntary organizations, (e) a major global program. The last commends for support by governments and people of every nation the world-wide five-year Freedom from Hunger campaign of the UN specialized agency, the Food and Agriculture Organization. In both purpose and scope this program is commended to our churches and their members. National and international church organizations thus lend their support to individuals, to national and international political agencies contending that America's temporary embarrassment can be a boon to world development. And through this use of her resources the long-run purposes of the nation itself are best served.

The Consumer—Power
or Pushover?*

When President Johnson established a President's Committee on Consumer Interests and made Mrs. Esther Peterson the Special Assistant for Consumer Affairs, responsible directly to the White House, a half century of work on behalf of consumers' interest was crowned with success. This act may not guarantee the full realization of the ends desired by those who have championed the cause of the consumer, but it does represent an advance toward their objectives. The irony of this accomplishment lies in the fact that every one of the 195 million persons in this country, as well as the 3.5 billion persons in the rest of the world, is a consumer. Why has it taken so long for the interests of the consumer to be recognized as an important part of the structure of government? One answer is that we assume a free market and a free choice on the part of the buyer. He—or more likely, she—exercises freedom of choice in purchases and thereby determines what products shall be produced and the price that shall be paid. This in itself, it is hypothesized, should provide protection. What the champions of the consumer have been trying to say for at least half a century, however, is that freedom of choice does not exist and that the consumer is in need of protection against those who can control the market and, through devices of their own construction, beguile the buyer into accepting inferior products at dishonest weights and measures. There is much evidence that were he not protected by government-established health standards, his life itself could be

---

* I am especially indebted to Dr. Leland Gordon for his excellent paper on "The Role and Responsibility of the Consumer," prepared for the Fourth National Study Conference on the Church and Economic Life (November 1962).

in danger. Quickly it must be added, however, that devices to protect the consumer are also valuable in protecting the preponderance of honest manufacturers and distributors who hold high standards of integrity and public service.

The Economic System and the Ultimate Consumer

The economic system exists to provide goods and services for the satisfaction of human needs and wants. Within that system the consumer theoretically determines what is produced and the price paid. If the costs exceed the value to him, he declines to buy; if the return is too low, the producer declines to produce. This seems to be an almost ridiculously simple explanation for an economy which also spends almost 50 billion dollars a year for armaments. In our economic system we assume that if the consumer did not feel this was justifiable, he could, so the free-choice theory goes, decline to spend his money in this way. By contrast, for example, the Communist system needs no such justification or endorsement. Its directors have determined that a specified percentage of their national income must be used for defense purposes, and in response to their judgment the Russian consumer seems to go along. (Of course, the Russian expenditures, too, are justified in their minds by the fact that the American consumer has endorsed the expenditure of so large a sum for "defense." And so the escalation continues.)

Freedom of choice for the consumer is not a uniform condition. Again, under the Russian system, overseers of the economy have determined that capital goods (producers' goods) take precedence over consumer wants, as a means of building up the capacity for industrial productivity. In the United States productive capacities have long since exceeded what the consumer desires, and the result is the well-known surpluses in grain and "inventories" in automobiles, refrigerators, and many other things. The exception, of course, would be in what is called the public sector—schools, roads, housing, and health resources. But here again the consumer has presumably voted, consciously or unconsciously, that his funds in the form of taxes shall go for space exploration and defense.

Meanwhile, the Russian consumer is informed that in the near future his productive capacity will have reached the desired stage and that consumer goods will soon become available.

Theoretically, then, part of the difference between the "free" and the regulated economy lies in the extent to which the consumer is permitted to use his earnings in the satisfaction of his wants.

On the face of it, it would appear that the consumer in a free economy exercises his freedom under the direction of a balanced judgment which comprehends total needs and what is best for himself and his dependents. He will secure what is ultimately best for his welfare in a way that the Russian consumer is not able to do. One quick look at the imbalance between the things that are purchased and the needs that exist would indicate that in the minds of many, at least, there is no unanimity of judgment in this matter of purchases. "Do all consumers know what goods and services will promote their welfare?" asks Leland Gordon. "If all of them know, does it follow that they will consume only those goods and services which are beneficial? Are consumers able to judge the quality of the thousands of items they find in the market? Everything consumers buy is priced on the basis of weight, measure, or numerical count. To what extent are consumer buyers able to check the quantity measurements of their purchases? Can consumers know whether prices are really competitive? To what extent are the prices of some goods and services determined by the collusive action of the sellers? . . . To what extent are consumers rational?"[1]

If the consumer were truly rational, would it make any difference in the allocation of his expendable funds? Our liquor and tobacco bill per capita is only slightly less than our outlay for public education.[2]* At present this is the way the consumer chooses to have it under the freedom accorded him in our kind of system. ". . . High expenditures for tobacco, alcoholic beverages, soft drinks and movies, for example, by families with 'inadequate' diets, 'substandard' housing, and 'insufficient' medical care have been taken by some people as evidence that consumers cannot be expected

* Expenditures per capita in 1963 for public education, $116; tobacco $42.70 (approximately); liquor $60 (approximately)

to choose wisely. Some proposals have seemed to imply that decisions as to what kind of consumption is more important should be left largely to specialists who have greater knowledge and wisdom concerning consumer needs. This tendency is at variance with the deep-rooted conviction in the American society that individuals should be free to explore and to decide what is best for them, and that consumer education to improve free choice is a sounder way than decisions by experts to direct the course of future consumption."[3]

The American consumer, collectively speaking, has a voting power of approximately 410 billion dollars (1964) which represents his disposable income. His government, using his taxes, makes an impact on the economy to the tune of 110 billion dollars—purchases which are also dictated by this same consumer. The question of primary concern, then, is: On what basis the consumer, either himself or through his government, makes the judgment as to what is best for him and for the country as a whole? There have been instances in which the consumer vote made profound changes necessary. For example, when the Food and Drug Administration was created, it was no longer possible for "patent medicines" to be distributed with advertising which claimed benefits the medicines could not provide. More recently, after long and bitter debate between "specialists" it was finally concluded that cigarettes were a factor contributing to cancer. The consumer, through a tax-supported agency, forced public recognition of the cigarette as a menace to health—although judging from cigarette sales, this public action has as yet had little effect.

What the Modern Consumer Assumes

Before looking at the forces bombarding the consumer, shaping his thought and conditioning his purchasing, it is necessary to consider a whole world of influences which shape the thinking of the consumer almost without his awareness. These lines are being written during the longest period of continuous upward movement of economic indices in modern times. But whether such a setting is the one best known by the consumer or not, the state of the economy in which he happens to be living affects the degree of confidence or pessimism he reveals. I recall spending an evening with a small-town banker whose bank remained solvent during the Great Depression when others all about him collapsed. His conservatism and stability were household words in his own county and far beyond. Then came World War II and the backlog of buying potential, which fooled many economists and business leaders whose memories of postwar situations told them to expect a collapse. A minor collapse came, but much later. Through all of this the small-town banker remained conservative and admonished his customers to do likewise. Everywhere the expansion-minded were making remarkable headway, and the conservatives, including this banker, were left behind. This practice was not, however, confined to small-town bankers, merchants, and farmers. A famous case is that of a world-renowned mail-order house whose leadership operated on the same principles, until they were outdistanced by competitors and a change-minded board of directors switched management. The psychology of confidence or the expectation of retrenchment is a powerful factor in shaping the decision of the consumer.

Affecting both the small consumer and the buyer of giant proportions are certain major economic changes which have become commonplace in the consumer world and whose influence is widely if not universally felt, even though the consumer may not be constantly reminded of their presence. We shall consider these one by one.

The first of these changes is the emergence of powerful corporations determining the welfare of their industry, their employees, and in varying degrees those who buy and sell their product. Where they have been efficient—and except for the jerry-built structures designed for quick profits by speculators, they have been efficient—they are able to market their products at an advantage over the smaller operator who cannot take advantage of the economies in large-scale purchases and distribution. But the strictly economic factor may not be the dominant influence of these giant corporations; for they require a bureaucratic structure. Individually and collectively they shape the mentality of whole communities and their institutional life. Though they stress the necessity of their employees fostering the image of community concern, their own principal objectives are not primarily the welfare of the consumer but the operation of the market. The giant corporation begets its opposite number in the giant union organization. They are dependent upon each other and in collusion may take such action as will enhance profits and wages irrespective of the public welfare. What is true for the giant corporations has its parallel in all other large-scale enterprises, whether in agriculture or in medicine. We accept these great combinations as an inevitable part of the American system.

Second, whereas a generation ago military expenditures were very modest, we take it for granted that they have now become an all-encompassing factor in our economy, as has been indicated earlier. But here again the major factor may not be merely the size of the portion the military represents in the economy but the impact on the mentality of the people who are themselves products of its training.

Third is the rapid change that has occurred in the method of merchandising, as we moved from the store salesman or door-to-door salesman to the presentation of goods in picture form in unlimited variety in one's own living room. Value and quality are not the primary concern of the agencies who secure extrance to whatever part of the house we use to watch television or listen to radio. The objective is attractiveness and capacity to lure the potential buyer without opportunity for comparison with other "makes and models."

The fourth revolutionary change, which has come unheralded but nonetheless has taken possession of the mind of the modern consumer, is the consciousness that somehow spending is a patriotic duty and that everyone is under obligation to serve the economy. The nation's well-being depends upon keeping the economy healthy. The important thing is not the merit or quality of what is purchased but that production shall go on so that employment be maintained.

Related directly or indirectly to these four major changes which have occurred within a generation are others which call for some special mention. Rare is the person reared in another day who does not shake his head perplexedly when the question of installment buying arises. Expectation of continued prosperity has lifted the private debt of this country from 60 billion dollars to almost 400 billion dollars in less than a quarter century. Financial analysts are constantly being interrogated, and their answers headlined, on the question whether we have reached a saturation point in personal credit. We have come to assume that both fiscal and monetary policy can be brought into action quickly enough to curtail excesses if such seem to be emerging. Young people do not expect to start a home with the limited equipment of their parents. With an easy credit situation they can enjoy a measure of comfort comparable to that of a generation of others who own similar gadgets and conveniences after a lifetime of saving. This has given rise to such a large business of loaning money for installment purchases that some merchandising establishments make more money in the loaning of money on time payments than on the sale of the merchandise. The convenience of having the equipment transcends anxieties over future capacity to continue payments. It adds up to the expectation of a plane of living equal to the best, at least in the areas of household equipment and automobiles.

Many who have come to maturity during the current period cannot remember the time when healing drugs were not available, so commonplace have they become. With them has come the resultant expectation of less serious illness or even the prevention of illnesses which at one time were a common dread. So gratified are consumers that these drugs can be readily obtainable, that there is little disposition to ask whether they are available at a price commensurate with their costs. The Congressional hearings on drug costs, chaired by the late Estes Kefauver, shook the drug industry with its sensational findings but apparently elicited no great public indignation.

What is true of drugs is perhaps even truer of food. Frequently have we been reminded that food takes a lesser percentage of the American budget than is the case in any other country, and therefore we do not ask the question whether it could be available even more cheaply.* The convenience of ready-prepared foods, so beneficial to the household where time for preparation is at a premium, has minimized the inclination to inquire about the costs of the food itself and the processing which makes it available so quickly. The facts that, though food is in great abundance, its cost continually rises and the farmer receives a steadily declining proportionate return for what he has produced, constitute one of the paradoxes of our time. Only recently has there been emerging at Congressional level the demand for a major analysis of this dilemma.

To any list of commonplace assumptions would have to be added the expectation of obsolescence. A productive society capable of manufacturing more than can be consumed must foster a disposition to purchase new models and to discourage repairs. The automobile industry is a major example of this encouragement of artificial obsolescence. Until recently there has been little serious resistance to the manufacturers' policy, but the importation of some durable foreign-made cars seems to have induced a disposition to concentrate on quality in the domestic automotive industry.

Nevertheless the widespread misgivings concerning doubtful claims for many products have undermined public confidence in many types of advertising. Noteworthy efforts have been made to achieve and maintain standards of integrity in offering certain goods and services, but that deviations are frequent is widely apparent. The current trend in self-regulation as observed in the area of cigarette advertising compares with the regulations resulting from the false claims at one time made for "patent medicines." Medical facts plus public indignation have combined to curb dishonesty. With so many reputable producers using honorable means to portray their products, it may seem harsh to concentrate on those who practice deception. As in every profession or type of work, it is the latter who bring discredit to the work of others. One of

---

* E. g., comparing Moscow work time as a percentage of New York work time in 1959: butter, 900 per cent (21 min. vs. 3 hrs. 4 min.); eggs, 800 per cent; beef, 400 per cent; milk, 400 per cent. (Source: The Conference Board Road Maps of Industry, No. 1275.)

the major frontiers of ethics in our time lies in the promotion of integrity in advertising.

INFLUENCING THE CONSUMER'S JUDGMENT

As a nation we believe so thoroughly in the old slogan "it pays to advertise" that we are willing to spend 12 billion dollars, or 2.8 per cent of our national income, for that purpose. This can hardly be condemned as an exorbitant expenditure toward keeping the economy healthy. With considerable truth the defenders of advertising contend that this very large business makes a substantial and necessary contribution to our economic well-being.

In any area of life involving so great a sum of money it would be strange if there were not a proportionate measure of chicanery and outright fraud. Techniques for manipulating the minds and dispositions of others are a constant temptation to dishonesty and give rise to profound ethical problems. In a free economy, where the market is presumed to determine prices, those who practice the science of influencing purchasing decisions can assert with some reasonableness that "no one has to buy," that individuals are still free and can judge for themselves whether they are getting "value received." As was stated earlier when we were discussing the increasing importance of the three big components in our economy—government, labor, and management—it has become apparent that "the sovereign importance of the market is a thing of the past. Even if it were to furnish a perfectly equilibrated price structure the market would resolve few if any of our fateful dilemmas."[4] Also at the level of the individual consumer the market has a diminishing significance. This is not to say that changes do no occur because of changing tastes. Rather it is to suggest that tastes themselves can be created and also that in gratifying these tastes individuals can be induced to buy goods which are, if not inimical to their best interests, at least of poorer quality than others which they might purchase.

Caveat emptor—"let the buyer beware"—has been a cardinal feature of the free-choice system. Presumably, if the buyer has been deceived enough, he will change his purchasing habits. The burden, therefore, has traditionally rested with the buyer. When federal and state governments entered this arena, it was charged that this was interfering with the sovereign right of the buyer and also that of the enterprising producer. A higher standard was resorted to in this controversy—the standard of the well-being, the wealth of society, or what has come to be known as the common-weal. Regulatory agencies having jurisdiction over quality, contents, and weights and measures were set up to give protection to the buyer who himself could not know the content of foods and medicines or judge honest weights. Thus he became protected, in part at least, against the attractiveness of word and picture with which the advertiser confronted him.

Leaving the health aspect aside—for few would argue in this day that government should not protect its citizens against physical injury from food and drugs—the question still remains whether the buyer should not have the privilege of being fooled if he so wishes, or of satisfying his own personal desires as they have been stimulated through advertising media. If he chooses not to be a rational buyer, is not that his privilege? The answer would necessarily be yes if first the individual has been apprized of all the factors which enter into the purchase. If he knows he is getting less than his money's worth, it is certainly his privilege to pay as much as he wishes over and above the actual worth of the product. But if he has insufficient means for discovering the difference between the value of the product and the price being charged, whose responsibility is it?

This difference between cost and value of the product comes out with special clarity in the whole matter of packaging. The issue is stated in the report of a Senate hearing on the subject:

In our modern society good packaging meets many consumer needs, among them convenience, freshness, safety and attractive appearance. But often in recent years, as the hearings have demonstrated, these benefits have been accompanied by practices which frustrate the consumer's efforts to get the best value for his dollar. In many cases the label seems designed to conceal rather than to reveal the true contents of the package. Sometimes the consumer cannot readily ascertain the net amount of the product, or the ratio of solid contents to air. Frequently he cannot readily compute the comparative costs per unit of different brands packed in odd sizes, or of the same brand in large, giant, king size, or jumbo packages. And he may not realize that changes in the customary size or shape of the package may account for apparent bargains, or that "cents off" promotions often do not mean real savings.

Misleading, fraudulent or unhelpful practices such as these are clearly incompatible with the efficient and equitable functioning of our free competitive economy. Under our system, consumers have a right to expect that packages will carry reliable and readily usable information about their contents. And those manufacturers whose products are sold in such packages have a right to expect that their competitors will be required to adhere to the same standards.[5]

For many years Congressional leaders, social workers, and all who have a concern for the problem of individual bankruptcy have been pressing for a "truth in lending" bill. In one year (1961) 150,000 families declared themselves in bankruptcy, a rate ten times that of a decade ago. A person buying on credit may pay anywhere from nothing to 275 per cent for the privilege. Cash loans secured through commercial loan companies, or as a part of the criminal "juice" racket, range from 4 to 2000 per cent! Commercial banks and credit unions charge 12 per cent, while consumer finance companies get anywhere from 30 to 42 per cent. An informed borrower could calculate the rate of his loan, but the tragic fact is that many are unable to make this calculation and respond to the blandishments of those exacting inordinately high rates under the happy expectation of paying off all their bills in one lump sum or of taking a vacation free of worries. It is understandable that those in the business of exacting such rates of interest, including automobile financing agencies whose income from the time-payment sale of an automobile is greater than the profit from the sale itself, are vehemently opposed to "truth in lending" legislation.

Trading stamps have become as much the symbol of the American economy as the supermarket. They are also a symbol of joyous self-deception. Everyone (well, almost) "knows" that everything he receives with the trading stamps he has already paid for with the initial purchase.* There is the possibility of a slight bonus

* The price increase ranges between one and two per cent, depending on which of the fifty-odd trading devices is used.

here; the people who do not pick up the goods to which they are entitled through trading stamps leave just that much more in the treasury of the trading stamp company and may add a little to the value received by others who do. This gigantic scheme for "kidding oneself" that he is getting something for nothing seems to be a part of the economic atmosphere of our time. It is a painless and euphoric device to avoid having to make evaluations and to shop discriminately.

Manufacturers in a free-choice economy have tried repeatedly and with some success to institute "fair trade" laws by which their products could not be sold below a stipulated figure without penalty to the seller. Some manufacturers hope that prices would be increased and their standards maintained by legislation better than by the competition of the market. Small merchants find this practice desirable as protection against big merchandisers and discount houses whose greater volume give them advantages. As a protection for the small businessman there is something to be said for the idea. Its major weakness lies in the fact that the free economy is disrupted because costs to the consumer should be going down as improved and more economical methods of production are adopted. When the manufacturer is able to protect himself against giving the benefit of these lowered costs to the consumer, he is less inclined to seek better means of production. The National Recovery Administration fostered price-fixing on a national basis, but it was declared unconstitutional. Then state laws were enacted which supported prices, but before they had been fully tested the World War II created a scarcity which temporarily eliminated the need. From 1941 to 1961 the consumers price index rose from 62.9 to 127.5. This included the years of wartime control. But from 1955 to 1960 the index continued to rise at the average rate of 2.6 points per year. Thus competition even in times of great surplus has not consistently kept prices down. One qualifying comment should be made, however. Hopefully there had been a measure of quality increase which is an offsetting factor and which would have added something to the rise in the index.

The consumer is thus embroiled in endless gamesmanship. There is a way of winning, but he may not want to condition himself for the fray. The producers, processors, and distributors, on the other hand, do not take the game so lightly. They spend millions of dollars to analyze the tastes of the consumer, which they have every right to do, providing they have not indulged in outright fraud. Unfortunately the record indicates a great deal of fraud. The labeling which says "ten cents off" doesn't indicate what it is "off of." The label which says "serves eight" may really mean that it serves four. In the Senate hearings on this kind of fraud, Senator Hart commented: "That is a sign of moral deterioration. . . . You wouldn't want your children to adopt a philosophy like that. There's nothing good about this attitude."

Whether the total fraudulence in packaging and advertising is any greater than the collusion which marked the scandal involving the foremost producers of electrical appliances and equipment is beside the point.* It is all part of the same moral deterioration of which the consumer is a victim and to which he has wittingly or unwittingly contributed. It is also of a piece with the collusion between public officials and the suppliers of road materials and highway equipment to the states and the federal government; the collusion between Billy Sol Estes and the financing companies, which dare not expose him for fear their own houses of cards would tumble; the widely exposed cheating in television, bringing distinguished and honorable names into discredit; and on and on.

Ultimately it is the consumer who must bear the costs of the deception, chicanery, and corruption. Some of it is overlooked on the ground that people really don't mind being fooled. They enjoy the little game, and what little they lose they may get back

* The reference is to the collusion between General Electric, Allis-Chalmers, Westinghouse, and others in the sale of equipment both to private firms and to the government from 1951 to 1960. Government prosecution charged prices were raised as much as 900 per cent on some equipment and 446 per cent on other types. Rigging of prices produced hundreds of millions of dollars in excess profits. The companies were declared guilty by a federal court on February 6, 1961. Seven executives were given jail sentences, others were given suspended sentences, and twenty-nine corporations were fined $1,787,000. Subsequently $7,460,000 was repaid to the federal government and additional sums to others who had been injured by these unethical practices.

in excitement or pleasure. This same rationalization, of course, lies behind the pressure for legalized gambling, currently highlighted with the sanctioning of lotteries by the state of New Hampshire. The justification offered is that ultimately it doesn't cost anybody very much and the schools will be the better for it in terms of modernization of plant and improved salary scale. Whether it is the pay-off of legitimate businesses to the crime syndicate, or legalized gambling at race tracks, or the statewide saturation with gambling in Nevada, the implications are basically the same. The question fundamentally is whether the article bought is contributing something substantial to the physical and spiritual life of persons, and whether the money spent therefore contributes to useful labor. This is the ethical problem confronting the consumer. Whatever forces are playing upon his attitudes in one way or another, they must finally come under judgment as to their social usefulness.

RESOURCES FOR THE CONSUMER

Leland Gordon, out of his wealth of experience on behalf of consumers, contends that: "Consumers need to know their part in the economy. The motivation and operation of the economic system must be explained. Consumers must be acquainted with its virtues as well as its defects. They must understand that the persistence of fraud, misrepresentation, and other undesirable practices is possible because of their own lack of organized resistance. They need to realize the importance of substituting reason for emotion in the marketplace."[6]

Fortunately there is a very wide spectrum of resources available to the consumer in our time, illustrated by President Johnson's appointment of a Special Assistant for Consumer Affairs, referred to earlier. The manufacturer and distributor have vast resources to help them prepare for their market and to render the consumer more kindly disposed toward their product. Who is doing anything comparable for the consumer, enabling him to select wisely, thus increasing, in effect, his own income and benefiting the total gamut of the consumer's life? These are some of the resources available to the consumer:

1. Foremost are the standards established by many departments of the federal and state governments. At the federal level the Sherman Antitrust Act, the Clayton Antitrust Act, the Federal Trade Commission, and the Food and Drug Administration are instruments for his protection. Not only is health protected, but weights and measures are continually checked against deception. "U. S. Government Inspected" has come to be a symbol of integrity within the range and purpose for which products are appraised. Where health is involved, there is little temporizing. Though the cigarette-smoking contribution to cancer was long in testing, there were strong forces extending every effort to prove cigarettes uninjurious. Similar state and federal legislation to protect borrowers of money has not thus far been as uniformly successful, but gains have been made at state levels even though at this time federal support of "truth in lending" still has not been legislated.

2. The schools have been efficient teachers of making money but less diligent in training for intelligent consumption, which is a necessary part of the learning process.

3. One hundred or more cities have Better Business Bureaus through which the honesty of advertising can be checked and claims investigated. Fraudulence is thereby reduced and the scope of public conscience is enlarged.

4. Seventeen million members of labor unions represent approximately that number of household buying units. Labor organizations long ago realized that one way to increase family income was to encourage intelligent purchasing. To that end some labor journals have introduced sections designed to sensitize their members and families to ways of extending their earnings. Constructive guidance is also available from the American Home Economics Association, the American Dental Association, and the American Medical Association, which in their respective areas, serve to provide better diet and improve oral health and general physical well-being.

5. The foremost nongovernmental agency or movement in the nation concerned with the consumer is the cooperative movement. No other organization or cluster of organizations has done as much for the welfare of the consumer. Starting with the primary assumption that the role of the consumer is of first importance, the

consumer himself devises the kinds of organizations which will assure that his interests are protected. The result is too well known to require recounting here. Out of consumers cooperatives has arisen a host of producer cooperatives owned by those whom they serve. Members of consumer cooperatives have developed confidence in the quality and standards of the products for which they are primarily responsible. If there are deficiencies, there is immediate access to the source.

6. The phenomenal growth of consumer testing agencies, such as Consumers Research or Consumers Union, each independent of any advertising or product dispensing, has given to the buying public a yardstick for quality upon which it can confidently depend. With millions of people basing purchases on their advice, producers have now learned to keep one ear open for the voice of these testing agencies.

Increasingly widespread are the consumer-centered movements dealing with burial practices, life insurance, discount stores, weights and measures, health and medical care, and many other common needs. Central consumer information agencies are available for counsel on these and many other practices. This is but a small fraction of the great wealth of resources available to consumers who desire to know ways of using their incomes wisely and of enriching the life of the economy.

Organized Labor's Role

The American people do not like things that are too big. Our people have always restrained business when it would grow too big. And now they are face-to-face with an organization more powerful, more merciless, and more dangerous than anything that has ever existed in this country—the American Federation of Labor.

—SAMUEL HARDEN CHURCH, President, Carnegie Institute, former official of the Pennsylvania Railroad[1]

Little did the gentleman whose quotation appears above realize that he had either misread the signs of the times or misunderstood the American people, or both. Labor and management and government have, in their respective spheres, become bigger and more powerful both in themselves and in their relationships with each other, and short of stopping the whole technological development, there is even more bigness ahead. No responsible analyst of society dares to predict that there will be technological restraints and curtailment of bigness.

Though both labor and management face large and highly complex problems, we shall deal here primarily with the issues confronting labor as they arise in relation to management and to the whole of society. Though management also has serious problems in relation to its employees, it has many other concerns as well —sales, financing, stockholder relations, and all those decisions relating to the continuance and expansion of the business itself. But in many of these decisions there is increasing coordination with labor, so that actually most discussions of labor carry implications for management.

The labor union movement in the United States has never been a vehicle for class struggle in the Marxist sense. There have been unions which attempted to voice class differences and to represent economic ideologies, but they have been few and do not represent the mainstream. This is not to say, however, that there have been no protest movements; actually they have been numerous. But none of these protest movements developed into a major labor movement with sufficient strength to incorporate large blocs of working people. The Industrial Workers of the World (IWW) was strong enough to harass some communities and stir up strife, but there was neither consistently strong leadership nor sufficient ideological conviction to guide a major segment of labor through both prosperity and depression. Attempts to coordinate farm and labor protests have served to challenge financial power centers and secure public sympathy to the extent that political changes were forthcoming. This latter fact is possibly the key to the failure of numerous radical movements in this country. The American people have maintained a sympathy for genuine protest movements resulting from injustices. It is a well-attested fact that the political power which has been available to those working toward economic reconstruction and a steadily rising standard of living have served to remove the frustrations of oppressed groups that believed they had no escape from their economic and social strait jacket. (Such a statement would have needed modification until recently, but dramatic and far-reaching actions affecting the Negro in this country bear out the statement.)

Samuel Gompers, though a product of ideological movements in Europe, had the extraordinary insight to recognize that such patterns would not be effective in the United States. As one of the founders of the American Federation of Labor and its president (except for one year) from 1886 to 1924, he convinced his co-workers that the future of the labor movement in this country depended upon adherence to three fundamental concerns: wages, hours, and working conditions. Other organizations, notably the Knights of Labor, had diluted their effectiveness by pseudoreligious objectives and a broad front of economic concerns. The times simply were not ready for so inclusive a range of economic changes as the Knights espoused.

A program that is right for one period is rarely adequate, in its initial form at least, for subsequent times. After enduring bitter and bloody hostility from management over many years, with the courts sustaining management on theories of property ownership and power, labor finally developed enough strength to challenge the combination of economic and political power exercised by the owners and managers, and a modification resulted. The history of the labor movement has been recounted so fully and in so many ways that it is not essential to repeat it here. We would simply reaffirm the fact that it was around the focus of the three cardinal features—wages, hours and working conditions—and its function of providing members insurance that the strength of the labor movement developed. This fact and the necessity for changing it became of great significance in later periods as labor reconsidered its role and policy.

The story of the development of the labor movement would be incomplete without an account of cooperation with labor on the part of nonlabor groups. In no small measure can the vitality of the Social Gospel movement be identified with its concern for labor. Numerous organizations were formed within Protestant denominations and across denominational lines as a result of the convictions that power was being unjustly wielded by owners and that individuals were being deprived of their God-given rights through excessive burdens and long hours which taxed physical and spiritual resources. One of the most notable instances of the combined effort of the churches on behalf of oppressed labor was the entrance of religious leadership into the 1919 steel strike. The results and the settlement of that strike represented a watershed in industrial relations. Intervention by religious leaders was bitterly resented; but the eight-hour day was established in the steel industry, and the combined influence of labor organizations and religious leadership was made apparent. Though full strength of the labor movement in steel was almost twenty years away, a principle had been established.

Roman Catholic support of labor found its most substantial expression in an encyclical of Leo XIII, *Rerum novarum* (1890), and forty-one years later in another powerful plea for economic justice, *Quadragesimo anno* by Pius XI. Since so large a number of those arriving in this country and becoming employees of a burgeoning industry were Roman Catholics, this concern of their church for their welfare had far-reaching significance.

Any history of the movements supporting labor and its purposes would be incomplete if it failed to recount the work of the League for Industrial Democracy, which, though unrelated to any religious body, included within its ranks large numbers of churchmen and nonchurchmen alike. It has been a militant voice in behalf of justice to labor. Still another agency has been the National Religion and Labor Foundation (more recently, the Religion and Labor Council), whose purpose has been to acquaint seminary students with labor's history and objectives. These organizations and many others came into existence during the times when the labor movement was fighting for its life.

Traditional concepts of property and ownership included neither the formal obligation to provide continuity of work opportunity for the laborer nor the obligation to provide conditions of work which would be safe and wholesome. To these faults labor began to address itself with new zeal and power. The history of resistance to its efforts is now a part of history that will not readily be forgotten and of which many of us are properly ashamed. The record includes the bloody Homestead Strike, the Haymarket Riot, the May 30 Massacre in Chicago, and many others.

Union Strengths and Weaknesses

Thus the Wagner Act of 1935 came after a long history of hostility on the part of industry in particular and the public in general. A depression, a lessened confidence in business leadership, and a political administration sympathetic to labor's purposes wrought a major change in the nation's attitudes. Union membership soared, reaching its highest peak up to that time during the period of World War II. With the war over the pendulum began to swing in the other direction—this time producing the Taft-Hartley Act and subsequently the Landrum-Griffin Act, both designed to reduce the power that labor unions had acquired in the period of their greatest influence. At first there was deep resentment on the part of labor against the new legislation curbing union expansion. But as time went on, the consequences of the new legislation proved to be not as restrictive as anticipated, and labor learned to live with the new regulations, not happily but with acceptance. In spite of the hostility in the period from 1947 to 1951, unions won 97 per cent of 46,146 elections held for the purpose of securing union-shop provisions in contracts. The favorable response to unionism was so great that some firms, it is reported, did not even bother to enter into an election.

Money poured into the coffers of many unions, making possible an investment program which has been both a source of strength and a gross temptation to racketeers. At the present time (1965) union assets exceed 670 million dollars. At a meeting of the AFL-CIO Executive Committee in August 1964 a mortgage investment trust involving pooling of union funds for investment in government guaranteed mortgages was readied for functioning with "a number of millions of dollars" already committed.[2] Many of these funds were accumulated to provide a cushion in time of strikes; but where strikes did not occur, the funds piled up. Others are pension and insurance funds. "Business unionism" took on a new meaning. It had heretofore meant simply taking care of the business affairs of the union, making certain that dues were paid and that membership was intact, and negotiating contracts with employers. Now a new facet of the movement appeared: the need for professionals to handle the intricate business affairs of the unions. Among them were persons competent to invest the union's funds. A labor organizer does not necessarily make a wise investor, any more than the investor possesses the technical and legal skills to enter into intricate negotiations. Unions have had to become profession-conscious in order to secure the caliber of representatives who could attend to the complicated new areas of union business. The abuses of some of these funds have made front-page stories in the daily press, but Clair Cook, himself a labor union member and a clergyman, has commented: "The intensive probing by the McClellan Committee turned up a figure of $10 millions in union money misused for personal gain or stolen outright over the last fifteen years. That last year alone employers illegally kept $250 millions withheld from wages for income taxes and social security, failing to turn it into the federal government after they were entrusted with it."[3] *Life*, in appraising the ethical climate of business, estimated that 5 billion dollars annually is the toll for bribes, kick-backs, and other unethical business expenses.[4] The labor racketeering and misappropriated funds, though bad enough are small by comparison with the scope of corruption in other phases of our national life.

A slackening of pace in the labor movement's expansion and aggressive action cannot be attributed primarily to its increased economic security as indicated by its investments. Having won its right to exist and having demonstrated that harmonious and helpful relations can exist between labor and management, each has come to accept the other (in the major industrialized areas at least). Now they can fulfill their respective functions without having to spend energy in securing general recognition of those functions. It must be added that clean-cut definitions of those respective functions will probably remain elusive. For the time being, with its major objective—recognition—attained, the sense of mission and need to survive is less intense.

One of the reasons American labor has been unreceptive to political ideological programs conflicting with the enterprise system can be seen in the vast program of welfare activities conducted under the auspices of labor unions. The list is much too long to incorporate into this brief space, but it includes housing projects, total health coverage, vacation opportunities, and insurance programs of a wide variety. Many of these programs are in addition to similar programs of the corporations and supplemental to government programs. All of this is in addition to the principal functions which the labor union was originally designed to serve. With all these benefits compounded, one might be inclined to ask why all persons thus eligible for participation in labor unions have not eagerly accepted the opportunity of doing so; for the fact remains that less than 20 per cent of all workers are enrolled in labor organizations.

Some of the reasons for nonparticipation can be seen as a result of the very success of the labor organizations themselves. Having achieved security—in many parts of the country, at least—the sense of being a movement has steadily declined. Since, as we have seen, unions have themselves become major businesses, a criterion for remaining in office is the capacity to operate the business successfully and with a minimum of friction within the organization. Eric Sevareid, no hostile critic of unions, says:

There is today, among some labor bosses, the same child-like fascination in finance, in deals, in handling big chunks of money that was true of successful businessmen in the booming wonderland of the 1920's; Beck and Hoffa are prime examples of wide-eyed wonder at the reproductive capacity of money. . . . Little of political ideology remains to organized labor; the goals are almost exclusively material in nature and limited in degree. It is a vast, vested interest, the other side of the identical coin of capitalism. . . . Little wonder that the public talk today centers on labor's responsibilities to the general society. Little wonder that the same laws that gradually regulated the once unregulated power of business are slowly creeping up on organized labor. . . .[5]

In consequence there is lessened anxiety over the large number of those not enrolled in unions. To compound matters for those responsible for conducting the business of the union, there is the fact that because of automation unions have been declining still further, as was pointed out in Chapter 4.

Another factor contributing to labor's declining sense of mission is, for good or ill, its collaboration with industry's objectives. To maintain themselves with the minimum of internal disorder, unions of many different types have entered into close relations with employers, who formerly were their opponents. In steel, electric power, and coal, for example, unions have supported the companies in their development programs, many of which would make necessary increased prices to the public. One paradoxical result has been the unofficial support of private power programs while the official position of the union supported public power.

As job opportunities contract and the peril of losing out in the business administration of the union looms larger, any expression of opposition to the organization becomes suspect and unions think they must be curtailed. Some labor organizations, historically democratic in their roots and committed to a theme of human brotherhood, feel themselves under the necessity of suppressing all opposition. The result has been a tendency toward self-appointing hierarchies, with all the temptations accompanying such practices.

Under a system of self-defense and the maintenance of the *status quo*, it is hardly to be expected that unions will become the champions of long-range plans and committed to the development of programs designed to protect the consumer and foster the far-reaching purposes of the nation as a whole in its total economic outlook and its world obligations. Yet it must quickly be said that there are labor leaders capable of this sort of leadership and that they have made a contribution in the nation's life far in excess of what could be expected from their constituency. They have run the risk of being in the forefront and thereby endangering their own support. To their great credit it must be asserted that they have labored diligently to arouse the interests of their fellow members in plans and programs whose ultimate ends are in the best interest of the nation as a whole while in the short run they are less desirable.

Because of Congressional hearings and widespread dissemination of information in the nation's press, labor unions have come into serious condemnation for their seemingly rigid insistence on certain archaic work practices. The sin of which they are guilty, in the public mind at least, is that they are placing an undue burden upon the economy by demanding wages for work not done and thus imperiling the economic health of the industrial organizations forced to continue these dubious practices. "Feather-bedding" aptly illustrates one of the fundamental dilemmas of the economy and of the role of labor unions. As technological improvements are made, certain jobs become unnnecessary. There has been emerging over the generations a reluctant acceptance of the fact that a person has an equity in his job. Unions have fostered this conviction and have won new recognition for this right. Where a job is to be eliminated in a society where other work is unobtainable, unions have stressed the responsibility of the eliminator to give assurance that the worker's livelihood will not be destroyed.* The insistence upon job protection or compensation for job loss constitutes one of the major contributions of labor unions in a period of adjustment. Because some unions have had greater success in defending their members' rights to their jobs than others, the issue has been lifted into full view.

Public indignation has also been aroused over the feather-bedding charge because of a suspicion that the unions fostering the practice are not willing to share the responsibilities for technological changes. Because unions have been in a position to protest job changes, the onus of the defense has fallen on them. Unorganized workers, suffering similar work modifications, have lacked equally vigorous defenders. Behind the charges and countercharges is the preservation of jobs. The rapid disappearance of jobs, with other work unavailable, has caused unions to stress the retention of jobs. Devices to retain jobs and keep members employed have included deliberate inefficiency and "slow-downs," not because of a depreciated sense of quality, as had occasionally been charged, but because it is the most available means of making the work "go around." From the workers' point of view the the slow-down is not loafing; it is a modification in the unit of work, designed to help guarantee a job.

LABOR'S NEW PROBLEMS

A part of the genius of the labor movement has been its ability to adapt to the shifts in the industrial situation. By concentrating on wages, hours, and working conditions, labor was able to make gains proportionate to the expanding economy and the requirements for added workers. Its strength has always been among those classified by the census as "blue-collar workers." At one time they were the majority of employees, but during the past decade a major shift has occurred, and as has been noted earlier, today the white-collar workers predominate. With them the labor movement has been singularly unsuccessful.

* The result of the arbitration process involving the railroad firemen and the operators, with encouragement from the White House, would indicate at least tacit acceptance of this idea.

The reasons for labor's inability to organize the growing number of white-collar workers are not unrelated to the role of labor itself and the image it has projected—that of a worker with hands and tools rather than with pencil, cash register, or typewriter. Even though labor has never identified itself primarily with a socialist ideology and has itself noticeably gone up the economic scale in an open society, there still remains the class stigma and the aversion of white-collar workers to identification with an historically lower-class movement. It may well be that as white-collar workers discover that they are in need of the kind of job security which helped to give impetus to the labor movement itself, there will be an increasing disposition among them to look favorably on organizations for this purpose. Already there is strong indication that AFL-CIO and unaffiliated unions are mounting major efforts in this direction.

The greatest increase in the labor movement's membership was reached just prior to the passage of the Taft-Hartley Act. Since then a leveling off has occurred, with a slight decline in the early 1960s.* Present membership may represent a more stable constituency than the swollen roster of members who joined the unions during and following World War II. But the leveling off and decline are not simply the defection of lukewarm members; automation is a more serious "culprit." Figures change so rapidly that they are out-of-date before the ink is dry. The fact of the serious decline in membership of major unions does not change, however, and every indication suggests that the decline will continue. It may be offset in part by new members recruited from white-collar ranks, but technological developments in many types of industries will account for further reductions in some unions. The issues presented by automation are not those which can be resolved through collective bargaining. No one can reasonably expect management to continue employing unneeded workers, but neither can one reasonably expect unions to concede that they and their members have become superfluous. What about those disemployed? Who will absorb the costs of moving and retraining them? The workers themselves? Management? Who? "And so the problem of automation and particular unemployment cannot

---

* The AFL-CIO reported a gain of 360,000 in the first six months of 1964.

be kept inside the confines of traditional collective bargaining; the government must share the responsibility for its solution, and perhaps assume the major share. True, machines have made workers unemployed before but it has never happened at such a rate."[6] An electric coal shovel doing the work of one thousand coal miners in a Kentucky strip mine is a vivid illustration of technological advances in steel, autos, meat-packing and many other areas. In an earlier era the Luddites and their counterparts in other times and places smashed the machines which took their jobs. Today the stripping-machine digging coal for TVA power is not opposed by the United Mine Workers. The machine pays a levy to the union treasury, benefiting welfare funds of union members as well as those unemployed, but the levy does not equal the union dues or put a thousand men to work.

Industry-wide bargaining has been a moot point with labor and management for many years. Management opposes it. Labor once saw advantages in a uniform scale, but now it is unsure. The necessity to abide by a single decision applicable to diverse situations can both create confusion and possibly work hardships. It is easier to confront management with the specific problems of a given plant than to have to abide by an action covering a multiplicity of plants. Unions would rather negotiate with one railroad at a time than with the entire railroad industry. Efficiency might dictate changes in work practices applicable on a nationwide basis, but efficiency as the principal criterion would work havoc in job security at a local level.

Organized labor contends that one of its strongest contributions is its support of democratic principles. But the question widely asked is: Can democracy and efficiency be reconciled?

The essence of technological change and the justification for acceptance of its consequences is the concept of efficiency. But efficiency and job security are largely mutually exclusive. The rapid acceleration in automated activity is justified on grounds of efficiency, while job security disappears. Fundamental to the democratic principle is the right of the individual to exercise some control over the political and economic processes in which he has a large stake. While industry was expanding and there were jobs enough for almost everybody, insistence on democratic practices and rights seemed reasonable. But now there emerges in the name of the sacred concept "efficiency" a set of requirements which call for the reduction of jobs and the minimizing of the democratic process. For this labor has been for the most part unprepared. It should be quickly added, however, that labor is not alone in its unpreparedness. There is apparently in process as these lines are being written a diminution in the ranks of middle management in even greater porportion than the losses in labor ranks. Efficiency is no respecter of status, collar, or color.

Securing and protecting the right to organize and negotiate has long been a justification of labor's participation in politics. New conditions have made political action continually necessary. Length of the work week and minimum hourly rates are established by legislation. Since one obvious and available means of providing jobs or spreading the work is the shortening of the standard work period, labor believes it should use its influence on legislatures to secure this benefit. The same is true for accident and employment compensation, and a wide range of activities in which labor has been interested for itself and the community at large. Recently a concern for retraining of workers has emerged as a necessary service. Probably no group would be more sensitive to this need than organized labor. Political action is required to institute and finance such programs.

Labor's formula of "reward your friends and punish your enemies" has paid off well in the political scene. Labor has learned the necessity of making its wishes known at the national political level as well as the local. A new phase of government relationship has come into the scene, however, complicating life for both labor and management. It is the fact that much of the new work now employing hundreds of thousands of workers is government-supported but privately operated. Contracts are made with private corporations, but the work being performed is government-initiated and in most instances fully government-sustained. Much of the work being performed is authorized by the Department of Defense, and therefore a controversy over wages confronts labor with the delicate question of conflict with our national security and possibly at the same time impairing the relationship of good will with the taxpayer. Nothing illustrates more sharply the intricacy of current economic life than the total dependence of large brackets of industry upon government support and the anomalous, if not paradoxical, relationship of labor as both taxpayer and employee. Traditional collective bargaining takes on new meanings and renders old patterns obsolete. Issues involved here cannot be resolved by traditional bargaining relationships between labor and management. The key is held by government, and each of the other parties is beholden to the "third force," government, for its very livelihood. No amount of brave proclamations about the enterprise system or the rights and dignity of labor against a tyrannically oppressive management can bring a solution to this vast and growing problem.

Closely related to the problem of labor-government relations is the tough and increasingly troublesome problem of our national relationship to foreign markets, balance of payments, tariffs, and the health of our own national economy. The statesmen among labor leaders know that there is no future wholesomeness for American economic life without increasing correlation with the economies of other nations, and now particularly with the "Inner Six" and the "Outer Seven," the European Common Market and those nations most closely related to Britain. Will the rank and file of labor which ultimately elects these statesmen among their leaders understand when concessions in tariffs are made which may further shift employment in our own country? Though American industry has faced this problem before, it has never been under these conditions and under the pressure of the competition of other nations' mounting efficiency.

NEW ROLES FOR LABOR

Economists may disagree over the contribution labor organizations have made to the improvement of working conditions and the rights of working people. Albert Rees in his *Economics of Trade Unions* contends that "the studies to date must be regarded as highly inconclusive; no union effect on labor's share can be discovered with any consistency. . . . By far the most fundamental point, however, is that a successful union will not necessarily raise labor's share even in its own industry." Then he adds: "There are many other aspects of union activity yet to be considered, and an economy has other and perhaps even more important goals than the most efficient allocation of resources."[7]

Possibly the most recent and also the most definitive study of the subject to date, that of H. G. Lewis, estimates that "the average union/non-union relative wage was approximately 10–15% higher than it would have been in the absence of unionism." The author comments further: "These figures imply that recently the average of union workers was about 7–11% higher, relative to the average wage of all workers, both union and non-union, than it would have been in the absence on unions. Similarly, the average wage of non-union workers was about 3–4% lower relative to the average wage of all workers than in the absence of unionism. . . . I conclude tentatively that unionism has had a small impact on the relative inequality of the distribution of wages among all workers. The direction of the effect, on presently available evidence, is ambiguous."[8]

Some economists have gone so far as to suggest that wages have actually been kept lower in certain completely unionized work than might have been the case had they been free from contract arrangements. Whether this is true or not does not constitute our principal point of interest. Possibly labor's greatest contribution to the life of this nation and subsequently to many others as well lies in the achievement of a standard of decency and justice for wage earners. What is of primary importance is the distinctive contribution which labor has made to the well-being of its own people and many others who have no specific identification with the labor movement.

The fear of bigness, which is another way of expressing a fear of power, as indicated in the quotation at the beginning of this chapter, stems from apprehension over the misuse of power. But the very term "misuse of power" is one which does not readily lend itself to clear analysis. Usually it means the way in which the other person is using his power against me. From this perspective labor has been feared by management, and the entire history of the labor movement gives evidence that labor has had just cause to fear the power of management. Now within a comparatively short period of history labor has emerged as one of the major power configurations on the American scene able to provide a check against business maltreatment. In its capacity as a defender of human rights it has served as one of the major instruments for ethical achievement, and in this function it has contributed richly to the physical and spiritual well-being of an entire nation. Coincidentally, it is significant that the areas of the nation where labor has been unable to organize and make itself felt are the areas of greatest poverty, where human welfare is held most cheaply.

With their history of contribution to both the ethical and economic life of a people, the question must now be raised whether labor organizations in their individual or federative forms have a function to perform in the present situation of this nation. It is recognized that the geographic areas referred to still need the kind of humanizing and experience of justice which labor has brought to the more highly industrialized areas of the land, but with the legal and moral protection which has already been built into the economy of the major parts of this industrialized nation, is there still a function for labor organizations?

Business unionism, as indicated above, has obviously become highly successful. Union leadership is a matter for professionals and is no longer the prerogative of those who were most effective with the brass knuckles in a day when force had to be met by force. Children of union leaders and of the rank-and-file are encouraged by the unions themselves to move up into new brackets of economic and educational attainment. Labor journals delight to picture the children of their members who have earned Merit Scholarships and Phi Beta Kappa keys. An open society has made possible upward mobility, and the same talents which make for dynamic leadership in the union are also praised when they lead the second generation into other forms of leadership in society. The assumption behind all of this is that labor leaders—and, by imputation, labor itself—are not simply concerned with their own rights and prerogatives. To the extent that it is an ethical movement concerned for the opportunities of all people, labor has an obligation to share with society at large the convictions it holds or has held about the worth of man and the kind of a society he must build.

If such a picture of labor's expectations seems naïve and over-idealistic, one does not have to go far back into the history of the labor movement to discover a large element of this kind of emphasis. Has business unionism undercut the far-seeing intentions of those who in another generation saw the labor movement as primarily an instrument for human betterment? Obviously there are many in the impressive ranks of labor who still regard labor as a movement and conceive of it as a continuing instrument for society's welfare. Having won earlier battles to bring labor to its position of relative security, many of its more thoughtful members are asking whether its work is over or whether there are frontiers as demanding in this period as those which characterized earlier days. One world-renowned labor leader, when asked on the occasion of an anniversary of his leadership of the organization what the greatest thing he had accomplished for his union was, pointed to the bank which had been formed by and for that union.

Solomon Barkin, who writes from the inside of a labor organization (he is the Director of research in the Textile Workers Union), but who also has maintained a high degree of objectivity about the role of unions, comments that "few social thinkers would now look to unions for the leadership needed to revitalize our economic and social system."[9] Barkin is writing primarily from the standpoint of the ability of unions to offset communist influence and of the decline in general respect which liberals have expressed toward labor as it became so heavily preoccupied with itself and its privileges.

The incontrovertible facts remain that there are still vast areas of injustice in American life and that there are the problems of national and international relations upon which hangs the future health of our own economic existence. Unemployment has been hovering at or above the 5 per cent figure for several years. No other major group is going to speak on behalf of the unemployed, unless militant organizations are formed around the interests of that group alone. No single body, however, has as much knowledge of organization and as much wisdom about the nature of the economy itself as the combined forces of the international unions. With 108 research directors (at last official count) hired by these unions they have at their fingertips data in a quantity equaled only by the federal government itself. Seeking justice for those who are without adequate voice and pressing for the rights of all who may be disadvantaged do not necessarily involve the kinds of organizational procedures upon which labor itself originally came to power. Today its position of eminence on the national scene as a respected wielder of power gives it a leverage in the national political picture second to no other major pressure group. This is not to say that whatever labor wishes can be brought to pass. Obviously the record of labor's advocacy of various measures belies such a claim. But in terms of the actual numbers potentially involved and the record of concern for the totality, the power for civic good on the part of the collective labor organizations in the AFL-CIO is unexcelled.

No longer, however, are contracts limited to wages, hours, and working conditions. Many of the bargaining activities in the current period are less concerned with wage increases than with "fringe benefits." It is these that provide a stability and security which wage contracts alone have been unable to provide. They include such items as life insurance, accidental death and dismemberment insurance, job accident and sickness or disability payments, hospital care, surgical care, obstetrical care, home and office medical expense, and pensions. Most of the contracts negotiated in our times provide for these benefits. Approximately 12 million of the 17 million members of labor organizations are covered by plans including many if not all of these items. This is a phenomenon primarily achieved in the past decade.

During the World War II decade much attention was given to the guaranteed annual wage. Widely publicized plans were developed in a few industries (shoes, soap, meat, etc.). With the advent of unemployment insurance and the large-scale demand for universal income maintenance there has been less pressure for the guaranteed annual wage as such in separate industries. In its place supplemental unemployment benefits have been instituted to cushion the severance from employment. The amounts available vary according to the kind of settlement negotiated with the respective unions.

Illustrative of a technique for labor's securing of advantages in the area of pensions through political activity is the experience of the United Automobile Workers in requesting further assistance in pensions. Management replied that pensions were a state function. When the UAW attempted to get further assistance at this point, management lobbyists registered vigorous opposition on the assumption that the increased taxes would be too burdensome. Shortly labor sought a minimum monthly pension of $100 with the companies paying the difference between social security and that amount. Industry's opposition to the tax increase ceased.

Collective bargaining, which involves the long-range future of both labor and management and ultimately of the economy as a whole, cannot be left to amateurs. A major contribution from all three of the leading parties in this triumvirate would now require that participants take account of the total welfare as the only sure means of protecting the best interests of each one of the participants. Any catalogue of major areas of service for labor in our time would include its concern for sound justice. The record to date is both good and bad. Industrial unions have been opener and readier to include all races. The craft and railroad workers have a less honorable history in this regard. It must be credited to the national federation that officially it has attempted to open the ranks of its international union constituents to all qualified candidates. The fact remains that at the time of this writing there are craft unions and railroad brotherhoods which could greatly strengthen their contribution to the forward thrust of American life by changes in their racial policies.

No single idea can incorporate the full range of possibilities for labor union contributions to the national life. One objective, however, encompasses so broad a scope of possibilities that it deserves special mention. It is an area in which labor has already made a rich contribution to society at large: its sense of obligation to the community. For many years union leadership has recognized that good will is a prime asset of both local unions and the national organization. Community specialists thus became an integral part of locals, if they were strong enough, or of the central organization for the larger area. Membership in community fund organizations and on school boards symbolized this sensitivity to good will. But essentially more than that was involved. What affected the community affected union members, and vice versa. With a background of organizational know-how and a collective body capable of exercising pressure, the unions stood in the advantageous position of being able to secure benefits for the community at large. Here is a vast area of union contribution which fulfills the long history of union objectives for welfare and gives the union a usefulness far beyond the plant and its own membership. At an AFL convention prior to the merger with the CIO the executive council reported to its delegates that it had been "mindful of the responsibilities that American labor must meet in this critical period of world history. Today our duty goes far beyond the building of a powerful trade union movement in our own country. Today our tasks go far beyond those of strengthening our trade union movement as a dynamic voluntary organization, as a pivotal force in, of, and for our free society and American way of life."[10] Then at the 1955 convention of AFL-CIO actions were called for which "include support of child labor laws and other measures in the interest of childhood and youth; federal aid to medical schools, hospitals, and medical research; health insurance; improved facilities for the handicapped; federal aid to education; revision and liberalization of the McCarran-Walter Immigration Act; amendment of the Refugee Relief Act to insure admission of the full number of refugees authorized in the law; provision for federal flood insurance; enactment of a fair employment practices law; approval of the Supreme Court ruling on segregation in schools; and provision for peacetime use of atomic energy."[11]

Indications of labor's commitment to a wider range of community and social involvement is indicated by the changing structure of the AFL-CIO itself. Recent among these indications are the additions of such departments as social security, international affairs, community service, civil rights, and political education.

The life of communities and of the nation includes broader

issues than those which have traditionally been labor's immediate concern. Alert union leaders have long since recognized that gains made in the plant can be wiped out by forces determining the life of their workers in their community and family spheres; for utility rates, rents, housing, and the cost of living are just as important as wage contracts and sanitary washrooms. "To give the worker more than make-believe protection," says Gus Tyler, "a modern union must be concerned with influencing the legislation that goes to make up our legislated economy."[12]

Anyway you look at it, the American labor union has been and will undoubtedly continue to be a powerful force in the economic life of this nation and consequently in other nations as well. Though the record contains both good and bad, the destructive factors are infinitesimal as against the vast good accomplished by all of the bodies related to organized labor. Throughout its history the principal function of organized labor has been collective bargaining, and this will continue to be its major activity. But organized labor, too, will increasingly face the fact that its collective bargaining must take place within a setting even larger than the plant where decisions are being reached through bargaining.

Today adversaries sitting across the table from each other, engaging in what is traditionally known as "labor-management relations," have suddenly found themselves in a strange new world. Where government at one time had to wheedle and cajole to secure a settlement, it now has become involved in a large portion of the economy, and it has become the determiner of policy for an even larger part. To this anomalous situation is added the fact that the welfare of the citizenry is intimately identified with the decisions made at a national level by a central government in relation to other governments and their economic life, upon which we are dependent and which in turn are dependent upon this nation. It is in such a situation that labor organizations through their rank and file and their leaders are compelled to make judgments and arrive at decisions harmonious for numbers far in excess of their own membership. The reality of the integration of ethics and economics has become clear for all but those who will not see.

9

Disarmament and the Economy

The Problem

The expression "having a bear by the tail" aptly describes the situation of the United States and its armaments program. We lay claim to a capacity to "overkill" every Russian industrial metropolitan area 1,250 times, with an estimated one-tenth of the labor force or approximately seven and one-third million engaged in military or related activities in 1965. Moreover, one-tenth of the U. S. production of goods and services is allocated to defense.[1] Yet we continue to increase military production. Jitters in the stock market follow an official suggestion that it might be advisable to reduce the flow of military hardware or atomic fission supplies, both of which are in great oversupply. At the same time the United States Arms Control and Disarmament Agency recognizes the danger of a decline in defense expenditures impairing the long-term stability and growth of the economy, even though present defense expenditures appear to be far in excess of strictly defense needs.

Heavy commitments have been made to our gigantic commercial industrial plant in the form of large allocations of both personnel and equipment. Much of it has been moved to new locations, resulting in the establishment of entire new communities with all the institutions and activities attendant on the formation of a community. Disruption of these arrangements would inevitably work hardships for the persons involved, necessitating readjustments in employment activities as well as closing down manufacturing and research facilities until their services could be put to civilian use.

Comments from members of Congress and the executive branch and the Congressional voting records indicate little if any disposition to attempt seriously the conversion of any military production activities to civilian use. Repercussions from constituents whose livelihoods depend either directly or indirectly on the military production program quickly discourage legislative representatives from any inclination they may have toward economy or converting unneeded military production to the provision of some of the many dire needs required by a wholesome civilian economy.

Whatever may be one's attitude toward the defense program, there can be no denying that as a nation we are deriving substantial economic benefits from the arms race, and our participation in it has stimulated the national economy. In addition, there are many indirect and beneficial effects of this research upon the economy. As Emile Benoit says:

Most of the important technological break-throughs of recent years have originated in defense research, including radar, atomic energy, jet engines, and space exploration. These in turn have had important effects on the development of new civilian products and services. For example, space research has yielded improvements in basic materials, in water purification, and in techniques for the automatic measurement of body changes. A major drug for the treatment of emotional depression was developed from one component of a rocket fuel.[2]

The question is inevitably asked, "Why rock the boat? We have a very gratifying state of prosperity, don't we?" Unquestionably the economic indices do reveal a recognizable state of prosperity. What they do not indicate, however, is that fact that so large a percentage of the products whose creation accounts for that prosperity are without any use or benefit to this nation or any other, once full capacity for protection has been achieved. No representative of the legislative or executive branch of the government could deny that we already possess many times over the capacity for deterrence—which is the basic reason for our military production in the first place. In sum, the warfare state has become our national condition, and for the time being at least we are both unwilling and unable to reduce our dependence on an economy sustained so largely by military defense.

Scope and Consequences of Defense Economy

The 46 million dollar budget for defense represents approximately 9 per cent of the Gross National Product (GNP). In view of the total production, this may not be unbearable, and if it were required by a genuine need for defense, it could be wholly justifiable. As Benoit points out: "The burden is, of course, only a fraction of what it was during World War II or the Korean War. While defense expenditure absorbs resources which would otherwise be available to the civilian economy, it also contributes importantly to that economy."[3] In comparison with other nations Yugoslavia, England, and France have defense burdens of 7 per cent of the national production and come closest to that of the United States. For the most part, in other nations the figure is nearer 4 or 5 per cent. The reason for the greater U. S. percentages is obvious.

The problem is not only the size of the defense budget but also its allocation. Uneven placement of defense contracts, made possible because of superior jockeying and pressures from Congressmen and/or advantages because of geographical and climatic conditions, have produced temporary benefits for some sections of the country but at the same time have contributed to potential disruptions and complications. In 1959 San Diego, for example, had 82 per cent of its manufacturing employment in aerospace production; Wichita, 72 per cent; Seattle, 53 per cent; and the Los Angeles-Long Beach area, 27 per cent. Fourteen states are included in a bracket "above average dependence on major procurement for their employment, and nine additional states with exceptionally heavy dependence on Department of Defense payrolls to sustain their income."[4] Out of a total of 22 billion dollars of industrial orders placed by the military in 1960, the preponderance went to five states.[5]

The day of reckoning for such heavy concentration and for the failure to anticipate transition to civilian production is typified by the experience of the Republic Aviation Corporation on Long Island, when it was contended that this plant was no longer necessary. Involved were 13,000 jobs and a trail of 990 subcontracting firms, with a total loss of employment of 80,000 to 90,000 jobs.[6]

Not only have industries been meshed into the total military production program, but universities have likewise become dependent on the military budget. A combination of direct payments to universities by the Department of Defense, the Atomic Energy Commission, and the National Aeronautics and Space Administration (NASA), plus funds received from manufacturers engaged in military production, brought the total of defense-supported and aerospace research activity to more than 50 per cent of university research work in 1960–1961.[7]

Since Sputnik we have been voluble in our discussion of the need for training scientists, though our concern hardly began at that point. We simply became more highly aware of the need. Whether to attribute it largely to the danger, real or imagined, created by Sputnik, the fact remains that from two-thirds to three-fourths of all American scientists and engineers are at present engaged in work related to military and defense activities. Redirecting the activities of these highly skilled and useful individuals constitutes one of the major problems in converting to civilian activities.

Few people are aware, for example, of the extent of the atomic installations alone, as one part of the total military production program. Fred J. Cook reports: "The five nuclear installations (Oak Ridge, Hanford, Paducah, Portsmouth, Savannah River) together form the nation's largest consumer of electricity, coal and water; they require more machine tools than General Motors, Ford and Chrysler combined. The Savannah plant (more recent than Oak Ridge and Hanford) cost $1.5 billion, four times the cost of the Panama Canal. It uses more electricity than the entire state of Delaware."[8] The Atomic Energy Commission consumes between 5 and 10 per cent of all the electrical energy produced in the United States. Were any of its plants to cease its contribution to the defense program, it could bring increased tragedy in unemployment and hardship to communities around it and to far-flung points of supply which are dependent on the defense program in the plant.

Not all of the productivity of these plants, to be sure, can be attributed to immediate defense needs. There are health-producing concomitants and contributions to the civilian life which can go on regardless of the defense program. But without the defense program nothing like the present size of operation would be required.

Paralleling and closely tied to the development of fissionable materials and our capacity for overkill is the size of our aircraft industry. In 1964 there were in service 1,855 commercial planes, and approximately 30,000 military planes. Any curtailment in defense production would cause serious dislocation and hardship for many who have identification with aircraft manufacturing.[9]

The program of Research on Economic Adjustments to Disarmament (READ) sponsored by the Center for Research on Conflict Resolution at the University of Michigan estimates that net displacement might amount to between 500,000 and 600,000 employees per year during the first stage of disarmament. It expressed the belief that this would not be unmanageable but that it would increase pressures on a labor market already in difficulty because of large numbers entering that market for the first time and because of technological displacement.[10]

The extraordinary increase in defense appropriations and the manufacturing plant which came into existence out of defense needs is not the result of any sudden or crash program; it has been evolving steadily. "Expenditures of the Department of Defense have risen from $19.8 billion in fiscal year of 1951 to $43 billion in 1961, or by over 100%, a growth rate far in excess of that of any other major area of the American economy. At the present time, Defense Department purchases of goods and services are equal to almost one-tenth of the gross national product. The proportion reached peaks of 48% during World War II and 12% during the Korean War, but was, of course, lower during the interwar period. . . . An abrupt change in the nature of the external threat would probably cause another major shift in the proportion of the country's resources devoted to armaments."[11]

With the capacity to more than match anything that any potential enemy might do, there is ironically not now, nor is there likely to be in the immediate future, a scaling downward in defense resources in terms of plant, highly trained engineers, skilled technicians, or office force required to keep the enterprise in motion.

RESISTANCE TO DISARMAMENT CONVERSION

The Arms Control and Disarmament Agency Report expresses the apprehension that the chief danger of a steep decline would be psychological. Adjusting to a series of defense cuts over a period of a decade would confront us with a situation unparalleled in our history.[12] There have been other experiences of adjustments following wars, but none in which the economy of the nation became so dependent on war and defense preparations. After World War I, for example, business was eager to get back to a peacetime basis; after World War II there were great peacetime needs to be met by a civilian production program. Today those needs have been met, for a large part of the population at least, and we have not yet envisioned the ways in which our economy can meet the very real but insufficiently defined needs of the new industrial society.

It is all but inevitable that as a part of the psychological consequences a stock market decline would accompany any major diminution in government support of military manufacturing. Ironical though it be that stock market enthusiasm is dependent upon artificial and unneeded production, the fact remains that the fear of inability to convert, or in some cases to reconvert, to civilian production would have depressing consequences. As many economists and social analysts working on this problem contend, however, such consequences are not inevitable. With adequate preparation for transfer to other types of manufacturing and production, there is little likelihood that a decline and subsequent pessimism would result.

Social psychologists and anthropologists will, no doubt, engage in extensive studies in years to come to determine why so high a degree of resistance to conversion to a peacetime economy marked the attitudes of the American people in the mid 1960s. Irving Horowitz asks: "Why should it be the case that, in the midst of this intellectual know-how, there is such a paucity of activity oriented toward the realization of that long-postponed and ephemeral phenomenon—a peacetime economy?"[13] He suggests the prospects for such a conversion remain dim because of social and political considerations, prominent among which is the fact that there exists so little awareness of the dangers involved in a military economy. On the other hand, such satisfying conditions already prevail in our economy that it would be inadvisable to introduce major alterations.

The inability of the general public to understand the nature of this problem is not alleviated by the attitudes and actions of Congress. Sluggishness of Congressional hearings reduces the tempo of public awareness and reinforces Congressional actions which perpetuate the *status quo*. Especially in a time when the economy is regarded as generally satisfactory, it is unlikely that lawmakers would approve actions which might even temporarily reduce the over-all contentment. Any extensive program for conversion must be soft-pedaled lest it imply that the present state carries any marks of impermanence. Some of the opposition to the test-ban treaty is undoubtedly (1) resistance to peacetime conversion, and (2) apprehension over Communism. Some opponents have not been above branding advocates of conversion as unpatriotic; because initiative for conversion must come in large measure from government sources, it has been labeled socialistic. The scene of an industry, wholly dependent upon government, caustically calling all attempts to foster greater civilian participation socialistic takes on an element of the ludicrous.

Among other factors influencing the reluctance to provide adequate offsets to defense cuts is the fear of inflation. The question becomes whether producers would be under such pressure to increase their production costs during a transition to nondefense economy that they would unwittingly create a spiral of inflation.

Traditionally we have been taught to abhor personal debt, and this attitude has carried over into our national patterns as well. We dislike budget deficits and feel compunction to reduce national debt. To that end there is strong pressure within the nation to achieve a budget surplus. Espousal of such a program makes election to office somewhat easier. At least the economic stability prevailing under a total program which includes armament costs can be recognized. Whether a similar degree of stability would exist if the armaments were reduced and a public works program were to replace it is uncertain. In the transition period it is doubted that incomes would be equally sustained. This uncertainty probably accounts for no small measure of the reluctance to support a major shift to public works programs. Also, opposition to government spending is deeply grounded in the public mind. Even the suggestion that the spending might be for the benefit of the citizenry is not enough to outweigh this reluctance to increase the public debt. This may be due to a suspicion that such spending implies a trend toward socialism or represents a national conservatism where public debt is involved.

A survey conducted by the University of Michigan Survey Research Center found that this general attitude toward debt was reflected in a strong disposition to using defense savings for national debt reduction.[14] Thus even the continuation of a doubtful defense program would be preferable to extending the national debt, if such became necessary, during periods of transition from defense production to civilian programs. We had such an experience between 1954 and 1960: "By reducing expenditures and holding up taxes, the Federal government, in four out of seven years from 1954 to 1960, inclusively, took more purchasing power away from private consumers and businesses than it restored to them by its own expenditure and benefit programs (that is, it ran a 'budget surplus on income and product account'). With the resultant deflationary impact, unemployment more than doubled, and the industrial output rose only 18% in the period between 1953 and 1960—in marked contrast to the 54% rise in industrial output and the reduction in unemployment achieved in the seven preceding years."[15] While the volume of government spending and taxes was by no means the only factor affecting the economy during this period, its impact was an influential one.

The cold war has become institutionalized, and institutions rarely liquidate themselves. Instead, they find new reasons for their existence and rationalize their continuance. Anticommunism has become a major "cause" for a very large number of Americans, though the "thaw" has undermined its vigor in some quarters. The study of the true sources of support for the anti-Communist crusade has yet to be made, but one does not have to look far for likely sources of its spiritual and financial assistance. The areas of the nation which received the largest measure of government assistance in the form of defense programs are at the same time centers for the most vigorous anticommunism campaigns. That there is a connection does not require super-sleuthing.

Lacking a forward-looking national purpose in the period following two world wars and being confronted with an ideology which momentarily at least seemed to have its people on the march, it is understandable that the American people should have settled for an anticommunist rationale as its own national purpose. It paid off in the form of vigorous scientific-industrial activity, but the result was that the ideology against which it had been generated was itself similarly consumed by fears of opposition and kept from the advances it also might have been making in civilian progress. By a creeping fear that democracy was not capable of organizing itself adequately for civilian pioneering, our nation has been moving from the enterprise system in economics toward a military-dominated centralization.

Happily some of the participants in the total defense program who are most aware of its crippling consequences to democratic life and the freedom of the human spirit, have been most vigorous in urging that the nation recognize the import of the direction in which its policy is pointed. "The increased demand of nuclear scientists for freedom of movement and less secrecy is an indication that one major veto group is cognizant of the relation between secrecy and coercion."[16] What these men, in addition to some economists, philosophers, theologians, and others, have been contending is that the consequences of the excesses of the defense system are destructive to more than economic life, that they inhibit the freedom of the spirit, making its own forward movement less likely. These are results of preoccupation with defense economy, and behind their supporters lies the resistance to its conversion to constructive peacetime ends.

Proposals for Modification and Their Consequences

Central to any viable suggestion for scaling the defense economy downward is the proposal contained in the Arms Control Disarmament Agency's report: "To do the most good, therefore, offsetting measures should, if possible, be initiated at the very time that defense contracts are cancelled and before defense expenditures—not to speak of actual production and employment—begin to drop."[17] The report goes on to suggest the necessity on the part of the Congress to grant the executive branch authority to initiate measures which would accomplish the desired end, especially in the form of stand-by public works or tax reduction. In view of the public misunderstanding of the function of tax reductions, there is little likelihood that such authority will be readily given to the executive branch. The fact that tax reductions would have to be in an amount greater than the reductions in government expenditure complicates the problem of public acceptance; but only reductions of these dimensions would accomplish the desired purpose.

Getting down to specific proposals in terms of adjusted appropriations, Benoit explains:

Our disarmament model involves a reduction over the full twelve-year period of United States defense expenditures from $56 billion estimated for 1965 to $10 billion estimated for 1977. Offsetting this would be a rise to $7 billion for the United States contribution (assumed to cover one-third of the total) to the annual current costs of the judicial, administrative, inspection, police, and deterrent functions of a World Peace Authority. . . . It is also estimated that the NASA space program, and the civilian Atomic Energy programs (both of which have been closely associated with the defense program) will rise from $4 billion to about $11 billion over this period. Thus the net cutback of all security expenditures (taking account of these offsets) would be from $60 billion to $28 billion—or about $32 billion. Of this total, however, over $21 billion is estimated to occur in the first three years. It is during this period that the maximum economic impact will presumably be felt.[18]

Reductions of such magnitude are not made simply by decree. Curtailment of defense spending and corresponding tax reduction call for a vast array of projects in both the public and the private sectors. Specifically involving the latter is the need for the replacement of more than 10 million substandard dwellings. In the former, the public sector, we are short some 600,000 classrooms; every major city is calling for a solution to its transportation problem; the steady and rapid urbanization of the nation has placed a strain on the available water supply which is bringing some communities to the brink of anxiety. Projects such as these and many others cannot be left to small or segmented planning. They will necessitate a scope comparable to that involved in the development of the TVA, the MVA, or the unifying of resources such as was required in wartime.

Resistance to centralized planning and execution of plans adequate to offset the temporary impairment from defense conversion is probably inevitable. Political capital is to be made of the charge of centralization, even though the defense program itself is more highly centralized than the program which might be substituted for it. Melman suggests that appropriation of funds from national sources could be made with full consideration of local needs. It is possible to avoid the dangers of centralization, he contends.[19]

In the general range of large-scale attacks on the total problem, it would be essential to devise fiscal and monetary policies capable of influencing aggregate demand but sufficiently flexible to affect allocation of resources among competing needs. The ACDA report proposes that "the balance struck between tax reduction and increased Government spending will be governed by the relative importance accorded to private demand for such goods and services as food, clothing, housing, recreation, health, higher education, machine tools, research, and development—as against public demand for school construction, teacher training, roads, space exploration, urban renewal, area redevelopment, public health, and social services."[20]

Even such large-scale proposals as tax reductions, fiscal and monetary policies, assistance to both public and private sectors, will not of themselves be sufficient. There still remain a large number of other possibilities, such as lowering the retirement age, raising the age at which youth undertake jobs, increasing vacations, and other programs specifically designed to influence the working arrangements of individuals. Uniform requirements in such areas as those mentioned could, in the aggregate, make possible a large number of additional jobs. Nevertheless, with the increasing utilization of automation it is unlikely in the immediate future that jobs will be found for all of those who are released from defense production. It is to these that reference is made in Chapter 3, where it was suggested that in an economy capable of providing for all of its people, without all of them having to work full time, there will be many for whom new types of creative expression will have to be found in lieu of the traditional concepts of constructive work.

Despite the complications and dangers involved in a positive effort toward disarmament, there is much that is hopeful in the picture, too. Kenneth Boulding has convincingly contended that the military organization ("milorg") does not make for increase in civilian common markets. It only stimulates its opposite number in some other nation. Therefore if the civilian economy is to thrive, there must be free activity on the part of the business firms and those organizations which exist by serving all of society.[21] With the diminution of the milorg and with various efforts to meet the civilian requirements, full employment is not an impossibility.

Analyses looking toward the reallocation of workers from defense-related activities to civilian production have already been undertaken.[22] Such proposals must necessarily be inconclusive until serious effort has been made on the part of all of the various industries involved to ascertain what other types of activities they might undertake as a part of the civilian production program. Less vague, however, is the insistence of the planner for conversion that, instead of individuals being transported to jobs created for them or available to them in other areas, it is far more satisfactory both from the standpoint of the industry and of the workers that industry wherever possible be brought to the communities which have been reducing their defense activities. Uprooting and dislocating families has social consequences and long-term deleterious effects for the life of individuals, communities, and the nation.

Not least among the consequences of disarmament adjustment will be the reassignment of the large army of scientists and engineers whose services have been available to the many phases of the defense effort. About one-half of all our scientists and engineers engaged in defense work are involved in research and development. "Although scientists and engineers will probably be harder hit by arms reduction than any other occupational group (save military people), it is not likely that unemployment of scientists and engineers will be more than a very short-run problem."[23] In view of the vast needs in the civilian economy the talents of these highly skilled individuals can be adapted with facility to other than defense activities. Thus presumably the 97,000 engineers now employed in government-supported electronics work would be available for work of civilian importance.

Finally, the ACDA proposes some particular programs upon which a start can be made in the near future. They would include: strengthening of our system of employment offices and the unemployment insurance program, a workable retraining scheme, and government attempts to influence industry to provide more liberal pension rights, group insurance, hospitalization, and similar perquisites, and to provide employees with company-wide rights of transfer, etc.[24]

The discussion of the theme "Disarmament and the Economy" began with using the figure of the perplexed person who had a bear by the tail and dared not let go. A person who has possibly done as much as anyone in our time to study the intricacies of this complex problem is Emile Benoit, to whom, as is obvious, we are deeply indebted for much of the foregoing material. He asks the question in another way: "Can we have roast pig without (at the least risk of) burning down the house?" He answers in the affirmative, providing we not only organize "a 'moral equivalent of war' but an 'economic equivalent of defense.'"[25]

From the standpoint of those responsible for this volume the disarmament issue is a profoundly spiritual as well as a technical economic problem. Here our concern has been not primarily the problem of disarmament itself. That is of course a deeply ethical issue. As has been noted, however, our concern is with the significance of disarmament for the economic life of this nation and inevitably for other nations as well.

We believe it is basically unwholesome for a nation's people to live in an atmosphere of suspicion and in expectation that its unprecedented power may be used whether in retaliation or in warding off anticipated blows. The piling up of defense materials in excess of any use to which they could possibly be put constitutes unjustifiable and deleterious action by any nation or people. Its consequences cannot but be inimical to the nation's well-being, and it will serve to delay facing the nation's fundamental needs. Returning to a wholesome civilian economy presents vast and complex problems, but the sanity of the world requires it. Economic considerations, in the traditional sense of the term, are not likely to provide resolution to our dilemma. In its larger sense, implying the fullest meeting of man's needs, there is more reason for confidence. Hence I included this theme in the roster of areas for which a dimension of faith is essential.

10

International Trade and Aid

Two conditions transcend almost all others in their implications for the immediate future of our world: (1) the fact that two-thirds of the world is hungry, and (2) the economic strength and stability of the United States. That these two conditions are closely related constitutes the basis for much of the foreign and domestic policy of the United States, the other industrialized nations, and also the lesser developed nations. Nowhere are those policies more effectively revealed than in the areas of international trade and aid. In them are to be seen both the ethical values of the nations most involved and the way in which their economic life is conceived.

From the days of the Apostle Paul, those in the Hebrew-Christian lineage have recognized that their responsibilities do not end at the nation's boundaries. All persons everywhere are God's children and our brothers. But the limitations of our human vision cause us to have a descending degree of concern as our thought moves outward from those closest and dearest to us. To most of us, foreigners are "they and theirs" as distinguished from "we and ours." The main reasons for this feeling probably are that for the most part *they* have different languages, attitudes, and cultures and live at greater distances from us, and that *they* are subject to other governments and legal jurisdictions.

The foreign missions movement rested on and stimulated a powerful vision that helped Christians overcome these parochial limitations. Businesses, too, have been interested in other peoples, but the chief motivation has been that of economic gain. Governments also have international interests. In part these have been to support the work of the missionaries and businessmen. In part the national economic interest is involved. Also, there are political and security interests to be defended and promoted through the exercise of persuasion and power and through alliances and international organizations.

Our approaches to our responsibility to people in other countries involve all aspects of human relations. The two principal economic concerns are international trade—including investment —and foreign aid.

International trade consists of the exchange across national boundaries of goods and services. Foreign aid is the provision of assistance by the government or people of one country to those of another. Except from a short-run point of view foreign aid has an important aspect of mutuality, benefiting the providing country as well as the receiving country. Seen in the longer perspective, as Paul G. Hoffman has pointed out, "the term 'foreign aid' is illusory. It is neither 'foreign' nor 'aid.' Realistic appraisal of the forces stimulating revolutionary change, and of United States' vital interest in orderly progress suggests that what we really mean by the term is 'mutual development.' "[1] Thus while designated as "aid," its fundamental purpose is to strengthen the governments, economies, and morale of the new nations so that they may more readily rise to that position in the world of nations where interchange and cooperation may go on without condescension and with mutual benefit. Foreign aid, therefore, though it does have a strong humanitarian implication, is fundamentally a preliminary step toward the achievement of dignity and self-support by both individuals and nations.

International trade is of vital importance for many industrial nations in order to supply the goods and services that they could not produce except at relatively great cost, if at all. Even as self-sufficient a country as the United States finds in international trade a source of great economic benefit. International trade is particularly important for the less developed countries, as a source of earnings to finance the importation of capital and other requirements for industrialization and economic development. Foreign aid is a supplementary source of finance for the less developed countries which cannot earn enough through trade.

International Trade With the Industrialized West

In its trade with the industrialized countries of the free world the United States is unusual in being a major exporter both of temperate-zone agricultural products and of finished manufactured goods, many requiring a high level of technology. Its imports from these countries are predominantly manufactured products. Despite the mutual economic benefits flowing from international trade, most industrialized countries place some restrictions or burdens on imports, usually by levying customs duties (tariffs) and sometimes by imposing quotas. Perhaps the most common reason for this is the clamor of certain domestic industries to be protected from foreign competition, but the maintenance of industries that are deemed to be of key importance for national defense also is frequently given as the reason. In some situations, moreover, restrictions on imports may be used as a method of holding imports in balance with exports to avoid disruptive deficits in the country's balance of payments.

After a half century or more when its dominant policy was the protective tariff, the United States in recent years has been promoting agreements with other countries for the mutual reduction of tariffs and other trade restrictions. This effort to liberalize trade was supported by the Section on the World Economy of the Fourth National Study Conference on the Church and Economic Life, which affirmed: "We agree unanimously that the engagement of the United States in a program of mutual development and trade involving the whole world (eventually including the Soviet bloc as soon as international conditions permit), is irrevocable and full of promise, despite the risks it brings to some sections of our economy. The consequences of withdrawing from freer trade with the industrial nations of the European Community (The Common Market) and the British Commonwealth, or of failing to cultivate the development of other nations by trade and aid would be disastrous and unthinkable."[2]

International Trade With the Less Developed Countries

Traditionally the less developed countries have produced and exported agricultural products and raw materials and used the proceeds to buy manufactured goods from the industrialized countries. The pressure of rapid population growth, the high rate of unemployment and underemployment, the failure of the markets for their products to expand with sufficient rapidity, and the "demonstration effect" of economic development in other countries have brought great pressure in the less developed countries for rapid economic development and particularly for industrialization. This has placed a heavy financial burden on these countries to pay for the machinery, equipment, and other resources for industrialization. To some extent the burden is being carried by private foreign investment; to some extent it must be borne by foreign aid, as we shall see. For the most part, however, dependence has been on international trade.

The trade policies of developing countries are protectionist, aimed at helping infant industries develop substitutes for foreign imports. The special need for such protection has been recognized in general by the industrially advanced countries.

As Chase Manhattan Bank economist William Butler writes:

How important international trade is for the less developed nations is indicated by the fact that it frequently accounts for 20% or more of their total economy as against 8% for the economy of the United States. Indeed, trade is much more important to them than aid. Total exports of the less developed areas amounted to $31 billion in 1960 while the total flow of financial assistance from the industrial nations (including private foreign investment) amounted to $8 billion. For all these reasons it would appear that one of the major economic objectives of free world nations should be to promote an expanding volume of trade between the industrial and less developed nations. . . . Their share in world exports has declined steadily from 31.5% of the total in 1953 to 24.7% in 1960. Since 1956 total exports of less developed areas have been growing only 2% per annum as against 6.5% for the industrial areas. The lag has been particularly severe in the case of Latin America where, excluding Venezuela, exports have been rising only at one half of 1% per year.[3]

INTERNATIONAL TRADE WITH THE COMMUNIST BLOC

The long-continued emphasis on economic autarchy in the Soviet Union, on the one hand, and the difficulties of carrying on trade with Communist economies, on the other hand, have kept down trade between the industrial West and the Communist East. In addition, the United States has largely boycotted trade with a number of Communist and Communist-oriented countries, including China and Cuba, and pressured its allies to refuse to sell military equipment and certain high-technology machinery and products to the Soviet Union and the Communist countries generally.

The relaxation of East-West tensions in the 1960s, the competition for markets among the Western industrialized countries, and the recognition that the restrictions were no longer achieving their goal of weakening the defense potentials of the Communist world, have resulted in a movement for increased East-West trade which seems likely to continue. On this Roy Blough has commented: "Whether any useful economic purpose is served in further efforts to keep communist countries from Western trade is very doubtful. After all, trade has advantages for us and our friends, as well as for the communists. We have forced the communist countries to become self-sufficient in some commodities when we might have served our security interests better by keeping them dependent on Western supplies."[4]

ISSUES IN INTERNATIONAL TRADE

Much of the American misgiving centering about our foreign economic programs stems from a fear that any resulting imbalance might be injurious to this nation's economic welfare and that we cannot stand the persistent strain. The ideal arrangement would be to effect a proper balance through exchange of raw materials or finished products. The sooner the use of goods can replace the cash outlay, obviously, the sooner the healthy state of genuine trade can be attained. And not the least of the gains recorded thereby will be the national self-respect achieved by the nation which has been on the receiving end.

The need for initiative and constructive action is not confined to the economically advanced nations. Generosity and good intentions on the part of organizations and governments of industrially advanced countries have met with uncooperativeness and injury in developing countries so frequently that caution to the point of wariness attends consideration by the "have" countries of new trade relations. Instability or even hostility on the part of resentful political groups has jeopardized many good intentions. A primary condition for facilitating stable trade relations is the willingness of the nations seeking investments in its productive facilities to encourage the ventures and to understand both the problems of the investors and the need to assure stability. There may be years of chaos before the developing nations can meet the need for that stability which alone can bring economic benefit to their people. Freedom from disruption and unnecessary loss is a *sine qua non* of wholesome trade relations.

Relieving the hunger and overcoming the economic weakness of the world are of course not solely the responsibility of the United States. As a result of the extraordinary recovery after World War II (due in large measure to the Marshall Plan) nations which had been decimated by war now enjoy a prosperity exceeding that of their most satisfactory prewar years. Because of this prosperity they are able to share in alleviating want and helping to build the domestic economies of the less developed nations.

Foreign trade inevitably involves an attempt to bring exports and imports into favorable balance. With industrialized countries it means the ability to sell finished products; for the lesser developed countries it means selling raw materials. Herein lies a dilemma for the United States, since it has both manufactured products and agricultural products which must be sold if its own economy is to remain stable. But hunger and need in the less developed countries require that agricultural products be consumed at home, and so there is less credit for buying the industrial equipment to enable them to become industrial nations and to give their population more productive employment than substitution for beasts of burden in agriculture. According to economist Egbert De Vries,[5] means must be found whereby those countries can expand imports to 50 billion dollars. An import program of those dimensions means, of course, an export program which is commensurate, and it cannot be in soft currency valid only within its own boundaries, for world trade must be conducted on a currency basis which permits transfer of credit.

The conditions under which agreements for trade liberalization can be negotiated have been greatly modified in recent years by the emergence of several new intergovernmental organizations. Most notable and far-reaching, both for their economic and political significance, are the European Coal and Steel Community, the European Atomic Energy Community, and particularly the European Economic Community,* which bring together, in commerce and manufacturing, nations which had but recently been at war with each other. So recent is this development that it cannot be said that all difficulties in relations with nations not in the EEC have been harmoniously resolved. Each nation in the EEC had its own internal arrangements, with special consideration for coal miners or farmers or other types of producers, or for merchants. Internal political stability depends upon maintenance of these established agreements. To break them would mean the downfall of the very governments which entered into this imaginative collective venture at the international level. And not only is there the necessity for reconciling differences within the EEC but also for an attempt to arrive at harmonious relations with the nations outside it which have done business with its members or would like to do so. For the British Commonwealth, the Scandinavian countries, and the United States, therefore, whose economic health depends upon ability to trade with the EEC nations as well as others closer at hand, there are delicate issues portentous of trouble as well as promising benefit.

The formation of such organizations as the European Economic Community and the European Free Trade Association presents the United States with a brand-new situation. Since the emergence of the United States as a dominant world power during the early years of this century, no single nation or combination of nations presented serious competition. Now suddenly powerful trading blocs emerge to challenge United States preeminence. The nations participating in these blocs have been strengthened by the same forces of industrialism which underlay

---

* This is usually referred to as the Common Market.

the growth of the United States into a world power. They have been the beneficiaries of scientific and technological advances, and their people have demanded ever higher living standards. But the smaller ones among them—Belgium, the Netherlands, and Luxembourg—could not within themselves support the total fabric of resources, trade, mutual benefit, and economic defense which a larger collectivity of nations would make possible. To this consideration must be added the fact that the nations individually, and now collectively in their respective trading blocs, must constantly face the fact of the massive economic and military establishment of the United States. These nations have been protected or opposed by American military and economic resources in two world wars, but after what had been defeat for some of them, they have sought to put aside centuries-old differences and to develop a common power which no longer left them feeling inferior. The fact that they have become bound together in a pact of mutual defense, the North Atlantic Treaty Organization, does not obligate them to include in their economic structures all of the nations comprising NATO. As of this writing the EEC (France, Italy, Germany, Belgium, the Netherlands, and Luxembourg) have not included in their roster the United Kingdom or the Scandinavian countries. The group outside is known as "the Outer Seven" and the EEC as "the Inner Six." But as John W. Hight of the Committee for a National Trade Policy has pointed out: "Any union has two aspects; it brings the participants closer together while it pulls them away from those outside the union. One effect of the European Economic Community has been to cause consternation in the other countries of Western Europe over the prospect of losing non-discriminatory access to the markets of the Six. This, of course, led in the beginning to the creation of a loosely-structured European Free Trade Area, spearheaded by Britain and Sweden and designed to act as a countervailing force to the Six."[6]

Development of the EEC has implications for other nations than its European neighbors. The United States, for which European nations have provided mutual trade relations, is forced to make serious adjustments also. Charles P. Taft stated in 1962:

"In the case of Europe we face the immediate danger of exclusion from a market just as large again as our own U. S. market. This concerns only $6 billion of our exports and a gross national product of $550 billion, but it happens to be a critical $6 billion. It includes $1.3 billion of agricultural products and $800 million of that last are subject to variable levies."[7]

This combination of trade organization and nation cooperation created for the United States a totally new confrontation with which it had to deal in such a way as to avoid injury to itself as well as to its former allies. The General Agreement on Tariffs and Trade (GATT)* forms the foundation for mutual trade action by all the nations involved. The United States Trade Expansion Act (TEA) of 1962 hopefully has paved the way for negotiations in GATT that will liberalize trade relationships between the United States and the European blocs. It delegates to the President of the United States the power to make adjustments without Congressional ratification, within limitations fixed in the Act.

What has occurred in Europe in the establishment of combinations of nations for mutual support in trade and defense has been paralleled by the initiation of the Central American Common Market and the Latin American Free Trade Association, and the prospects are that still other blocs for similar purposes will be formed in Africa, the Far East, and the Middle East. Until now the preponderance of United States trade has been with Canada, the European nations, and Latin America, but the new combinations of nations bid fair to change the patterns of trade.

FOREIGN AID

Economic aid and technical assistance are today going only to the developing countries. These countries have vast needs that are not being met. A great new field for trade expansion lies in

---

* All the principal non-Communist trading nations are members of GATT. Its members have agreed to give to all other members equal consideration in tariffs except when such organizations as the Common Market require otherwise.

the economic potential of those nations, many of which are new, which are to be classed as the "less developed" or "developing" nations. This takes us from the question of trade to the complicated and puzzling problem of aid. Here a new factor has been emerging in recent years: nations lately in need of an economic "shot in the arm" are themselves now able to use their resources for cooperative investments in lands which are just beginning to enter the industrial era.

If aid to the less developed nations were simply a matter of giving funds or materials, the process would be greatly simplified. The fact is, however, that benefactions from nations with surpluses can leave the receiving nation in a penurious condition forever, unless some portion of the benefits are utilized to build self-supporting instruments in the developing nations.

The problem becomes that of finding the kinds of manufacturing which are most suitable to the newly developing nation and which can be sold to the benefactor nation at a price which does not make the sale primarily a charity transaction and which in turn enables the selling nation to invest in further expanding means of production. The word "charity" is used here in an ambiguous sense, for in all probability it will become necessary for the advanced nations to make concessions both as to price and as to product, even though its own production resources and personnel are temporarily impaired. This, of course, is one of the most delicate and difficult decisions for an advanced nation to make. Here the problem is twofold: (1) whether the developing nation can sell its product at a price which yields a profit, especially when the developed nation with higher efficiency in its manufacturing can produce the same article for less, and (2) whether the developing nation may have so low a wage scale that it will impair the economy of the purchasing nation which has made an original investment in the developing country. It is axiomatic that those who are disemployed because of favor shown a nation which needs to expand industrially are not going to be kindly disposed toward the party in power which makes such a decision.

The Fourth National Study Conference on the Church and Economic Life issued the following statement:

In the face of some doubts about the effectiveness and value of aid by the United States government to develop countries we would like to assert the conviction that it is and must be a lasting part of the responsibility of an economically developed country for nations less advanced in this respect. . . . We cannot shirk this burden because other industrialized nations are not doing as much as we think they ought. Foreign aid is necessary in order that aided countries may develop the capacity to support themselves by their own industrial and agricultural production and make their contribution to the world economy. It can be justified by a long-range view of the self-interest of the giving country, for a developed economy is a good customer and a satisfied people contributes to world peace. But this rationale will always need the support of a particularly Christian perspective which emphasizes that we are responsible for our neighbor's welfare as far as we can serve him regardless of the reward we may receive.[8]

There is no hiding the fact that a substantial measure of American support for foreign aid derives from the conviction that this is the means for containing the expansion of communism among nations which in the years ahead could provide trade opportunities but which, if communism were to prevail, would in all probability not exist. American foreign aid, therefore, is compounded of a genuine idealism and also what some might term "hardboiled realism," the guaranteeing of future trade opportunities. It is the contention of a large number of sensitive, ethically minded people that these two elements are not mutually exclusive. Relieving hunger and at the same time guaranteeing that a whole nation shall not be permanently trapped in an international web whose purpose is to serve one principal nation and its ideology can be ethically realistic. However, effecting these policy objectives is much more difficult than appears on paper. While cooperation may be possible, unforeseen problems have arisen at both ends to inhibit the success of the aid program.

The fundamental problem is hunger. Beyond assuaging hunger lies the need for constructive action to prevent hunger and to begin establishing a decent standard of living. Hungry people cannot put their minds to work at learning the skills and techniques required to eliminate hunger, but unless educational levels rise and skills increase, hunger will not be alleviated. So at the heart of all aid programs in the developing nations is improvement of agriculture, with the subsequent reduction of the numbers engaged in agriculture; thereby an adequate supply of industrial labor can be freed to make the products that will increase the national income and with it the standard of living. This is not usually a politically acceptable conclusion in the developing country, where the pressure is for rapid industrialization and agriculture tends to be neglected.

The fact remains, however, that "one-half of the world's people live in countries where the average per capita income is less than $100 per year. In contrast the 15% of the world's people who live in the United States, Canada, Western Europe, the United Kingdom, Australia and New Zealand, enjoy about 75% of the world's income. The United States alone with 6% of the world's population, enjoys more than 40% of the world's income."[9]

Paul Hoffman's *World Without Want* is a documentation of the plight of nations whose people know "the eternal compulsory fast and where misery and squalor are the accepted, though resented, conditions." In this emotion-arousing portrayal of the tragedy of living in underdeveloped nations, Hoffman discusses some of the agencies working to eliminate the conditions now endured with bitterness because the people know they are no longer inevitable. He admits that mistakes have been made in the decade of experimentation: one was to assume that benefiting these nations through assistance programs constituted a program of charity or "give away."

Development programs are investments in people and prosperity—and investments in peace and freedom as well. They benefit both the giver and the receiver. . . . Closely allied to the charity mistake has been the continuance of the "donor country-recipient country" point of view. These terms were perfectly acceptable in describing international relief programs, but they outlived their usefulness when attention shifted from relief to recovery and then to development. As this change occurred the relationship between the nations changed into a partnership—a partnership in an international joint venture to relieve human misery and expand the world economy.[10]

To catalogue here the great variety of forms of aid and the manifold types of projects sponsored by aid-giving countries and agencies is not possible. For the most part, however, they come under these general categories: (1) disaster relief, (2) aid to shore up countries which are not stable in their own economy but must be fortified against communism, and (3) long-range aid. Under both of the latter two, aid may be extended through technical assistance, loans, or grants, or even a combination of all three. In any event, the nation extending the aid is primarily concerned that the result shall be an increase in the ability of the recipient nation to sustain itself and to increase its own capacity for trade. Here again the economic stability of the assisting nation, if it is the United States, is of ultimate importance. "A recession in the United States and Western Europe during 1957/58 depressed the demand for and the price of such products as coffee, tea and cocoa. This decreased the export earnings of the under-developed nations by some 7%. Since the prices of manufactured goods continued to rise the under-developed nations lost about $2 billion in import capacity. This was almost as much as all the economic aid they received during the recession year."[11] The sum total distributed under the Mutual Security Program of the United States is unquestionably very large. Nevertheless, the fact remains that in no single year has our participation in the development of other nations amounted to as much as one per cent of our national production. Those who contend that even the one per cent of our gross national product is more than we should allocate to other nations must realize that the recipient countries spend 80 per cent of their aid money in the United States. Actually, increase in aid would even put some of our own unemployed to work.

Resistance to participation in aid programs has come from those who felt that this nation was bearing too high a proportion of the total costs and that much of the giving, whether in the form of goods or cash, went into the hands of individuals who fattened their own incomes and whose funds subsequently found their way to Swiss banks. Where money and goods in such large quantities have been hastily poured out, there has undoubtedly been opportunity for corruption. This does not minimize the need or the ultimate goal. It makes mandatory more careful supervision and intelligent allocation.

That there are insufficient funds to meet the needs of every developing nation is obvious. Some selection must be made, but in doing this international feelings are bruised among both the giving and receiving nations. Even with the best of criteria there remain some who doubt the wisdom of sending assistance outside the country when there are still those within it who are themselves in need. There can be no end to this argument, since there will be at least relative need in our own country as far into the future as anyone can see. The question is rather whether the proposed aid will serve to lift the level of competence and capacity for self-support on the part of the receiving (or partner?) nation. All of this requires a capacity to sense and weigh the respective needs both of other nations and of one's own and to envision potential future relationships. It is the failure to think inclusively which gives rise to Gunnar Myrdal's thesis that as nations become welfare-minded, they decline in their acceptance of international responsibility and become instead increasingly nationalistic. This is the ethical and spiritual dilemma of the nations which are already advanced and capable of doing more for their own citizens than can the nations which are still in the "traditional," or at the "take-off," stage. Confronting its own citizens with this fact constitutes one of a government's primary responsibilities.

A nation's life transcends that of its citizens. The future well-being of a whole nation may depend on the mutual trade relations beginning with an act of beneficence. Speaking of this in reference to the delicate problem of increasing exports in the developing nations, even at the cost of embarrassing and disrupting imports, William Butler suggests that "painful though they may be, such adjustments work in the long-run interests of the industrial nations, which will be able to obtain consumer goods at lower costs, while shifting their production to the more highly technical products where their international advantage is greater."[12]

U. S. foreign aid from July 1, 1945, through June 30, 1962, totaled approximately 97.1 billion dollars. This includes 30.7 billion dollars in military assistance and 66.4 billion dollars in grants and loans to 112 foreign countries, territories, possessions, etc. Of the amount of economic aid, some 31.5 billion dollars went to Europe and Japan, and 31.5 billion dollars to the underdeveloped countries. Through the year 1963 the grand total was 101.1 billion dollars. In allocations of such magnitude it is almost inevitable that there should be certain failures, and they cannot easily be tossed off. There has not been time to develop a large and tested staff of administrators, rich in wisdom and experience in the nations to which allocations have been made. This fact does not excuse the failures, unless there has been a little learning and constructive experience while nations and people have been relieved, in some measure at least, from want and given hope for future development. To give aid to less developed nations means inevitably some form of interference with their political, economic, and social life, but to insure that the interference is constructive and designed for the best interests of that nation requires specialists who understand the life, customs, and needs of the developing nation. Only thus will viable economies emerge and future harmony with the contributing nations be assured.

Out of the welter of new experience has emerged a single organization responsible for most of the civilian operations in providing both relief and solid instructive programs, the Agency for International Development (AID). Its structure and program have become well known both in our own nation and around the world. One indication of its extent is the fact that it is manned by some 13,000 workers, more than 6,000 of whom are United States nationals overseas.

The American people have been bombarded with a wide variety of arguments relative to foreign aid. A U. S. Senate special committee to study the foreign aid program reported that "foreign aid has been justified at one and the same time as the answer to the prevention of further Communist expansion; as a key to the national defense; as a lid to cap explosive political situations like that in the Middle East; as a vehicle for the expression of our friendship and our humanitarianism; as a means for keeping or winning the less developed nations to freedom; as a principal bulwark of world peace; as a stimulator of trade, investment and free enterprise throughout the world; as the answer to the problem of agricultural surpluses and other lesser economic dislocations in this country."

The committee goes on to suggest that this confusion "has resulted in distortions to the purposes, cost and potentialities of particular types of aid. This misconception was bound to lead, as it has led, to increasing disillusionment and hostility toward foreign aid in this country."

John Nuveen, investment banker and former U. S. minister and chief of this country's economic mission in Greece and Belgium during the Marshall Plan period, commenting on the consequences for communism under the Marshall Plan program in Europe, says that in Belgium there were forty Communists in the Parliament prior to the Plan. In 1950 there were ten, and by 1958 three. True, this was the nation which had known a healthy economy and cannot be compared accurately to the developing nations. But as Nuveen goes on to point out, after eliminating military aid figures, the United States is attempting to cure the economic anemia of the underdeveloped countries with one-sixtieth of the strength (on a per capita basis) which produced results in Europe.[13]

Communist competition has loomed large in the justification for foreign aid, and correctly so. The well-being of the people of an emerging nation may be the concern of the people of nations providing assistance, but at the national level the expectancy of future trade benefits constitutes the principal rationale. Potential exclusion from the benefits of trade confronts nations which must project their life long into the future with the possibility of impairment in economic relations. Evidence of Communist gains already made justly give rise to apprehension.

The increase in Communist aid to the under-developed countries has been matched by an increase in Communist trade. The Soviet Union itself has been taking the agricultural surpluses of those countries— Egypt's cotton, Burma's rice, Uruguay's wool—and sending in return, arms or capital goods and raw materials needed for development. Between 1953 and 1956 the Soviet Union nearly doubled its imports from the under-developed countries and increased its exports to more than five-fold. Other members of the Communist bloc—Poland, Czechoslovakia, and more recently, Communist China—have also increased their trade with the under-developed countries though by lesser amounts. By the end of 1958 Western businessmen were talking about Communist China's economic invasion of Asia and Africa.[14]

The United States' answer to this challenge is first, of course, the maintenance of economic strength and stability in this nation.

But beyond that lie the various kinds of assistance to which reference has been made above. As the people of less developed nations and their leaders discern the fact that assistance from the West carries with it no mortgaging of their future or bondage to a rigid political system, they will evolve in their own self-respect and note in the history of their national life the fact that the aid given them did not carry crippling requirements.

Stipulations as to agencies and specific programs are unnecessary at this writing, for they must change in accordance with evolving needs. The principle underlying participation in economic assistance has not altered nor is it likely to be altered in the foreseeable future. Conditions in developing nations do suggest, however, some variations to be taken into consideration. The development of traditional societies presents different requirements, in contrast to those of the nations aided by the Marshall Plan, and the patterns found so successful immediately after World War II cannot be exactly duplicated. This may be illustrated in the comment of an Indian official: "The Germans have built us steel works but we are the hostages of their technology. How can we get our people trained to replace them, without adequate elementary schools to give any grounding? Give me 10,000 teachers."[15]

Aid in the form of loans, grants, food, schools, technical assistance, and many other forms is indispensable. To these, however, must be added substantial help in the form of control of population growth. As stated earlier, most of the benefits accruing from assistance, however unselfishly motivated, could be minimized if not destroyed by a rate of population growth too great to permit the nation to develop itself for holding its own with other nations in the world of trade. It becomes obligatory upon the assisting nations to find means for convincing the receiving "partners" that extensive measures must be taken to limit their population increase.

No small clue to economic development for the less developed nations lies in the attitude of the American people. Development of living standards in the United States exemplified the forces which have aroused the aspirations of those living in underdeveloped lands, aspirations which can never be quelled. It is difficult for middle-class Americans to understand the realities behind the standard-of-living figures of the nations now seeking an increasing measure of the things Americans take for granted.

U Thant, secretary-general of the UN, says: "The truth, the central stupendous truth, about developed countries today is that they can have—in anything but the shortest run—the kind and scale of resources they decide to have. . . . It is no longer resources that limit decisions. It is the decisions that make the resources. This is the fundamental revolutionary change—perhaps the most revolutionary mankind has ever known."[16] This is the attitude which has permeated the thought of a large percentage of people in the developed nations.

Because the future health of world economic relations depends upon a recognition of both its own fortuitous situation and the possibilities for increasing world economic health, it is recommended that "the United States in cooperation with other rich countries of the world, take an unlimited commitment to provide the developing countries with all the financial resources which they can usefully absorb and which can be effectively used. In other words, the Commission recommends that a lack of financial resources should no longer be allowed to hamper programs of aid to the developing countries."[17] It is estimated that to accomplish this purpose it would require only 15 per cent of the annual increase in income which could normally be expected in the nations participating in the giving.

Finally, it becomes apparent that motives for participation in foreign aid are a compound of genuine generosity and national benefit. There is nothing derogatory or reprehensible in this combination. Here economic well-being of our neighbor is inseparable from the consequences of concern for him as neighbor. In the whole issue of foreign aid the mutual involvement of mankind is illustrated with convincing evidence. As the Fourth National Study Conference on Church and Economic Life stated: "A basic condition of truly effective aid is a sense of mutual purpose and shared responsibility among the countries and people involved."[18]

11

Government Power and the Economy

The proper role of government—the most inclusive of all organizations—has, except in totalitarian states where it is all-embracing, become a major issue in the consideration of problems of economic development.

—WILLIAM ADAMS BROWN, JR., in *Christian Values and Economic Life*

If Alexander Hamilton and Thomas Jefferson could witness what has occurred in their country a century and a half after their famous controversy over concentration of government power, they would be surprised to learn that each had won his point: the powers of the central government have increased steadily, and the rights, privileges, and security of the citizens have experienced parallel increase. Thus the fundamental intentions of both men have been realized. The paradox is that it has been the mounting insistence that the federal government provide for the well-being of the individual citizen which has been so largely instrumental in concentrating power at the national level.

Hamilton's interest in a strong central government was hardly motivated by a zeal for establishing a welfare state; in fact, if some historical analyses of that period are correct, the Federalist Party espousing strong centralization went out of existence in part because of its reputation for indifference to the common man. Jefferson's fear, on the other hand, was that aristocrats wielding power would be insufficiently aware of and incapable of protecting the interests of the overwhelming majority, the ordinary citizens. Thus not only did the two men not foresee that the nation would ultimately focus major attention on the welfare needs of its people (and that of other nations as well), but that in consequence the stability of the economy which both men so eagerly desired would be realized.

GOVERNMENT EXPANSION

Seemingly unlimited opportunities for geographic expansion and a conviction that material salvation was the assured result of hard work spared a new nation the necessity for clarifying its central economic policies. An unlimited frontier could give substance to Horace Greeley's admonition, "vote yourself a farm," at least until the closing of the frontier around 1890. The maxim "that government is best which governs least" had special meaning for all who stood to gain by their diligence or skill in appropriating the resources of the new country. The psychology of the whole nation supported their efforts. Courts, reflecting the dominant tone of expansion and optimism of the nation, upheld their actions and property claims. The Federal Land Policy, expressed notably in the Homestead Act of 1862, likewise reflected the national temper. Land was the symbol of property. Independent and self-reliant citizens would acquire it either for agricultural purposes or for speculation. Government's role was to facilitate the acquisition of land and to foster the type of citizen Jefferson believed was the backbone of the nation.

As the new government sought means of facilitating the nation's expansion, prior to its encouragement of railroads and land disposal, it entered into various business ventures. In 1791 a national bank was established, though later abandoned; canals were dug in many states, and a national road was constructed. State governments also undertook the initiating and operating of ventures designed to increase their own functions and to expand the economy within their borders. In addition to roads, canals, and banks even some manufacturing was undertaken. At least one state, North Dakota, continues to operate banks and grain elevators, not so much, however, to expand the economic activities of the state as to protect its citizens from injury by outsiders.

Then came the greatest decision since the founding of the nation itself. It emerged from a casual land policy and forced a government heretofore unchallenged in its land disposition to decide whether newly opened areas should be operated on a slave economy. A war with England in 1812 united a new nation in the common defense but left unresolved the major question whether the central government had the right and power to coerce its own people into uniformity where a fundamental ideological difference still remained.

With the Civil War issue resolved, at least on the political and legal levels, the rebuilding of a devastated southland and the continued westward expansion of agriculture, transportation, and mining, major government controls were delayed more than a generation. Government resources poured into agricultural production through the land-grant colleges, direct aid to farmers, land gifts to railroads, high tariffs to protect "infant industries," judicial discouragement of labor organizations, and through many other means supporting unrestrained individual and corporate aggrandizement. All this presumed that an ultimate harmony of individual and social needs would result if restraints were minimal. The hypotheses of John Locke, the influence of David Hume and his utilitarian school, and Jeremy Bentham and his laissez-faire philosophy, all of which had so richly informed the thinking of the founding fathers, remained the cornerstones of political and economic philosophy.

But Locke, Hume, and Bentham had not envisioned the misuses to which their advocates might direct their theories. Though the ability of the federal government to maintain the union had met its greatest challenge, there remained the necessity for defending the one group of citizens who benefited from the government policy of land disposition against another group who also benefited but in the form of railroad franchises. The result was "The Green Rising," or Populist Movement. Intimately related to the injuries done the farmer by fraudulent grain-grading programs and excessive and discriminatory charges for hauling of agricultural products was the conviction that the farmer was the victim of money rates and interest charges making it increasingly difficult to pay off land mortgages. This protest produced the beginnings of the farm organization movement which in turn enhanced the power of the agricultural states to secure from the federal government both redress of grievances and a measure of special consideration which has prevailed until very recently.

Industry had experienced no such necessity for securing its objectives; a government already kindly disposed toward manufacture and trade did not have to achieve its end through consolidated opposition to powers already installed. Though labor had long since attempted collective pressure, it had not won the public support and sympathy accorded agriculture. After all, the farmer was an indigenous American embodying the very essence of the American system, the "Protestant ethic"; he worked with his hands, but he was also an entrepreneur, and he represented that pure type which Jefferson thought could be trusted with the destiny of the nation.

Labor, on the other hand, represented massed power, and many of its dissident leaders as well as its rank and file bore names which were other than English or North European. Massed power in the form of labor unions was regarded as a vulgar threat to the persons who, through initiative, diligence, and personal economy, had arrived at their places of distinction. A government traditionally founded on the qualities associated with Calvinistic virtues was not yet disposed to come to the rescue of those who were judged to have failed to exhibit these virtues and to take advantage of the opportunities supposedly available to all. Thus it was no violation of fundamental tenets of American life to organize the forces of government on behalf of its most exemplary citizens, the farmer. By protecting him this same benevolent government was merely extending the action originally taken to provide the nation with a solid core of loyal independent citizens on the land. It is therefore consistent that when this particular exemplary citizen fell upon evil days in the maturing of the total economy, it was around his needs that major rescue programs evolved. They were the forerunners of those systems which ultimately had to be devised by an increasingly centralized government to rescue the entire economy.

A greater factor, even, than the plight of agriculture in creating the necessity for increasing the central power of government was the process of industrialization and technological development. This theme was dealt with more fully in chapter two. Here it must be affirmed that concentration of government power is no more a devious plot than is the centralizing of power by industry and business. It is an inevitable consequence of utilizing the scientific gains whereby efficiency is enhanced and living standards raised. One may question whether the consequences are universally desirable, which introduces a question of relative values. But it can be unequivocally insisted that if we continue the technological advances which have produced concentrations of economic power, a commensurate governmental power becomes necessary and inevitable if a democratic society is to survive. This nation has assumed from its inception that economic enterprise is subordinate to the common welfare and is not, therefore, autonomous. The rapid advances in technology and industry have created the confusion and tension attending the formation of corresponding government responses. Some of this results presumably from sheer resentment against government expansion, but much if not most of it is the consequence of trial and error in ascertaining the most appropriate and effective instruments for government action in our evolving industrial society.

WELFARE AND INCREASED CENTRAL AUTHORITY

Since the founding of the nation there has been no serious denial of the central government's authority to initiate the defense program and to manage the finances of the nation. Protests on either score would hardly be taken seriously. Though there are still a few individuals who would like to have the postal service placed under private management, they attract little serious support. Control over corporation abuses against the populace as a whole has been reflected in "trust busting" activities under the Sherman Antitrust Act; because the scandals of corporate abuse and defiance of public good were so widely portrayed, the public was prepared for the restraining action. For similar reasons, the food and drug legislation found acceptance. Not so readily accepted, however, was the legislation establishing the federal income tax. A wartime income tax of 1861 had been repealed in 1872; another tax levied in 1894 was declared unconstitutional. Finally, in 1913 the income tax amendment was adopted. There was intense opposition to the tax by business and higher income groups who attacked it as being socialistic; small but noisy outbreaks of such opposition continue to exist a half century later.

Support for the nation's citizens whether in need or in return for service rendered their country found no place in the earliest stages of the nation's life. Veterans of the Revolutionary War and the War of 1812 were given grants of land in the newly opened areas of the country, but this was not in the form of continued payments or pensions. The granting of pensions, both to meet actual need and as tokens of gratitude, began after the Civil War. Therewith began the policy of providing through the national government for unmet needs of the nation's citizens.

Private charitable agencies, the traditional method of meeting need in this country, were unable to cope with either the causes or the consequences of unemployment, with hunger and suffering. Public welfare measures were the province of the states, but under the impact of nationwide and world-wide need state programs were inadequate. Not until the depression of the 1930's, however, was the scope of government's role as sustainer of the well-being of its citizens fully realized.

Though the agricultural dilemma had been handled—not wholly successfully, it is true—with proposals for sustaining farm incomes, there was no acknowledgment of responsibility on the part of the federal government to assure income maintenance for individual citizens. Finally, the lag between capacity to produce and ability to purchase the goods produced became a recognized issue in the total economy. A government which heretofore had been responsible for sustaining industries in difficulty because of production costs or inability to sell competitively either in this country or abroad, was now confronted with the fact that millions of its citizens were unable to sustain themselves within the resources of the then current economy. European nations had long since experienced the evolution of "the welfare state." It now became apparent that the same forces which had fostered the sense of governmental obligation in European countries were inevitable and were operative in this nation. Though the range of newly accepted responsibilities is essential documentation, the spate of legislation produced by this new awareness of government responsibility is too well known to rehearse here. Those responsibilities include: (1) alternative action where private resources and enterprise are deficient; (2) establishing levels of decency below which persons shall not be expected to descend and providing them the resources to maintain themselves in dignity when private resources fail; (3) fostering conditions for full employment and, where this is not available, stabilizing the income of those temporarily or even for longer periods forced into unemployment; (4) providing for those whose physical condition no longer permits them to take their full and vigorous part in the life of the economy, i.e., the aged, the dependent, and the ill, so that their well-being becomes a responsibility of the nation as a whole; (5) specifying the conditions of work, lest hazards and unsanitary surroundings impair the physical or mental condition of the worker; (6) requiring a basic education for the entire populace, so that the nation as a whole might be freed from the deleterious effects of illiteracy and hampered in its own opportunities to play an effective role in the world of nations; (7) and finally, taking such steps as may be necessary to give impetus to the total economy, in order that the health of the nation and the well-being of its people shall be assured.

All of this was not a vast movement on behalf of those at the bottom of the economic scale; rather it furnished a broad base for the entire economy. It included in its range the Reconstruction Finance Corporation and such income maintenance projects as the Works Progress Administration. Here was a revolution in assumptions about the role of the state and its obligations to its people.

Would any political party seeking to reverse this trend of federal responsibility for the well-being of its citizens be taken seriously by any appreciable number of voters? Most individuals with sufficient literacy to read a newspaper know that the economy of the nation is increasingly dependent on the kinds of decisions made at its center. No major corporation would expect to go it alone in the economy independently of any and all government coordination. As civilization itself evolves and establishes ever higher minimal standards for human decency, it becomes apparent that some major force must assure those standards of decency, since unconnected and inchoate bodies uncommitted to any common standard are incapable of maintaining such levels.

This is not to suggest that the activity of a central government in devising programs designed to sustain its people and maintain harmony in the life of the state is the product of deliberate intent over an extended period. Many of the devices and instruments established for benefiting the citizens have emerged out of pressures, agonies, and needs occasioned by the exigencies of the times. Only as an accumulation of these needs appears has there arisen the awareness that something much more consistent and comprehensive had to be instituted. But even that may fall short of full and comprehensive organization. As Gunnar Myrdal has expressed it: "In the same way as the 'created harmony' of interest in the welfare state of the western countries was never planned, and thus never created in the strict sense of having been purposively attained, so the actual large-scale planning, which is today a major explanation of the high degree of harmony that actually exists, has remained largely unprogramatic."[1] Relative to the whole concept of the welfare state he adds: "It can even be seen that, to many persons, the term 'welfare state' has negative, not positive connotations—not, of course, because they do not appreciate welfare, but because they are bent upon protecting themselves against realizing that welfare has not come into being by itself, as a result of the unhampered play of market forces, but through public policies which are all under the ultimate sanction of the state."[2]

That a central government does not expect its welfare programs to go forward solely by accident and exigency is attested by the formation of the United States Department of Health, Education and Welfare at cabinet level. It has become accepted in the total national life that health, education, and welfare can no longer be left to mere fortuitous development. The life of a total people is too important to be left to the unregulated activities of an uncertain economy. To this department has therefore been given the commission to engage in the kind of planning over both the short and long future and to assure to the nation that its most humane interests be protected.

THE GOVERNMENT AND BUSINESS

A major product of the technological age is the large corporation. It may be nationwide or, as is increasingly the case, international in the scope of its activities. Oil companies have long operated on a multicontinent basis; more recently the automobile business has extended its areas of sales and manufacture. Because of policy established in the earliest days of the nation, each of these nationwide corporations or international organizations operates under a charter issued by and in a single state, not by the national government. Despite this fact no corporation chartered even in a single state, if doing business in other nations, may act independently of the policies and requirements of its own central government. Thus, though the fiction of responsibility to one of the fifty states is maintained, the ultimate controls over any corporation with international business interests are established by the national government. Many corporation activities even strictly within the national limits must likewise be constantly reviewed to insure compliance with the stipulations of the national government.

As corporations and markets become nationwide, with similar products required or available in diverse areas of the nation, a regulatory body with comparable authority becomes essential. Distances are of little importance with almost instantaneous communication. Thus policies and practices of corporations operating nationwide and affecting the population in many areas require oversight by the one agency responsible to the total population, the national government.

With increasing demands at the national level and the realization of the necessity to preserve common values, not only corporations but also states once regarding themselves as sovereign have faced the need for common controls. "Abdications of power to a central unit are designed precisely to defend all that can be maintained of the autonomy and individuality of the surrendering group. Much of the success of the American federal experiment rests on the aptness of the federal instrument in just this respect. The federal system can recognize, preserve, and defend diverse individual and parochial values at the same time that it unites forces necessary for the common welfare and the common defense."[3]

For each major area related to industrial activity, such as transportation, petroleum, steel, and finally aircraft, there have been brought into being either agencies or major policies for regulation and control to protect the public and to prevent injury to the economy of the nation and to the industries themselves in the process. Here, however, the governmental regulation is both direct and indirect and for a variety of reasons. All of these industries are privately owned and operated, yet their health and vitality is heavily dependent on the federal government. For example, 95 per cent of all aircraft production is sold to the government, and, presumably, the government market for fissionable materials is even higher in percentage than that of aircraft production. While substantial supervision over some areas of industry and technology can be required because they owe a very large percentage of their business to the federal government, this does not constitute the principal reason for exercising control and providing directions. A more fundmental reason is the significance of the operating practices of the industries involved as they bear upon national welfare. Disharmonies through unbridled competition with subsequent personal losses and community injury can and should be avoided. Examples are prevention of profligate waste from undue competition through production quotas (oil) or regulation of monopoly power (public utilities and transportation systems) and, more recently, labor standards of firms doing business with the government. Increasingly it becomes mandatory that a power of adequate magnitude shall enter into the decisions of organizations whose activities deeply involve the national welfare.

A. A. Berle contends that five hundred corporations control

two-thirds of the nonfarm economy of this nation; and of those five hundred corporations a comparatively small group determines the major policies of each. This, Berle says, is the highest concentration of economic power in recorded history. "Since the United States carries on not quite half of the manufacturing production of the entire world today, these 500 groupings, each with its own little dominating pyramid within it, represent a concentration of power over economics which makes the medieval feudal system look like a Sunday School party. In sheer economic power this has gone far beyond anything we have yet seen."[4] Ownership and control of these corporations represent one of the major confusions of our society. It is illustrated by the historic remark of a General Motors official who, on being asked to open the books of the corporation to a labor union, remarked, "We don't even show our books to our stockholders." The agonies through which some stockholders have had to pass in order to get changes made in the management reveals the slight and often unimportant role of the theoretical owners.

Kenneth Boulding points out that there are some corporations which are larger and affect the lives of more people than many of the nations of the world.[5] Many of these corporations in their local units determine the existence of whole communities, while collectively they influence the lives and destinies of more people than some of the fifty states in the United States.

Almost any time in the last half century it could be reported that a plant had closed and moved to another location, bringing despair and economic tragedy to a whole community. More recently it could be added that where a plant had chosen to move to another community for purposes of tax advantage and lower labor costs, a federal court has intervened on behalf of the workers. In at least one instance such a move was not permitted, and in a number of others the government ordered compensation for those who could not move and other jobs made available to those who would be willing to accept employment in the new location. At this writing there is no uniform policy, but both practices have been recorded.

In the field of communications a single industry, the American

Telephone and Telegraph Company, so penetrates the life of the nation that it enjoys a status tantamount to a public agency under private ownership. What is true at A. T. & T. is also true, even though in lesser degrees, of many corporations which do not enjoy such a near monopoly. It is no longer possible to make clean-cut distinctions between public and private agencies. Even privately owned corporations not enjoying those concessions made by a central government which are necessary for utilities are under such a measure of public jurisdiction and the consequent necessity for maintaining the public good will that they must presumably conduct themselves with a high degree of circumspection. The broad field of communications—radio, television, newspapers, wire services of many sorts—has been increasingly recognized as enjoying special governmental privileges, though without the more rigid regulations of public utilities, and is therefore under the obligation to conduct itself in a manner evidencing consideration for the national well-being.

The operation of these semipublic and private corporations may not be as intimately related to the health of the economy as, for example, would be the operations of fiscal and monetary policy, but there can be no doubt that with the total harmony of national life and the stability of individuals and organizations at stake, each of these corporations has an intimate tie with the total economy. Thus, much of the insistence upon authority and control over the public and private corporations has arisen for reasons which are at the same time economic and ethical.

GOVERNMENT AND THE NATIONAL ECONOMY

Earlier it was suggested that a watershed in the role of government was reached during the great depression, when the nation first realized that the welfare of its people was a national concern and that only measures taken at the national level could guarantee proper subsistence. Functions of a government are never isolated from each other, and however much one would like to have the welfare aspects of government identifiable and operated strictly within their own range, they cannot be separated from the forces which affect the total economy.

Fiscal and monetary policy* have a direct bearing on the problem of employment, gross national product, expansion or growth in the economy, and everything else affecting economic life.

National monetary policy in the United States may be said to have had its principal development with the passage of the Federal Reserve Act in 1913. Fiscal policy, however, was an activity that began with the depression in the 1930s. Because industries lacked the liquid resources and could not secure funds at a sufficiently low level of interest to launch major expansion programs, the federal government undertook the now famous pump priming program under the Works Progress Administration, Public Works Administration, Reconstruction Finance Corporation, any many others. Under a monetary policy of reduced interest rates and more adequate supply of funds through the Federal Reserve Board, encouragement was given to industries to start expansion. The income maintenance provisions of the social security programs not only protected individuals and families but served to increase effective demand. However, during the first few years of the decade repeated efforts were made to balance the budget by increasing taxes, always without success. Influenced largely by the British economist J. M. Keynes, the Roosevelt administration after 1937 moved toward the policy of federal spending as a positive means of accelerating the economy's growth. Meanwhile, taxes were not further increased lest this should offset the stimulating economic impact of the increase in expenditures. The result was a moderate increase in the national debt, a fact reluctantly accepted as a necessary consequence of the other steps. Major developments in the use of fiscal policy were made during and after the war.

Obviously, such actions can be taken only at the national level, for the integration of the economy is so complete that only nation-wide use of governmental expenditures, taxation, and interest rates can have the necessary impact. It is significant in this instance that through the exercise of both fiscal and monetary policy the results could be felt immediately not only by those at the lowest

* Fiscal policy is designed to influence the economy by changing the volume of demand in the economy through measures of taxation and government expenditure, including deficit spending. Monetary policy is designed to influence the volume of demand and accordingly of economic activity by changing the supply of money and its cost to the borrower.

level of income but also by the most powerful corporations in the nation. It was total economic therapy.

That not everyone is pleased with the use of fiscal and monetary policy as means of stimulating the economy is revealed by vigorous opposition to tax reduction as a means of putting more money to work in the expansion of plant and increase of buying power on the part of individuals. So accustomed are we to thinking of the finances of the federal government in terms comparable to the finances of a family that it is difficult to make convincing argument that going further into debt as a means of stimulating economic life is at times justifiable. In 1963 former President Eisenhower said: "I say that the time-tested rules of financial policy still apply. Spending for spending's sake is patently a false theory. No family, no business, no nation can spend itself into prosperity. Any way you look at it, a nation is nothing more than a collection of families—about 47 million of them make up the United States—and it is their money that the government is spending."[6] Nevertheless a year later a government which had witnessed the longest continued span of prosperity in many years voted a large tax reduction as a means of assuring the continuance of what appeared to be a healthy economy. This was done with the encouragement of the President's economic advisors and large sections of the financial and industrial leadership of the nation.

In addition to the protest against a "spending for prosperity" theory there should also be mentioned the objection to the use of taxing powers for the general distribution of wealth. This is regarded by many individuals as "socialism."

Fiscal and monetary policies are tools to be used in promoting the growth and stability of the internal economy. Their use is determined or stimulated by many factors, among which is the balance of payments with the rest of the world. Paradoxically a deficit in balance of payments may result from rising internal demand achieved by successful fiscal and monetary policy. Its remedy may come from still further changes in those policies, through, for example, the deflation of demand and the increase of interest rates. Doing so may, however, cast a cloud over the economy's health, as a reduction of levels in business and employment may result. Obviously, the making of fiscal and monetary policies is an extremely delicate matter and, to be effectively applied, requires the utmost in governmental responsibility. The point being made here is not a defense of or an opposition to the practices described but a warning that in so complex a matter as the total economy of the nation only a central administrative force can exercise the initiative and fulfill practices required to meet what are deemed the fundamental needs of the nation.

EMERGING GOVERNMENT FUNCTIONS

At this writing the federal government, in fulfillment of its mandate to provide for the general welfare, has envisioned a vast program for the reduction of poverty. In magnitude it is comparable to some of the programs initiated during the depression, though the circumstances are by no means identical. We are mindful of the paradox that extensive poverty exists when the economy is enjoying a degree of health unknown before and unparalleled in its duration. Not only are public works being initiated to provide employment, but also retraining programs made necessary by the obsolescence of certain industries and types of work are under way. Responsibility for implementing programs designed to strengthen the economy does not lie solely with the federal government; nevertheless much of the difficulty can be overcome where government exercises such initiative in cooperation with private agencies.

Roy Blough proposes some measures to speed readjustment in the economy impaired or inhibited by technological, psychological, or cyclical factors: "One positive approach is to take the kinds of steps that will speed the necessary re-adjustment to technological change. Among these are maintaining a high level of general economic demand, improving labor mobility, enlarging and improvising educational programs, and encouraging the development of new industries."[7] He goes on to discuss proposals that have been made for government programs to support employment, shorten hours, and share work, which make for wider and more nearly equal distribution of income. Again, though these are not entirely a government responsibility, they can be substantially implemented through joint government-private agencies or institutions. "The imaginative creation of new institutions and relations between governments and private groups is a critical need of our time."[8]

No full classification of central government actions or responsibilities is here intended or possible. What have been suggested above are essentially illustrations of the fact that government action is necessary to assure national viability. In his *American Capitalism: The Concept of Countervailing Power* John Kenneth Galbraith developed the thesis now popularly identified with him. The power structures in contemporary life are so great that there must be a comparable force to provide checks against misuse of power. Such countervailing powers tend to come into being to meet great power structures, but when this does not happen, the duty rests on government to perform the restraining function of countervailing power. Thus labor unions have become a countervailing power to management, but the power of government sometimes must be exerted to restrain the overzealousness of both labor and management. It was on a similar thesis that the founding fathers established a government with three major centers of power and control, each capable of correcting the excesses of the others. It must be pointed out that in the present period of history the defense aspect of the government looms so large, both as strictly defense activity and because of its increased involvement in the total economy, that it has come to be the most significantly determining influence in the total life of the nation. The countervailing power in this situation is obscure. Labor, management, and the legislative and the executive branches of the government are so much under the pressure of the reputed defense requirements that they are apparently reluctant to exercise their countervailing competence. As will be explained later, this phenomenon has found its rationale in the need for maintaining the stability of the economy. The thesis being put forward here, however, is not impaired by this phenomenon. It simply exhibits even more pointedly the role of the federal government in its maintenance and regulation of the economy.

Inherent in all of the functions to which reference has been made is a phase of their existence which perhaps is taken for granted but which is increasing in scope and intensity; it is the area broadly designated as planning. When the Beveridge Plan came into prominence in Britain at the conclusion of World War II, substantial resistance was recorded in the United States, because planning, as implied in the Beveridge Report, was taken to mean socialism. The emergence of the National Planning Association has met with approval by many organizations and individuals that might have been alienated by the imputation of socialism, since the roster of those identified with the NPA constituted the bluebook of American industry.

Countervailing power of itself is inadequate to give balance and to provide direction for the life of the economy. Earlier in our history much that characterized the relationship between government and business was the result of a policy or the product of a theory that things would work themselves out satisfactorily. Obviously that day is gone. "More and more we are asking," says W. H. Ferry, "whether it is possible to organize matters better—perhaps with planning as a central means—to serve the ends of a liberal republic. More recent concern with what these ends may actually be is exemplified by the appointment of a Presidential Commission on National Goals."[9]

Every organization making significant headway has a planning body within it, analyzing its past and projecting for its future. All corporations have such units in their structure if they expect to survive. The State Department has a policy planning staff, and unions, educational organizations, professional groups, and many others have come to realize that planning is indispensable.

One concomitant of the development of planning programs is the realization that such brand names as socialism and capitalism have become outmoded. The enterprise system is dependent upon planning in the organization of its life for the long pull. Capitalism, having long since departed from its original laissez-faire ideology, accepts the role of government supervision and coordination as integral and essential to its existence. Meanwhile, the public as a whole may not be as kindly disposed toward the term "welfare state" as it has been ready to accept the changes involved in order to maintain the enterprise system. It is the same desire for the over-all well-being of the nation which has produced acceptance of the fundamental necessity of basic planning. Apprehension over increasing power of centralized government has provided a rallying point for one major political party in our time and is a source of concern to many individuals, whatever their political affiliation. We have come to accept the fact that only confusion and anarchy would result if central planning in many aspects of the nation's life were to be abandoned. One issue seems to be whether a responsible citizenry will undertake at local levels those activities which can best be effected there and thus help determine the range and areas of national action.

The central objective of planning is to make certain that the best interests of the whole society are preserved, and this means increasing responsibility of the actions of government at all levels. This does not necessarily mean that governmental intervention as such will need to increase.

Planning is needed to make consistent and effective use of intervention. To some authors, notably Gunnar Myrdal, an objective and hoped-for achievement of planning in the welfare state is to simplify the character of intervention and to reduce the need for it. Under this conception planning would seek to substitute a few general policies for a growing mesh of detailed and specific ones, and in particular would restructure the national economy to the end that for the most part cooperation and collective bargaining would determine the norms for people living together.

There is fear on the part of some individuals that in the process of planning, power may be used for the purpose of manipulating the lives and interests of persons irrespective of their own best interest. This is indeed a risk, but there are options open to a responsible electorate for its protection. Willy-nilly, we will have some kind of government. The question is simply whether it will be a humane government, sensitive to the interests of its people or responsive to the will of those who may stand to gain most for themselves. David Bazelon puts the issue thus:

An advancing technological society cannot exist ungoverned; without more coherent government than we now have we will end up crushing each other—eventually physically, as now psychologically. With more and more people living together in increasingly complicated and inter-dependent patternings made possible and imperative by the technology and its astounding historical pace, fewer areas of social life can safely remain free of governing. Each time we wait for problems to solve themselves we deny the probable world around us, thus seeking a disaster we must ultimately find. Health, education, employment and organization of our living and working areas along with the development of the scientific technology which is the source of all our blessings and troubles—all these require some decisive support or control by the national government, some positive use of central power.[10]

The suitable figure of speech for the kind of society which has been emerging in the United States and in many other nations of the West is not that of a pendulum swinging from the extreme of corporate domination to the opposite extreme of consideration for individual welfare. Perhaps a better figure would be the circle including within it both the welfare of the component economic units and the rights and well-being of individuals. Whether this is to be called the welfare state or the security state or the enterprise-economy state or what-not is immaterial. Sidney Hook has suggested that whatever may be our attitude toward the name and the direction in which it has been moving, "it's only alternative is the ill-fare state."[11]

CONCLUSION

Thomas Jefferson's misgivings about concentration of power in the hands of a few stemmed from his misgivings about the ability of a people to resist their oppressors once power was concentrated in them. If we do not fear the state as oppressor in this country, it is for reasons which can be identified with historic ideological roots, religious origins, and the opportunities for personal and economic developments provided by a beneficent continent. A free public school system has taught the people of the nation that no class is superior and that power may be exercised only by those who earn the right to use it in the free market place of ideas.

The result is that despite abuses of this option and occasional distortions of freedom resulting in malevolence, government is regarded as man's servant and not his master.

Throughout this discussion of government power it may seem to be implied that power will be used impartially and beneficially. The record should disabuse us of such a notion. But even where such an application of power as is conceivably possible has been effected, there are some individuals who are restricted and whose intentions are frustrated. In our immediate period of history the conflict over civil rights has intensely illuminated this problem.

The rectifying of many decades of economic and political disadvantage inevitably impinges on practices and customs which under canons of human decency should never have come into existence. Regional regulations obviously cannot be counted on to protect human rights, hence only the larger power of a government serving the entirety of a nation can be efficacious. Where regional courts cannot be relied upon to administer justice, a court with nationwide responsibility is utterly essential.

The ethical use of power cannot be decided by majority vote, but fortunately, with respect to deprivation and injury because of race, the majority has, though belatedly, made progress toward ethical goals. Ethical norms in a pluralistic society cannot be posited upon the standards of a single religion. They can, however, find opportunity for expression if freedom in the market place of ideas is assured. Here government has dual involvement. It can be the defender of such freedom and at the same time can become the instrument and trustee of increased power. It is in this way that it functions constructively in the economy.

The New Meaning of
Leisure and Work

Books, studies, and articles about leisure are, like spring, "busting out all over." Our accelerated interest in the subject parallels in rate the changes resulting from technology; it is almost a one-to-one relationship for the very obvious reason that it is technology which is increasing the measure and availability of leisure.

Leisure was a subject of debate even in the time of Aristotle. Greeks who lived on a slave economy had time to ask themselves why they were permitted the experience of leisure as against the experience of the toiling masses of slaves who made such leisure possible. Now with mechanical slaves many who are not philosophers have a degree of leisure comparable to those who in earlier periods had time to ponder the question. Consequently the meaning and role of leisure has once again emerged as a subject of discussion.

Observers of developments in industrial society foresaw the changes which were to result in increased leisure long before cybernation alerted us to them with new clarity. In 1880 the Presidential candidate James A. Garfield, addressing an audience at Lake Chautauqua, proposed that human history could be divided into two major parts. "First the fight to get leisure; and then the second fight of civilization—what shall we do with our leisure when we get it?[1]

WHAT IS LEISURE?

We have chosen to link work and leisure together because leisure is a corollary of work. It is a state of existence which results from work and which can be enriched by work. Though in a work-oriented society they are often confused, leisure should be more than idleness; idleness may be destructive or disintegrative of self-hood, whereas leisure can be constructive. This creates for our generation one of its most fundamental problems: whether shortened hours of work will produce only idleness, or hours free from work will make possible a health-giving leisure?

"Not everything one does in one's free time qualifies as leisure," says Robert Lee. "Of course, free time may be converted into leisure. Hence, free time is only potentially leisure time. Non-committed or free time may well be idle time. The mood of leisure is affirmative whereas the mood of idleness is negative. . . . Leisure need not be viewed as subordinate to work or as a restorative for work but may be seen as an end in itself, something valued for its own sake."[2]

A debate on the nature of idleness and leisure could be interesting, but it is not our fundamental purpose. We will settle for the fact that free time is becoming increasingly available and that the use made of that time is an all-important question for industrial civilization. It is with the use of that time that we are primarily concerned. Marion Clawson says: "By leisure we mean all time beyond the existence and subsistence of time . . . so defined leisure closely resembles discretionary income, a concept which economists find very useful even though there is some ambiguity about some items that might be included in it. Leisure has well been called 'choosing time' because one can choose what to do with it. . . ."[3] Our concern, then, is with what is in fact chosen to constitute the substance of leisure activity.

Many people are compelled to work at tasks which are not their first choice as a way of living. Thus what they do in their free time becomes of great importance. It is during the period of leisure that they can become what they really are. This is the time when they may be at their best and fulfill their true potential as human beings, but there is also the alternative option of using that time at a level lower than one's potential.

Some fortunate people find their work more interesting than anything else they could do, and would do it even if it were not necessary for their livelihood. For them idleness is no problem; they are the ones whose work time is increasing while the hours spent at remunerative labor for most others is decreasing. Scientists, some individuals engaged in what are commonly termed professions, and independent creative workers will be unaffected by the forced free time of the rest of society, though even they must have respite from a too steady occupation at a single task. What they do by way of diversion may also contribute to their general well-being. Of greater concern, however, are those whose educational equipment, training, or background does not prepare them to take advantage of the increased leisure forced upon them. It is they whose idleness can be most destructive to themselves and to the rest of society, and for them increased free time can only create a downward spiral of disintegration.

Those deprived of education are not the only ones for whom forced idleness can be disintegrative. In 1900 the average life of a retired person was three years beyond retirement. At present it is somewhat over six years, and in another third of a century the average is expected to be nine years. Will the time be spent in vegetating, or will it add richly to the potentially "golden years"?

The established fact is that the shift from a production to a consumption economy, with an increasing number of workers available for a productive process requiring fewer and fewer man-hours, is confronting mass society with the problem of a constructive use of its leisure to a degree of breadth and importance unparalleled in history. With more free time available a very large percentage of the population is, paradoxically, subject to pressures demanding or coaxing them to utilize what free time they have in a manner primarily beneficial to others, who have a stake in their choice. The term "choosing time" therefore takes on added meaning. It is not simply the time one chooses not to work but the time in which he decides for himself what he wants to do.

EXTENT OF LEISURE

During World War I steelworkers in the United States worked 84 hours per week, and paid holidays were few. Not all industries were on the twelve-hour day, but the 70-hour week was normal less than a century ago. Now we take for granted the 40-hour week, and the 30- to 35-hour week is no longer idle talk. since in some industries this has already become a reality. It was estimated by the U. S. Bureau of Labor Statistics in June 1961 that the average hours of work per week per employee in 1976 will be 35.4, that the average paid vacation will be 2.8 weeks, and that the average number of holidays will be 8.5. When the increase in life span is added to these figures, the total is 22 more years of leisure in an average individual life, 1,500 free hours per year, or some 33,000 additional free hours for a lifetime.[4] Of course this is not universally applicable throughout the country. People who are in a position to determine their own hours of work and who may be engaged in service activities or creative work of many kinds will actually be under pressure to *curtail* their disposable leisure because of demands made upon them by those who have more leisure!

Anyone who has been on a public highway from Friday afternoon through Sunday evening, or during a holiday, does not have to be told that increased leisure has created whole new industries and expanded others immensely. Boating and fishing equipment and the do-it-yourself trend for home repairs and construction attest a phenomenon unknown a generation ago.

Reduction in the number of hours in a workday and "the long week-end" are but two of the sources of increased leisure. Another is the growing acceptance of and insistence upon designated holidays. Labor Day is now an established day of freedom from work, marking the end of the summer, and for families with children the last free time before school begins. Veterans' Day (formerly Armistice Day) gets increasing attention as a day of respite from work, just as Memorial Day has come to have significance as the end of the spring period and the beginning of summer. The leisure they provide thus carries a dual role. Christmas as a combination of sacred and secular holiday is taken for granted by almost everyone. St. Patrick's Day and Columbus Day have special meaning for certain ethnic groups, involving the closing of some establishments, as is also true of Good Friday in some communities. It is more than likely that observance of some of these now partially observed days will increase and that new ones will be added.

As suggested in the chapter on labor organizations, negotiations center increasingly around free time, both in addition to and as a substitute for wage increases. This does not imply a lack of interest in added income but a realization that wage increases may spiral inflationary movements and thus suggest insensitivity to the economic condition of the particular company or industry. Similarly, shortening hours without decreasing wages would also have an inflationary effect of the "cost push" variety much the same as would result from wage increases.

Shorter hours and additional free time in the form of holidays and earlier retirement represent concessions to a society which already has the minimal necessities, at least in its highly industrialized areas. Free time under these circumstances means a benefit to the worker who prizes it. With his added mobility and increased resources for enjoying free time he prefers the extra hours for personal satisfactions.

Parenthetically it has to be added that not everyone chooses to take this time for purposes of personal enjoyment. Whereas in 1950 approximately 3 per cent of those employed in nonagricultural pursuits were "moonlighting," it is estimated that more than 7 per cent of all nonagricultural workers in 1964 were engaged in one or more jobs in addition to their main occupation. On the long weekends, for example, school teachers, salesmen, and clerical workers may find employment in merchandizing organizations.[5]

THE HISTORICAL RELATION OF WORK AND LEISURE

"In the sweat of your face you shall eat bread" (Genesis 3 : 19). In accord with this biblical injunction man for centuries has assumed that his lot is to work in order to sustain himself. But the Bible does not say that man shall do nothing but work. Even God himself, the biblical writers tell us, "rested" on the seventh day, and a "day of rest" has been incorporated in the calendar as an integral part of our routine of life.

When men worked from sunup to sundown, whether in a hunting or agricultural economy, there were times between seasons and even during seasons when they took time out to revere the source of their livelihood. Out of such occasions grew the holy days and subsequently the holidays. When religion and livelihood were inseparably intertwined, secular holidays were unknown. As nations evolved and required esteem and praise, they set aside days for that purpose. The intermingling of sacred and secular holidays rendered some of them indistinguishable. Regardless of the sacred or secular nature of these days of leisure, industrial society, evolving its own rhythms of work, found it necessary to establish times for respite and recuperation.

With the emergence of industry long hours of continuous labor for both children and adults were rationalized on the grounds that busy hands were not engaged in mischief and that the productivity of those hands contributed to the character of the person. This was pleasing to God and at the same time made for economic stability. Max Weber has characterized these qualities by the term most frequently associated with his name, "the Protestant ethic."

As the industrializing nations evolved and extended their influence beyond their own national boundaries, a premium was placed on effort and frugality. Work was characterized as noble because it helped to offset the misuse of time and the consequent injuries to the working powers of those whose labor was needed in the burgeoning industries. This excessive emphasis on the virtue of work has been erroneously branded as a "Puritan" attitude, largely because of the continuous diligence required by Puritans in America, of whom the rigors of existence demanded persistent labor. But it was the Puritan's realistic understanding of himself as a child of God and responsible to his Maker which determined his attitudes toward all of life, his family, his neighbors, and the use of his time in work and leisure—not work for work's sake. Any attempt to comprehend "the Puritan mind" must include his own sense of obligation to his Creator and his desire to be worthy of salvation if such should be accorded him.

Thus periods both of work and of leisure were occasions for glorifying God. But this is vastly different from self-mortification.

It is not difficult to understand, however, why eventually a preoccupation with the virtues of work for its own sake did emerge from a background of Puritan industriousness. A fear that individuals would lack the capacity to use their freedom wisely made continuous labor seem preferable to a leisure which could be misappropriated. Religion came to occupy itself more extensively with the virtues of diligence and work than with training for creative use of such free time as might be provided in a system not so regimented. A "gospel of work" was extolled. It was easier to monitor and regulate life under a work program than to inspire its constructive use outside of work. In either case, the real question was the value of time and the use for which it was employed.

Then there came to our industrial civilization the unprecedented experience of finding it impossible to engage full-time in productive labor even if one wanted to. A society which found its meanings and values for life in productive labor was now faced with the necessity for discerning the fundamental meanings of life in its leisure-time activities. Now, only in their leisure are most people fully able to be themselves. Paul Weiss of Yale has commented that leisure "is a time when men can be at their best, making it possible for them to make the rest of their day as excellent as possible—and thereby discerning a new value and perhaps a new objective to whatever is done."[6]

If leisure is "choosing time" and the period in which the individual can be at his best, the basis for his choice has far-reaching implications. It is here that he gives evidence of his own understanding of himself. In effect he asks, "Is this the ultimate end toward which my life should be directed?" Here he has an opportunity both to discover and to express what is of ultimate importance. Not all persons are able to pursue the type of work activity which most truly fits their capabilities and dispositions. Even though there is greater opportunity for preference in the selection of one's work than was true in some preceding generations, there are still millions who must work at tasks which have little inspiration or appeal. Many such tasks are still necessary. That does not make them exciting or uplifting. Fortunately, however, less and less time will have to be spent in our industrial economy at such tasks. We work at them in order to have the leisure which work affords. This is what makes of vast significance the kind of activities in which we engage during leisure and is actually determinative of the very quality of life itself.

Fortunately people are not without extensive resources for guidance in the wise use of the increasing leisure time available to them. There is a mounting wealth of such resources. Any cataloguing of these resources would be far too cumbersome to include in these pages, but it is significant that educational institutions, foundations, governmental agencies, and institutions of all sorts have turned their attention to this important phase of human existence. One symbol is the comprehensive series of Reports to the Outdoor Recreation Resources Review Commission, surveying the country's outdoor recreation resources and measuring the present and likely demands upon them over the next forty years. It is a report made to the President and the Congress by a Commission staff of the National Planning Association and by the Bureau of Labor Statistics of the U. S. Department of Labor. Never before in history has a people been provided with such resources with which to plan for constructive use of its increasing leisure. Studies 23 and 24 deal with projections in economic growth, population, labor force, leisure, and transportation, and No. 24 also deals with economic studies of outdoor recreation. What these monumental reports and projections do for outdoor activities, other agencies are doing to prepare a total society for a new phase of its existence.

CURRENT ATTITUDES TOWARD WORK

"Primarily man works in order to live," says Emil Brunner. "The fact that he works in order to live, however, is something by which he knows himself to be a human being. . . . He cannot avoid asking himself whether he intends to work, why he does it, how he will do it, and what he intends to do. . . . All this means that work becomes an ethical question."[7]

Leisure and work are interdependent, but the solution of the one problem does not guarantee the solution of the other. Thus even if the problem of leisure were happily resolved, it would still leave unresolved the problem of the nature of work and its significance in an industrial age.

One overarching fact colors our consideration of work: the gap between faith and work. It is this gap which gives rise to our concern with the nature of work and attitudes toward it in contemporary life. Why, one might ask, cannot work be accepted for what it is, without having to confuse the issue by raising philosophical and theological questions about its ultimate meaning? Work, many assume, is what one does to make a living, and if it provides a satisfactory living and enables one to take care of his family and through insurance, social security, etc. to provide for emergencies and his retirement, is not that enough? Apparently it is not enough, if one is to judge by the very great effort being applied by industries, educational institutions, and government agencies to help men understand what it is that seems to be lacking in the kind of work that many of them are now doing and what would provide greater meaning for themselves and their families.

Industrial culture is dependent upon and shaped by the whole process of work. The basis of living in every industrialized nation is determined by the kind of work its citizens do and the meaning they find in doing it. If work is devoid of any significance in itself and is only meaningless drudgery, the whole life of society is conditioned by this fact and is thereby devoid of significance for a large number of its people during half of their waking hours. Even the reduction in working hours cannot reduce that fact. Fortunately for a substantial portion of our population, work is not as barren or bankrupt of meaning as the previous statements might imply. This is not to say, however, that there is rich significance in what they are doing. For most people the meaningfulness of their work ranges between the total commitment of a thoroughly dedicated worker and the vacuousness of one who goes through the motions simply for the paycheck.

There probably never was a time when everyone's work was religiously motivated, but there have been periods when many felt their work had some significance beyond themselves, that it contributed something to the total welfare of the tribe, community, or nation, and that in some sense it had religious meaning. The industrial revolution did more than rearrange populations, develop new governmental forms, and utilize new sources of power. It reduced the sense of meaningful work and in the process changed the relationship between the individual and his community. Early in the industrial age it was still possible for some people to acquire special abilities and to enjoy a status in their community as a result of their craftsmanship and skill. Many studies of industrial relations and the role of the individual in industrial society point to the change in that situation. Increasingly the individual becomes subordinated to the machine instead of the machine being subservient to the direction of the individual. In the automated industries he becomes an extension of that machine.

Contrasting again with an era in which the individual felt his work could be performed as a service to God, the industrial age places primary emphasis on the fact of work itself rather than its objectives. It is by participating in the act of work that one gets what is needed for himself and his family, and any other ends which may have constituted a part of the motivation of other generations become of lesser significance. Thus work has tended to displace an attitude of grateful response to a God who was the Creator and Sustainer of life.[8] Religion for such a worker is less likely to provide the integrating factor in his life. He is simply a worker earning his livelihood and maintaining himself as best he can from the results of his work.

When work alone becomes the objective, a new set of criteria for personal and social existence enters the picture. Craftsmanship may still be a factor for some who manipulate the machines still responsive to individual skills. But even for these persons, without a sense of meaning beyond the satisfaction of their own physical wants, preoccupation with work for its own sake eliminates any reference to the value of their work to society as a whole. Their objectives become those of status and prestige accorded them by their neighbors and devoid of any sanction or judgment by religion. For them and for most of our society it is not expected that religion will have anything significant to say about the nature of work, its importance, and its ultimate meaning.

But meaningless work is not simply a concern of religion but also a profound problem for the industrial system itself. Where meaninglessness prevails, it not only reduces the significance of the person but it is fraught with unfortunate consequences for the productive process itself. The rapid rise of organizations whose primary purpose is to offset the depersonalization which industry fosters, reveals the growing concern for this entire situation. Religion, having become widely discounted by industrial society for its inability to provide an alternative to this depersonalization, finds its place, temporarily at least, occupied by the industrial relations departments, human relations experts, and the numerous studies dealing with the impact of industrialization on the human self. Similarly, religious agencies, uncertain as to the role they should play in offering alternatives to the current emptiness of industrial life, have seen the initiative taken by a proliferation of secular organizations, notably labor unions and fraternal groups, which, though they may not have significant bearing on the nature of the industrial process itself, at least offer complementary or offsetting experiences. The attention to the individual which has been steadily disappearing from the industrial scene finds its support in those groups which fill the time of the worker outside his hours of employment. Thus the depersonalization of industry elicits other forms of activity which partially fill the vacuum caused by the meaninglessness of much of the work industrialism offers.

Are these fraternal groups, social organizations, extrawork fellowships, the only resource available to supply meaning to existence where it has been limited, if not eliminated, by the work experience of our times? Or is the concept of a divine calling to life itself so totally irrelevant that it cannot be considered seriously? This presumably is a fundamental question for religious institutions in an industrial era.

The Christian Meaning of Work

Work is dealt with often in the Bible, but in these few paragraphs it will be possible to present only in bare outline the essence of the biblical interpretation. The fundamental fact is that what is most important is not work but the person who engages in the work. This fact has far-reaching implications for what is considered the hierarchy of jobs in modern society. The important thing, then, is not what kind of a job one has but how each person conceives his relationship to God in the fulfillment of any job. Just as in the case of Adam, the primary fact of whose existence was his relation to God, so every one of Adam's descendants can fulfill his role in life only as he too understands that his primary obligation is to God as Creator and Sustainer and ultimately as Redeemer of man. The significance, then, of any job stems not from the way in which men regard it but "from its bearing on God's overarching purposes."[9]

The Bible's primary concern is the relationship between God and man, and the final criterion of man's life is the degree to which work is an instrument for the glorification of God. As Giver of life there is no phase of that life which God does not penetrate. The realization of that fact and the way the worker adjusts himself to it determines the ultimate meaning of life for him. This, then, makes requisite a consideration of what that life is; for it cannot be simply adopted and lived out apart from honest inquiry as to its purpose. Modern man may be freer of the necessity of asking such a fundamental question because he seemingly can sustain himself apart from any reference to life's ultimate significance. But eventually death comes to him, and in some measure, whether superficially or profoundly, he confronts the real issue of the purpose of that life which has been his.

The biblical interpretation says to the seeker after life's meaning that there is a harmonizing of God's work and man's work in which man can fulfill his true role. This understanding may come to him from a variety of sources, but significantly the individuals who shared this wisdom throughout the biblical record were often people who themselves were engaging in some kind of common and essential work, whether it was dressing sycamore trees, herding livestock, or carpentering. Aside from Jesus himself, the most renowned workman who became a vehicle for interpreting to men their dependence upon God for life and its redemption was the Apostle Paul. He remained a tentmaker so that he might be free to bring the message entrusted to him without being a burden to his hearers and new-found companions in the faith.

The term "vocation" or "calling" for the religious interpretation of labor did not acquire much prominence until the Reformation, but that meaning was there throughout the Old and New Testament periods. Persons and nations were summoned by God to fulfill their destiny in His service, and this calling had bearing on the total range of man's life. Prior to his actions he seeks the wisdom of God and attends to God's commands. These may come to him in an infinite variety of ways, through prophets, family, neighbors, and the far-reaching history of nations. The important thing, however, is that the person be open and ready for God's wisdom because he acknowledges the sovereignty of the Lord. God does not speak in broad generalities to empty spaces and trust to the wind to carry the message; He speaks directly to the hearts of the workers because it is the person who works and not a system.[10]

The Christian lives, as do his Hebrew predecessor and contemporary, to serve a God who Himself serves, and by this manner of life he shares God's way with man and in so doing discovers his own purpose in living. This is the continuing activity of both God and man. It means action, but action with a purpose which is more inclusive than the limited purpose of working only to sustain oneself and one's family. By summons or vocation or any other name, the joyous and willing response of the worker establishes his own identity and lifts his life to an ever higher level. "In this perspective there comes to new expression, with new force, the old Hebrew conviction that human life gets its meaning in and through a 'calling and election' by the Sovereign word of God. For Christian faith, that word is disclosed with new power and wisdom in Jesus Christ—at once a promise and an imperative demand for devotion to God and love to fellow-men."[11]

Stratification is a part of every society. Hebrew and Christian communities knew this fact, and obviously from the record they were not immune to class and status divisions. But basically there is no hierarchy of prestige in useful work, nor is there status to accrue from ecclesiastical affiliation in the true sense of *ecclesia,* the "called ones" who have answered God's summons to loving service. Neither is there a double standard of behavior for those who are professionally identified with the church and for those who are at work in the world. In the history of the relation between God and man and work these distinctions are meaningless, and instead of ennobling they have poisoned the minds of those who have been subjected to their artificial distinctions.

The Apostle Paul, confronted by differences in position and class, used the analogy of bodily interdependence to illustrate the irrelevance of class distinctions in the church. ". . . There are many parts, yet one body. The eye cannot say to the hand, 'I have no need of you,' nor again the head to the feet, 'I have no need of you.' On the contrary, the parts of the body which seem to be weaker are indispensable. . . . Now you are the body of Christ and individually members of it" (I Cor. 12 : 20–22, 27). Though there are diversities of gifts, there is but one Lord, and there are no levels of caste or class in his service.

Monasticism performed a service to humanity of immeasurable proportions as it dignified both manual and mental work and reminded the fellowship that they had one common loyalty and a common call. In the imputed simplicity of a monastic order it may have seemed simple to maintain such commonness of status, but it was discovered that even religious orders could be contaminated with the standards of the world and succumb to the temptations of power and prestige and indolence. If a "religious" organization is not immune, it cannot be charged that industrial society with its hierarchies and status systems are the only offenders and sinners.

From the Hebrew-Christian understanding of the meaning of

life emerged a new interpretation of the function of work. Just as all societies are stratified, feudal society, both in its sacred and secular aspects, reflected both the political and ecclesiastical gradation based on power. But power carries with it the seeds of its own corruption, and even the church fell prey to this common form of deterioration. The noble concept of the dignity of work embodied in the monastic system was not sufficient to maintain ecclesiastical purity. With the abuse of power in the church, a tendency to which no ecclesiastical tradition is immune, a reform movement took root. This was not the sole or perhaps even major purpose of the Reformation, but it was one of its major thrusts. The reformers challenged the power of the ecclesiastical structure in part because it made the ordinary citizen, the worker, if not a second-class citizen at least inferior to the church hierarchy and the nobility. In challenging this system Luther and Calvin, particularly, lifted to new levels of dignity the importance of work and the worker, contending that work done to the glory of God and on behalf of one's neighbor was not inferior to the work done in the church itself. Refinements of the distinctions made by the Reformers relative to man's participation in work are available in such profuseness elsewhere that they will not be delineated here. Suffice it to say that under the impetus of the Reformers a new significance was given to work and the worker. Under their fresh interpretation all men were enabled to realize what the Bible had indicated for centuries, that each man is called by God to work and that any useful work is a form of service to God.

Whatever distortion religious organizations may have perpetrated, the fact remains that for the Christian all work must be judged as it contributes to God's purposes in the world and for the measure in which it reveals our understanding that all of life is lived under trust. Work is service to God and man. The fact that so large a measure of work in modern times causes the question of its usefulness to God and man to be raised constitutes one of the serious dilemmas confronting all earnest people. Each can ask himself only whether his work is performed in order that love may be increased in the world or whether the work he does is inimical to human welfare. The decisions may not be as simple as it seemed to be in a preindustrial era, but this does not in-validate the question. The earth is still the Lord's.

Making Work Meaningful

Since work has become meaningless or of very limited signifi-cance for so many workers, the question must be raised: what made it meaningful at any other time? The answer is twofold. First, the work was needed by one's immediate community as well as oneself. This would include family, neighborhood, and possibly a recognizable community even beyond the range of neighborhood. We are, of course, here using the term community in its broad sociological sense as that body of individuals to whom one has a political or moral responsibility or both. Secondly, the conviction that one's life and the way it is used is of importance both to the community and to the Source of life itself. These two factors are not unrelated. It is the sense of responsibility to a power beyond oneself which gives meaning and vitality to the human community as well as to the individual. Work, then, becomes meaningful as it is performed in relation to both of these objectives.

When absenteeism and indifference in war production was undermining production schedules, human relations experts con-ceived the idea of revealing to workers the indispensable nature of their jobs and the tragic consequences where work was not ful-filled on time and with quality workmanship. Absenteeism dropped perceptibly. The same principle has been widely publicized in relation to the Western Electric studies by Elton Mayo and his colleagues.[12] Other studies of similar nature have been undertaken on the same theory, that individuals must know their work is important to someone and that they themselves have importance.

Cameron P. Hall states, "Through work our lives become in-volved with those of others. We work for and with, under and over, alongside of and—at times—against others. Each of these prepositions means that our lives are part of the lives of others. Together they add up to a relatedness which is complex and far-flung. The spirit and attitudes men bring into their work relationships are vital to the welfare of others, to the creating of community life, and to the inner strength of democracy. How an individual acts toward others is, likewise, central to Christian living: 'This is my commandment, that you love one another even as I have loved you.' "[13]

Work will become meaningful when (1) the significance of the human community is rediscovered and (2) as the source of the human community itself is recognized. Only then will the spiritual meaning of work be fully established. Surely there is a sense of calling in fulfilling one's obligation and performing useful work on behalf of the community around him, but the authenticity of that call or summons still lacks what in biblical history has brought a full and complete response unless the Source of the call is acknowledged.

Reference was made earlier to the declining importance of the individual in the industrial era. Paradoxically while the importance of the individual was declining because of his decreasing significance as a worker in the industrial complex, there was emerging an increasing insistence upon the importance of the individual in political and social life. Growing sensitivity to the importance of the human spirit gave impetus to political safeguards and the type of legislation which reduced human suffering. Now comes a whole new era for the significance of the individual. The alternative to the disappearance of individualism is the increased meaningfulness of the individual himself. This is a spiritual problem and one which industrial society is just beginning to comprehend.

Because community has been understood in too limited terms, there has been procrastination in discovering the significance of the individual himself within it. It was this awareness which the Social Gospel Movement, described in chapter one, attempted to explicate, but the sociological and theological tools were insufficient at the time. Today that excuse is no longer available. The total environment conditions the life of the individual and in turn enhances his sense of meaningfulness.

Finally, however, it is not the community which makes work meaningful. It serves principally as the tutor and the interpreter.

Meaningfulness is an intensely personal experience and under-standing. It is sustained and nurtured by faith, again not a com-munity possession but something deeply personal. Here then is the key to meaningful work—a faith in the source of the human community and of the lives which comprise it. It is expressed in acts of gratitude and love out of appreciation for the gift of this life which one lives in community. Such expenditure of effort out of gratitude and a love for God and neighbor gives a whole new meaning to the useful activities we designate as work.

CONCLUSION

Leisure and work constitute aspects of man's life experience in which his real self can be expressed, in which some of his fullest satisfactions may be known. Many kinds of work in industrial society make satisfaction unlikely if not impossible. Creativity, the satisfaction of performing a needed task or the achievement of a skilled accomplishment, may be denied in the very nature of required tasks. Fortunately an increasing measure of time, "choosing time" it has been aptly termed, is becoming available in a society wherein fewer hours are required to meet physical needs. It is this time of leisure which can be used to bring added enrichment and personal fulfillment. The use of that time carries with it profound ethical and spiritual significance for individuals and society.

13

Status and Stratification in Industrial Society

> The large complex society requires a system of prestige standards which can measure differences and achievement with some uniformity, measurements which can be clearly understood by the entire population so that all can appreciate the claims of persons not personally known to them. . . . Economic objectives and motivations are only one, though a very important group, among the large number of value areas which go to compose such a prestige system.
>
> —CLARENCE A. DANHOF in *Goals of Economic Life*

"Why," the reader may ask, "even a brief treatment of status and stratification in a volume dealing with the role of religion and ethics in industrial society?" The answer for the Christian lies in the very essence of his way of life. God took the form of a servant to reveal Himself. "He that would be greatest among you let him be servant of all." Jesus insisted on washing the disciples' feet.

In all forms of society role and rank are important. In industrial society status based on power and position is apparently of utmost importance. The devices used to attain rank may vitiate or supersede what the Christian gospel supports. In the end the motivations of economic life in general and industrial society in particular may, unless replaced by nobler purposes, come both to dominate the individual and warp the life of the very institution whose mission it is to make men servants of their fellow men, as was their Lord. The matter of status and stratification is thus a fundamental even if painful concern of the individual Christian and the church as a whole.

There is probably a correlation between the mass of literature and scientific studies relating to status and stratification in the social sciences and the rediscovery by contemporary theologians of pride as the foremost sin. Technology is forcing a readjustment in stratification, along with closer cooperation and coordination in society as a whole. These facts are demanding a reconsideration of human prestige systems.* The problems of status and human pride are basically the same, and they find expression in every age from nomadic to nuclear. Plato dealt with the problem of status in a slave economy; Jesus and the early Christian interpreters dealt with it in both its rural and preindustrial urban setting; Karl Marx sought to cope with it as industrialization threatened to crystallize the class system into two main divisions, the proletariat and the *bourgeoisie*. Each one suggested resolutions to this, one of mankind's most vexing issues. Plato's insistence that each man shall do what he was best fitted to do provides a partial answer. Jesus' conviction that all men are children of a common Father and that their role is to serve each other presents a thesis never fully accepted or renounced.

Karl Marx's theory of a rigid two-class industrial society has in the century since the *Communist Manifesto* been very effectively discredited. The division of all individuals into proletariat and *bourgeoisie* failed to take account of the rapid emergence of a large middle class, sharing in the gains in productivity and in social welfare. This does not, however, exclude the possibility that under the newer and rapidly accelerating forces of modern industrialism a new configuration may take place which can prove Marx more nearly right than some present-day facts would indicate.

Every society has its own form of stratification and status. It may be based on physical prowess, hereditary position, or the measure of one's possessions. Feudalism with its lords, knights, and vassals provided a complete form of social structure with each

---

* Community studies reflecting this development and achieving wide recognition are: Robert and Helen Lynd, *Middletown*; James West, *Plainville, U.S.A.*; W. Lloyd Warner and Associates, *Yankee City* and *Democracy in Jonesville*; Alison Davis and M. R. Gardiner, *Deep South*; and the "Rural Life Studies" of the Division of Farm Population in Rural Welfare of the USDA. In the field of theological writing no one has done more to sensitize this generation to the role of pride in individual and group esteem than Reinhold Niebuhr.

person contributing his part to the maintenance of that order. The lord of the territory, his status symbolized by his castle, held his property either under his personal ownership or as representative of some other political power above him. He, however, insured the safety of those who served him and worked on his lands. They in turn provided the maintenance and income for their lord in return for their peace and protection. The place of each was well defined and reasonably secure. The rudiments of this system were in evidence in biblical times, as is indicated by Jesus' reference to the evil and faithful stewards. The significant element inherent in the feudal system based on agriculture was the mutual dependence of the participants and their reciprocal obligations. This is not to say that everyone was happy under these arrangements. Peasant revolts were apparently not numerous, but as the feudal era was challenged by the emerging commercialism and the beginnings of industry, dissatisfaction with the lot of those coerced into the stratification of the system became so unbearable as to demand major revisions.

Industrialism could not provide the protection from want which the feudal order seemingly gave. The resulting protest challenged the status orders and the rights of those who claimed to govern their employees but who did not assume the responsibility for their total life requirements.

Despite its feudal roots England was more successful than some other nations in coping with the class struggle and its status structure because it allowed its newly emerging industrial leaders to participate in the political leadership of the nation. With political controls available the rigidity of class structure was less offensive and destructive of self-respect. Despite the fact that English life has not been an "open society" in the sense in which we apply the term to America, it has possessed the safety valve of eligibility for governmental office and therefore to business controls, making possible entry of lower status persons into the upper classes and even to the status of peerage or knighthood. Also significant is the fact that the British people, and the Scottish in particular, have traditionally been highly literate. Their familiarity with the biblical heritage, the partial regulation of their lives by biblical standards, and the capacity to relate their personal, religious, and political life freed "the People of the Book" from some of the restrictions imposed in certain areas of Europe. These biblical standards, too, served to modify some of the class hostility in other countries.

The earlier settlers came to the American continent out of societies free from some of the more vicious forms of class restriction. When still others, fleeing rigidities of class structure in their own lands, arrived on these shores, they found a system of openness which made unnecessary the kinds of protest they had known in their former countries, in some of which status was still ascribed by various forms of nobility and property transmission.

As Max Weber has contended, most forms of power rest on economic foundations. Property and lack of property are the elemental categories of class situations.[1] On arriving in the new land many immigrants were quick to realize that they were no longer bound by the status and class requirements prevailing in their former homeland, and that they themselves might now achieve a measure of distinction undreamed of in their former home. They recognized for themselves one of the fundamental insights which Weber has explicated, that a contrast in life's chances can be the result of the distribution of property or the structure of the economic order. In the acquisition of property a reshuffling of status occurred. It was no surprise, therefore, that the New England Yankees who had acquired real estate or were developing small businesses found offensive the questionable status of those who came to administer their affairs and make demands under their new rights. The continuing availability of property rendered the immigrant unreceptive to Old World types of formal society and rendered meaningless the authority such a society sought to exert. This manifestation of openness reduced the likelihood of class warfare and provided the foundation for a new social stratification, later to be challenged. Similarly, when rigidities of economic structure reinforced by class stratification made for violent protest in Europe, corresponding manifestations did not emerge on this continent except in very limited form, because of the opportunities available for challenging existing stratification.

STATUS IN CONTEMPORARY INDUSTRIAL SOCIETY

Status is the relative position a person holds within his class as a result of the esteem in which he is held. This, of course, may range all the way from very high to very low. Sociologists have long struggled to devise adequate definitions for the terms "status" and "class," but we will forego the more definitive analysis of those terms. For our purposes the term "class" is that company of people who have approximately the same life chances as a result of somewhat similar economic interests. Hence, the conclusion that in the United States the great body of the population belongs to the middle class. The upper class would comprise approximately 3 to 4 per cent of the population and the lower class the remaining per cent of the population.* A major factor in determining class membership is goods possessed, access to them, or reasonably justifiable expectation of having them. Status, however, is not the same thing as class. One's status is his position within a class. It is with status that we are primarily concerned, since in the American system of social life the overwhelming preponderance of individuals either place themselves or are placed by others in that broad band occupying most of the continuum and designated as middle class.

By contrast with the more or less open society of the United States, there are societies in which position is not determined by any amount of effort or diligence. In them position is ascribed rather than earned, which presumably is the case in the more nearly open type of society. This is not to say that there is no such thing as an ascribed position in American life. Obviously being born with a prestigious family name immediately begets a position of prestige. The important thing, however, is that others are not denied any position if they can fulfill the requirements for attaining it, and in American society one of the recognized means of attaining such position involves the acquisition of property.

* This very general division is derived from a synthesis of several polls in which individuals were asked to place themselves in one of these three classes.

As reading almost any newspaper or magazine will quickly reveal, status is not limited to birth or possessions. Robin Williams suggests that there are six kinds of criteria by which an individual's status may be recognized and his position in the stratification order documented: (1) birth, (2) possessions, (3) personal qualities, (4) personal achievement, (5) authority, (6) power.[2] Each of these may be facilitated by membership in a family or identification with a particular group, but with the exception of birth all of them can depend to a greater or lesser degree upon the motivation and effort of the person himself. Even so, there are obviously large handicaps which some people must overcome. Being born into a family where educational interest is low and incentive to get out of a particular level of life is minimal is a deterrent and a handicap. For one very large segment of the population, the nonwhite, the handicaps are greater than those suffered by others with the same economic or physical endowments.

It would be inaccurate to say that class distinctions do not prevail in the United States. We have had evidences of vicious distinctions, and in some instances class hatred growing out of those distinctions. The early period of the growth of the labor movement, the open warfare which prevailed in the anthracite regions, the Homestead Strike, and the Memorial Day Massacre in Chicago were all manifestations of deep class hatred as well as a demand for labor's rights and were in turn fed by the flames of resentment. The protest movements in the United States, whether in agriculture, mining, manufacturing, or processing, have had within them elements of class resentment. But they have been modified and the tension has been reduced because embedded in American cultural life is an equalitarianism which provided release through political remedies and exercise of alternative mass power which was available to the protesting bodies and movements. By this process forces making for resentment have been modified and temptations to use power and brutality have been restrained.

Most poignant of all illustrations of class antagonism and lack of mobility in the United States are the Negro, the Indian, and more recently the Puerto Rican. During the current decade we have seen the most massive eruption of movements growing out of protest against forced class subordination. Color alone has been the excuse for keeping almost one-tenth of the total population in the lowest class stratum. Despite repression many within the ranks of the Negroes have risen above their original class identification, achieving in many instances highest distinction for intellectual, professional, and economic attainments. Today the range of class and status among Negroes parallels that in all segments of society, though their movement into higher strata has been greatly limited by restrictions imposed from the exterior. Fortunately those limitations are being removed. As this takes place, however, it is unlikely that the patterns of class and status will differ from those within the society within which they are being increasingly integrated. The same elements which determine the status composition of the rest of industrial society will be evident among newly emerging groups.

Industrial society has traditionally implied manual labor. Within a decade this nation has moved from a preponderance of manual labor ("blue-collar") to a preponderance of white-collar work. Despite the attractiveness of white-collar work it does not inevitably bring superior economic rewards, since there are many blue-collar jobs which pay better than many white-collar occupations. Some of those blue-collar tasks involve very substantial skills, and the rewards are commensurate. For others the premium remuneration may be the result of pressure groups and a type of organization which keeps its ranks from being diluted and its wage scale reduced. By this process added status is attached to some kinds of manual activity which are more or less unattractive but which nevertheless are high in public recognition. Regardless of this fact, however, the evidence points strongly to the upward mobility of the children of high-pay, blue-collar workers.[3] Their parents' income is frequently sufficient to provide them with the quality of education which could make unnecessary their continuance in the blue-collar jobs and in many instances enable them to equip themselves for one of the recognized professions. The point we are making is simply that status, stratification, and vertical mobility are widely recognized social phenomena in this highly industrialized nation. What is true of this nation is also characteristic in varying measure of other industrialized countries.

FORCES REORGANIZING STATUS

Few facts are as visible in industrial life as the change in status of many industrial workers. Scarcely had we become adjusted to the shift from skills based on land labor to those involving hand-directed machines when cybernation rendered obsolete many of the skills so recently acquired. While we are still amazed by them, we have become accustomed to incredibly superior precision instruments producing a hundred or more times in volume what single individuals did formerly. Extraordinary as the production figures may be, their concomitants in the reorganization of status and the stratification of society are equally impressive. To neither of these phenomena are we reconciled nor adjusted.

Changes in the order of stratification are expected and accepted in industrial society, and the movement is not only in one direction. The slogan "Shirt sleeves to shirt sleeves in four generations" has its parallel in other nations and cultures. The implications have special meaning in the United States, a society which represents the ultimate in industrialism. Behind that slogan is a portrayal of industriousness on the part of the first generation and a decline of the third, as it fails to exert commensurate zeal in labor and acquisition. Thereafter comes the fall to the level of deprivation experienced before the original exercise of zeal. Behind the moralism of the cycle indicated in the slogan is the assumption that rising status is possible, if only the proper conditions are met. Sloth and carelessness account for the decline. Now, however, there comes into the scene a situation of which sloth and carelessness are not the cause. The acceleration of technology has simply been too great for most people to comprehend, let alone appropriate.

Increasing accessibility of education is a major factor in the upward mobility of whole masses of people. The change has taken place almost within a generation. Of those 65 years of age or older only 10 per cent had collegiate experience and only half graduated, while among the 25–30 year age group 25 per cent went to college and half graduated. In other words, higher education among the population has increased 150 per cent within thirty years. The figures for high school completion are even larger.

Education in an open society has permitted advancement on the part of many who in other countries would have less opportunity for status elevation. The British system, for instance, which makes a sharp division between individuals based on general intelligence as revealed at the ages of 10 to 11 years, has removed from possibilities of advancement through education large numbers who in the American scene would still have open to them channels for status development and higher rating on the stratification scale. British children may still have access to education, but the processes of division presuppose an elite group more likely to provide the leadership required in a less open society. The type of education required or made available in each nation indicates much concerning its status concepts and the function which education may be expected to play in reinforcing the stratification of society. It thus is either the great leveler, in the form of providing opportunity for all, or it helps to keep closed a society of privilege for a few.

In addition to higher wages for their parents rapid technological changes also decrease the likelihood that children will follow their parents' occupation, particularly in areas of manual labor. The unavailability of agriculture as a vocation for sons of farmers has been axiomatic, evidenced by the steady decline in agricultural courses offered in rural high schools. Sons following in fathers' footsteps in manual occupations were one of the sources of stability in society. Just as in agriculture, industrial occupations now suffer the same reduction in opportunities for livelihood. What does it mean to be a skilled coal miner when other forms of power have eliminated coal or when mechanical instruments can replace a thousand miners, as was suggested in a previous chapter? Obviously more is involved here than simply a reduction in numbers of those employed. It involves a major revision of the status of individuals in their home communities.

To all other factors is now added that of physical mobility. It is this which has made possible a substantial measure of social mobility as well. Park Forest, Levittown, Drexelbrook, and many other new communities owe their existence to the combination of physical mobility and social mobility. The pattern of movement required by corporations on the part of their executives at many levels makes necessary a type of living arrangement which corresponds to the short residence to be established in connection with a training period or testing period in the corporation. William F. Whyte has documented the implications of physical and social mobility in his classic, *The Organization Man*, which contains a study of one of these communities (Park Forest). The rapid changes in location, the "bucking" for position in the organization, the pressures for results on the part of the corporation, the evaluation of wives' as well as husbands' accomplishments—all constitute a part of the total complex whereby status and stratification are established and reorganized. These color the total life of a community.

We have been suggesting that the larger forces, such as technological change, new patterns of business organization, accessibility to educational resources, etc., are the influences contributing to the reorganization of status. It is apparent that no one of these is separate and distinct. They and all the allied forces around them are closely intertwined and interdependent. Similarly the individual who is subject to change in his status is not only the victim of this complex of forces but contributes to them as well. Witness the way in which physical mobility has accentuated social mobility. According to Lipset and Bendix's statement, "a person who moves up in the social hierarchy will tend to change his friends, join new organizations, move to a new neighborhood; perhaps he will even change his religious affiliations; in some instances he will change his name; often he will alter his political attitudes."[4] Each of these factors may be conditioned by others, but they also contribute to the shaping of the new status.

Probably no single factor has been more responsible for the over-all change in status and stratification than the rising income level of the population as a whole. Since 1947, for example, the level of income has been raised from about $5,300 per family to about $7,050 per family.* The ability to procure the gadgets and comforts which have become symbols of middle-class living have both reduced the pressures of protest and accorded to their possessors a sense of satisfaction. Thus the rising level of productivity which finds expression in increased consumption has steadily raised the living standards and income of most of the population. The resultant satisfaction in the realization that "progress" or advancement has been made provides assurance that mass improvement in status has been achieved. Though there may be marked differentials and discrepancies, they become less noticeable in the uniform elevation of most of the society. Weber contended that status groups are stratified in relation to their consumption of goods as represented in their styles of life. Where life styles are steadily improving, there is less resentment against others who may be improving even more.[5] Where general improvement in consumption levels and corresponding styles of life are occurring, there is general feeling of good will, even though interrupted by protests from special interest groups who desire additional advantages in the over-all development. The significant thing, however, is the fact that such development in style of life keeps attention from being called to crystallization or rigidities effected in the total stratification picture. To paraphrase Weber again, it is when there is a slowing down of economic development that the status structures and forms of social honor become intensified. It is to these that protest is made and against them resentment is expressed. Hence the importance of a steady rise in productivity and a corresponding increase in levels of income. Though Weber wrote before the Nazi era, he correctly designated the fears in loss of status on the part of the German people as their levels of productivity declined, and the massive protests of resentment took the form of Hitler support.

There are forces which are steadily altering the status and stratification picture. Some individuals are moving upward and others in reverse direction. Fortunately the total picture of pro-

* Road Maps of Industry, Nos. 1440, 1273.

ductivity is such that a general feeling of upward movement is experienced by the population as a whole, reducing potential resentments against the distinctions and levels of stratification even in an open society.

SIGNIFICANCE OF THE NEW STRATIFICATION

New lines of stratification follow lines of power. For centuries power has meant property and its control. In the rapid evolution of industrial society a new form of power is emerging. It is not unrelated to property, but it does not of itself involve property ownership. The kind of power which Adolf A. Berle, Jr., has been describing in his *Power Without Property—A New Development in American Economy* implies a control over the property of others. It is the new managerial competence for which property owners are willing to pay the highest salaries in history (General Motors, Bethlehem Steel, Standard Oil of New Jersey, et al.). In a business and industrial society the highest rewards are accorded those who can guarantee that the productivity for which they are responsible can be continued with the desired profits. (Of those being paid for services performed, they are surpassed only by a few entertainers.) The managers may not be the recipients of the greatest personal incomes, since those for the most part go with inherited wealth, but it is the inheritors of wealth who are willing to pay to the managers of their resources the kinds of salaries which indicate their appreciation of the managerial skill involved. Thus in the stratification of industrial society the manager of other people's money is near the top of the pole. Significantly, however, the very top of the status scale does not go to the managers. It goes to those who ultimately can decide on the rectitude and legality of the manager's actions, namely, the members of the Supreme Court.[6] It must be added that managers in the categories referred to above were not included in the list which was presented for ratings. Bankers as a class rank in the top ten, whereas the small store managers rate in the bottom half. Members of boards of directors of large corporations and nuclear physicists have the same rating in the top one-fifth. It is probably safe to surmise that with the mounting importance attached to space science more recent polls would record increasing prestige for those responsible for nuclear and space engineering.

Too much attention should not be given to the rank order of the various occupations, for much depends on who does the ranking. Presumably there would be differences by regions and by economic levels. Our principal reason for including the reference at this point lies in the fact that even though the major rewards of society go to those who are most effective in the production and distribution of goods, a high degree of importance is attached to those who engage in service to society. Next to the Supreme Court justices in rating is the physician, followed by governor, cabinet member, diplomat, mayor, college professor, and scientist. Judges, clergymen, and lawyers differ from the above by almost negligible amounts. For the present, at least, even in a highly technological era the serving professions and those which minister to the basic needs of individuals in this kind of a society are deemed to belong high in the stratification rating.

Without discounting unduly the fact that some professions have a higher status accorded them for historic reasons, may it not be inferred that in a society where status and stratification are subject to constant revision, recognition for distinction will be accorded to those persons who can bring to the lives of people an interpretation of their individual worth and significance in a way that enhances human dignity? With increased leisure and lessened importance in his work the individual thus affected seeks for the means whereby his own life and purpose take on significance to himself and his neighbors. The loss of position resulting from the elimination of his skills must be compensated through other and perhaps hitherto unknown experiences and interpretations. Discovering a useful contribution he can make, he is bolstered in his own self-esteem—a prime requisite for valid status with his fellows. At the same time the person who enables him to discover his innate dignity becomes a figure of major importance to the entire status structure of society.

Two polar forces, both the product of technological advances, are producing major tensions in this rapidly evolving industrial economy. One is freeing man from burdensome physical labor, which historically has given him his self-respect and status among his neighbors but which now threatens to place him in a position where nothing is substituted for the sources of his earlier self-esteem. The second force is making for closer integration of society and the mutual dependence of men, intra- and internationally. It carries possibilities for greatly enhanced human dignity and self-esteem. Technological gains may be utilized to increase the measure of harmony and coordination, or they can concentrate ownership and control in the hands of an ever smaller group, with others dependent on the bounty and generosity of the owners and managers of the new techniques. The issue of status and stratification in industrial society will be profoundly affected by the way this problem is resolved.

It is obvious that with controls residing in the hands of those who have paid for the major advances in the new technology, namely, the entire citizenry, this nation has committed itself to the retention of these fundamental controls. The contest for those controls is not yet over, but unless major reversals occur, they will continue to reside in the hands of all. Because there is at stake the management of ever increasingly powerful centers of control, the Christian cannot but ask the pointed questions "To what end are these functions directed?" and "What are the objectives of those who make the basic decisions?" If the replies, however subtly couched, reveal self-aggrandizement and acquisition of personal power, they may defeat the church's age-long concern for freedom for all men. Herein lies the contemporary test for the openness of our society, and at the same time it provides a clue to the status and stratification systems industrialism fosters.

If ours is to remain an open society, then the channels by which human dignity may be attained cannot be closed through artificial status, class, and stratification devices such as economic manipulation may provide. Opportunity to contribute usefully to the lives of one's neighbors becomes a first requirement of the economy and the institutions which serve it.

14

Ethics and Business

When Chief Justice Warren stated that "in civilized life, Law floats in a sea of Ethics,"* he stimulated sharp reaction from persons who pointed to illustrations seemingly contradicting his affirmation. The General Electric, Westinghouse, et al. collusion for which some executives went to jail, the Billy Sol Estes incident, the Bobby Baker case, rigged TV programs, the Hoffa scandal, and on and on could give the impression that American life floated on a sea of corruption. The cases mentioned and many others are significant, however, not because they illustrate corruption but because they were brought to the bar of justice. When an industrialist, then president of the National Council of Churches, J. Irwin Miller, was asked, "How serious do you think the ethical problem is in the American business community? If something has gone wrong, why?" he replied: "I don't think anything has 'gone wrong.' I've talked a good deal to my father and great uncle about what business competition used to be like. Today we would be genuinely shocked at some of the normal competitive practices existing in the days when Theodore Roosevelt thought it necessary to start 'trust-busting.' Business ethics and moral responsibility have improved substantially since that time. I feel your question really is: 'Has the improvement in business morality been as fast as it is necessary that it be?' "[1]

In the Middle Ages men were concerned about "the just price." It was a function of the church to alert its members to

* Earl Warren, Chief Justice of the U. S. Supreme Court. From a summary of Remarks at the Jewish Theological Seminary of America, Nov. 11, 1962.

the meaning of that term and to judge them when they defaulted. Though the church collectively in its manifold form says little about the just price in the twentieth century, it has had a good deal to say about the social responsibility of the businessman and the ethical role of the corporation. The church is not alone in these emphases; they have come in great volume from secular sources accompanied by philosophical and even theological interpretations. No single denomination is responsible for emphasizing this new concern, though many speakers on behalf of business ethics attest the fact that their interest and concern are motivated by a grounding in Hebrew-Christian foundations. Almost plaintively, it should be added, they ask for clarification and re-enforcement from religious leaders. In almost every chapter of a study reporting ethical issues in a number of occupations, the participants voiced their longing for ethical guidance in their particular vocational problems and lamented the lack of help from their respective churches.[2]

The series which the present volume concludes was initiated because of a deep concern for the level of ethics in our American business society. The late Chester I. Barnard, formerly president of the New Jersey Bell Telephone Company and later of the Rockefeller Foundation, discussing the origin of the Ethics and Economics Series, told the Department of Church and Economic Life that his interest in this theme stemmed from a conviction that the most fundamental problem confronting our civilization was the relevance of the Christian faith to economic life. He felt its relevance had not been made explicit, and it was essential that it should be. Impelled by that conviction he urged and assisted in initiating this series.

An ever-rising level of education and increasing freedom to ask fundamental questions has enabled individuals, whether in or out of business life, to evaluate economic practices as evidenced in modern business. Even more influential, presumably, have been the scientific and technological advances which have placed a premium on size and efficiency. A few giant corporations, dominating individual industries and collectively controlling a large part of the production and the corporate assets of the nation, give rise to questions of their responsibility to the nation as a whole and to those who are employed by them. Decisions made by a relatively small number of individuals affect the personal lives of millions. The question is inevitably asked: by what authority do these individuals possess such power and what are the controls under which they operate?

As industries and businesses increased in magnitude, their leaders found themselves in an equivocal position. Their prime functions were to expand the industry and to continue it as a profitable enterprise. But at the same time an ever more close-knit and interdependent society began to hold those leaders responsible for a contribution to society, and they naturally wanted to become known as accepting that responsibility. Thus a measure of conflict inevitably arose between the immediate requirements of the enterprise they served and the wider ranging claims of responsible citizenship. The two sets of claims are not easily reconciled. The dilemma of the business leader became the dilemma of his organization, the corporation, which also had to recognize its twofold responsibility. Not all of the business organizations which faced this profound issue were large ones, nor were all of the large ones asking such questions. Enough of both types, however, have become involved in this very basic inquiry so that industry and business are presumed by many thoughtful citizens to have a genuine concern for the ethical implications of their operations.

Schools of business connected with universities have served to inspire their students with a professional consciousness. One of the marks of a profession is its ethical criteria and standards. Bernard D. Nossiter, commenting on Adolf Berle's *The Twentieth Century Capitalist Revolution*, contends that corporations are leading the way to a modern "city of God," because their managers are tending to respond to the promptings of conscience or some inchoate higher law.[3] The university school of business finds itself the institution where the dilemma of the corporation and its leadership is most clearly defined. A part of its appeal lies in the fact that it can enable its students to provide substantial economic resources for themselves and their families, but at the same time the very business of the university is to enable its students to see the more comprehensive meaning of life in its totality. These two factors, though not necessarily mutually exclusive, are the source of an uneasy tension. "No one can serve two masters." If the purpose is self-aggrandizement, then the purpose of the university is defeated. If the student is interested only in the philosophical view of the business life, his place is not in the executive suite. The resolution of this ambivalence is an ethical, a philosophical, or, if you will, a theological problem.

The ethics of business must, therefore, include responsibility toward employee, stockholder, and consumer. The businessman becomes a steward of concerns far beyond what was conceived to be his field of responsibility even a half century ago. As Howard Bowen expressed it in another volume in this series: "The first and most essential condition, if social responsibility is to become a more effective force, is that businessmen must acquire a strengthened sense of vocation. They must accept the social implications of their calling. They must recognize that ultimately business exists not for profits, for power, or for personal aggrandizement, but to serve society."[4]

UNETHICAL PRACTICES

In his much-discussed study "How Ethical are Businessmen?" Raymond C. Baumhart, S.J., concludes that "four out of five executives giving an opinion affirm the presence in their industry of practices which are generally accepted and are also unethical."[5] Then he lists some of the practices which executives believe illustrate those categories: (1) seeking preferential treatment through lavish entertainment; (2) kick-back to purchasing department employees; (3) pay-offs to government officials; (4) price-rigging between supplier and contractor varying prices through favoritism; (5) collusion in contract bidding, underbidding with substitution of inferior workmanship or materials, etc.

Similarly, in his contribution to the group reports in *On The Job Ethics* William H. Cohea, Jr., finds parallels in the labor movement to the situations Raymond Baumhart reports from executives in industry.[6] In each of the other five reports of occupational groups similar ethical dilemmas are narrated by bankers, building contractors, business executives, personnel managers, and public relations consultants (in addition to labor unionists).

It would not be difficult to fill a book with instances of dishonesty and venality in business, labor, church, school, medicine, government, and every form of economic activity. Immediately it must be countered that just as quickly, if not more so, could a volume be compiled of honest, gracious, ethical actions by which man's spirit has been ennobled and whole communities have been elevated. The problem, however, is not to catalogue the diseases or glorify the state of health to the exclusion of all other realities. The problem is to examine the circumstances which give rise to destructive and injurious processes and which encourage decency and integrity.

While business ethics is so closely related to other forms of social life, it is impossible to consider business independent of all phases on which it impinges. For our purposes we shall limit consideration to the problems of business itself. Our culture is predominantly a business-industrial culture, and the standards which prevail in it are likely to influence strongly the qualities of the rest of society. This, presumably, is what underlies Chester Barnard's concern for the relevance of Christian ethics to business, indicated above.

Crudely but frankly stated, the express goal of business is to make a profit. But this is not its sole function or even its most important one, for it exists primarily to provide goods in response to human needs. But the individual economic incentive for providing those goods is the anticipated margin of profit by which the producer knows whether his product is in demand and is satisfactory to the consumer. Thus the quality of his workmanship, the attractiveness of the price, and the circumstances under which he makes his product available determine whether he stays in business. The producer and the distributor are rewarded, theoretically, according to the degree to which they meet those criteria. This is a grossly simplified picture of the "enterprise system," which is fraught with potential dangers and abuses, but which we in the West at least consider less vicious than those which attend a totally regulated economy where choice is limited and where caste distinctions are based upon political favoritism or conformity to an established ideology. (We have our ideologies, too, as will be shown shortly, but they are malleable rather than fixed in legal, creedal form, as Communism requires.) "Indeed, in America," says economist Harold L. Johnson, "corporate executives and the enterprises which they coordinate are expected to pursue profit goals, efficiency, innovation, and cost minimization. These items are key elements in the pattern of American business. There are nonprofit aspects to the business role, but in an enterprise system, strong emphasis remains on pursuit of profits, economy with scarce resources, and watching the dollar."[7] Business executives are not rewarded primarily for their civic-mindedness or their participation in nonprofit activities, though these may add to the public esteem of the executive. His primary function is to administer the work for which he is responsible in a way which is profitable to the total enterprise. If he can do this and contribute to the general well-being of his community, he may come to be regarded as a statesman. In the growing professionalism of business this designation becomes increasingly important. But it is not in the "statesman" areas of his activities where the ethical problems emerge primarily; it is in his profit-making activities.

The manager's ethical problem is compounded by the fact that his value to the corporation depends upon his ability to assure the continuity of the organization with an adequate profit rate. But what rate is proper? If it is too low, the company is imperiled and so is the manager's job. If it is too high, it has failed to distribute its earnings equitably among its stockholders and workers and is held to have taken advantage of customers and competitors. The dangers from the latter are less than the former, but nevertheless where social responsibility is taken seriously by the company, it must answer in good conscience for its earnings. Relative to the corporation's survival, management consultant and former Sears-Roebuck executive James Worthy comments: "Unfortunately this relationship between profit and survival is not generally understood. The social stake in profits is heavily obscured by the implicit equating of profit with self interest. This confusion of the two concepts is not only inaccurate; it places the business system in a vulnerable moral position and seriously weakens the claims of business for social policies that will foster its efficient performance. A more realistic and more defensible doctrine of profits will have to be built around the survival needs of the enterprise as an instrumentality of social service."[8] There is no formula for resolving this issue. The consciences of the managers and directors guided by their sense of responsibility to society and to the company for whose continuance they are responsible are the only criteria of decision.

The businessman and everyone else in his business relationships are confronted by the tension between self-interest and the values which might bring superior benefits to others. Writ large, this is the problem of the corporation as well. In both cases, whether individual decisions or corporate action, there may be a deep underlying conviction that what serves the best interests of the individual and the corporation in the long run may also be the best thing for society as a whole. This is the contemporary application of Adam Smith's "invisible hand" theory. Too simply stated, it is this thesis which underlies the American business creed, which will be discussed later. It provides self-justification for actions which "keep the economy going" even though they may have dubious ethical aspects. If rationalization is needed, it can be provided by the fact that profit-seeking can thus produce benefits to others through fostering the very system by which all may gain.

Numerous studies have revealed the fact that increased income or larger profits are not the only or in some cases even the most powerful incentive for activity in business. Though this may be true, there is enough evidence that economic gain has motivated many individuals to participate in ethically questionable activities. The bank clerk living beyond his means, though in the public eye he is a model citizen, provides a story which can be duplicated in almost any city. But this juggling of the books is hardly in the same category as collusion in the rigging of prices on the part of major corporations. We are merely contending that in both instances the incentives may be the same: the desire for self-enhancement or esteem either by the community or by the company which rewards accomplishment on the part of its employees.

In the corporation employee status may depend on many factors—the "right" school, friendships, personal attractiveness. Nepotism may also play a part and influence choices of many others. But fundamentally usefulness to the business depends upon capacity to increase profits and to extend the life and range of the company or corporation. Under such circumstances it is all but inevitable that the individual will do whatever is possible within the range of commonly accepted practices to foster his own present and future security in the organization. All of this is perfectly human, we say, and is no different from what prevails in every other walk of life. The difference, if any, lies in the fact that business is primarily engaged in the making of profit, and therefore it brings into clearer focus the consequences and temptations of profit-seeking. In the face of this fact the marvel would seem to be not that there is so much unethical conduct but that the forces in society at large and the consciences of individuals have created a climate with so high a degree of ethical quality.

THE CHANGING CLIMATE OF ETHICAL ATTITUDES

Debate over the source of industry's increasing sensitivity to ethical values may be interesting but not particularly helpful unless it adds to the present discussion, i.e., whether that sensitivity derives from a growing ethical consciousness of individuals or whether the nature of business itself makes increased ethical demands in our society. In the long run this question will have far-reaching implications. If, for example, the increasing cohesiveness of society is compelling men to conduct themselves with greater consideration of the rights and privileges of others, it may be that "secular" forces are accomplishing what religious morality and idealism have striven for much less successfully. For our purposes, however, the primary question is not who is more responsible for bringing this about but rather the implications of what is commonly accepted as an increasingly ethical climate in business.

For many years the corporation was a person in the eyes of the law. This fiction was slow in dissipation despite the inconsistency, if not ludicrousness, of attempting to regard the United States Steel Corporation, for example, as a person, where its self-perpetuating board of directors makes decisions and its independence in practice from its numerous stockholders renders it (and most other corporations) something quite different from an entity expressing the personal wishes of its owners. Whether person or not, however, the corporation, whatever its size, has gained a new role of responsibility in the life of the nation and more recently on the total world scene. As a legal person the corporation may have maintained the aura of privacy, but few corporations which seek support from a large investing public any longer regard themselves as solely private agencies. Every major corporation has become an institution with public responsibility and dependent upon public acceptance. Any distinction between public and private is at best inexact. This much is said concerning the corporation and its ethical role for the obvious reason that business standards are established and most visibly maintained by the large organizations. There are, of course, individuals in the smaller organizations who are keenly sensitive to ethical values and who may shape the patterns of their organizations more nearly in keeping with their personal ethical standards. The public, however, is more aware of the standards of A. T. & T., General Motors, Standard Oil, Sears-Roebuck, Swift & Company, and International Harvester as the determiners of ethical standards for industry and business. The emergence of the public relations profession, if it can qualify as a "profession," is intimately related to the desire of each industry to convince the public that it is honorable and ethical.

Having attained positions of eminence where their "image" is of great importance to themselves and to the public, corporations have learned what individuals who have been catapulted to great prominence have also had to learn, namely, that their objectives and standards are no longer merely their own but are made in part by their public and that it is of utmost importance that those standards be maintained. From the standpoint of business ethics, business leaders have discovered the truth of a comment made by the French sociologist Emile Durkheim more than a half century ago: "When one starts with a maxim that there are none but economic interests, one is their prisoner and cannot rise above them." This has been one of the most fundamental mistakes of Marxism, and accounts for a high percentage of the difficulties confronting the Russian economy in our period of rapid change. In its maturation American industry has had to discover that its interests have to transcend the limited meaning of "economics" and face its fuller meaning —the welfare of the entire "house." To the extent that American business has failed to comprehend the necessity for its own adaptability and responsiveness to public requirement, it has suffered and brought calamity to itself and those dependent upon it. Where this has been the case, the industry involved was guilty of the same rigidity that characterizes the Russian system. Ironically the latter theoretically forced a standard of equalitarianism upon its people but in practice provided differential rewards greater in some cases than exist in enterprise economies. Thus in an effort to rectify an unethical condition they created a new imbalance and a warping of creativity. The American system in its evolution as a product of industrial technology and grounded in Hebrew-Christian ethics was slower to coerce ethical equality, but by being free to respond to the trends in industrial society's evolution it has voluntarily created a situation infinitely more conducive to human creativity and mutual consideration.

Much of the grumbling that business does about government interference stems from its apprehension over fears of increasing control. Separating regulations from control in the minds of those who are actually or potentially subject to either makes for ambivalence. Regulation has served to protect industries from dangers in the conduct of their operations and has made for public confidence. But because the line between regulation and control is not clearly defined, the benefits of regulation are accepted with mixed feelings, tempered with the fears of possible control. This attitude toward government has become symbolized in the political party structure. The fact that the Republican party has consistently been supported by the majority of business leadership requires a more comprehensive explanation than simply to suggest that business has apparently had greater freedom from control under the Republicans. There are obviously ethnic and regional factors involved here also. The historic tie of labor (but not all labor) to the Democratic party may account in part also for management's identification with the Republicans. The point we are making here, however, does not deal with political preferences so much as with the reasons for hostility toward government on the part of a large segment of the business community.

It was stated above that the goal of business is to make a profit. The conditions under which that profit is made affects more than the business or industry involved. A government representing all people must be concerned with the balancing of benefits and injuries for the protection of all affected. Only thus can the private profit system be assured continuance. Thus despite restrictions and curtailment of opportunities for gains made against the long range of public interest, business realizes the need for government interference as a means of its own self-protection. It is to this situation that Secretary of Commerce Luther Hodges spoke when he stated: "If you studied the origin of these agencies (Federal regulatory bodies) you will have to draw the conclusion that all these things, troublesome and expensive as they may be, become necessary in modern, thoughtful government because a minority of people in professions, businesses and other groups act unethically, act illegally, or fail to do what the public—and responsible businessmen—regard as the correct and proper thing to do."

Regardless of how much times have changed and the public disposition to criticize business ethics has increased, it is extremely difficult for individuals and organizations engaged in business to regulate themselves in the interest of society at large. This is not a matter of human sinfulness and self-aggrandizement alone

—or even primarily. In a complex society there is insufficient wisdom in individuals or collectivities to inform and effect wise decisions concerning all those who are subject to those decisions. Allocation of wave-lengths to radio and TV stations is a case in point. The personal integrity of those seeking rights to the air is an insufficient guide to the granting process. And thereafter the judgment of what is good for viewers and hearers cannot be left entirely to the probity and wisdom of the station managers. Obviously there is more involved here than just competition. These are business-ethical decisions for which philosophical and/or religious values are required.

Though capitalism has historically espoused competition and gained its strength from the competing forces within it, the nature of our economy has become such that, for much of American business, competition is no longer the basic pattern. Technology has made competition of the traditional type difficult and perhaps impossible in whole areas which are now assumed to be effectively determined by it. The much-reported electrical industry scandal was a vivid illustration of the reluctance of giants in the electrical industry to engage in competition. The reluctance was in part a consequence of the nature of the industry.

Despite support of the competitive system competition between businesses is not viewed with enthusiasm. The situations anonymously related in the reports from the building contractors group in *On The Job Ethics* is a moving tale of the dog-eat-dog existence when open competition prevails. It is not difficult to understand why under these circumstances manufacturers enter into agreements with each other. Collusion or agreement on prices can enable some businesses to stay alive which would otherwise be forced out of existence.

The government has for many decades sought to promote fair competition by outlawing agreements in restraint of trade and unfair competition. The Sherman Antitrust Act, the Clayton Antitrust Act, the Federal Trade Commission, and the Robinson-Patman Act are some of the instruments which have been created to accomplish this end. The fact is that the problem is an enormously difficult one because of the very nature of competition itself and the necessity for maintaining the maximum of justice for all concerned.

Reluctance to face realistically the problem of government regulation may account for the fact that business administration, now being vigorously publicized as a coming profession, has been among the slowest so to regard itself. A characteristic of a profession is its capacity to evaluate itself and to justify itself in the mores and customs of society and to abide by the standards which that society espouses. Until recently business has been highly suspicious of intellectuals and therefore has produced comparatively few business philosophers. That condition is obviously changing. Some business leaders have recognized that their functions and the public weal must be in harmony. The rapid change going on in the technological aspects of society have confronted them with new ethical perspectives. Possibly because they have been powerless to halt those technological developments, they have resented those intellectuals both in government and in the university who have pointed to the inevitability of those changes. Meanwhile, the "statesmen of industry" face realistically the fact that a steadily rising set of ethical standards is demanded in the area most typical of modern existence—business and industry.

There is evidence that a new generation of business leaders is emerging, leaders who have been trained to take into account a wide spectrum of factors as they make decisions relative to company and community. Kenneth Underwood, out of extensive association with business leadership, contends that a new social ethic is to be observed in the health and growth of the corporate enterprise, based on the fulfillment of its useful function in society.[9]

If the level of ethical practices is steadily rising, one could ask, why become exercised? Will not the rational process of society's improvement take care of things? The incontrovertible fact is that man must ever be protected against the human propensity to seek one's own advantage. It is at this point that the forces of religion and ethics make their contribution to the well-being of society. As is indicated in the chapter on the consumer, producers and distributors need to be checked in their temptation to take advantage of the buyer. False and erroneous advertising and packaging are a constant temptation. When the public ire has been roused or conscientious individuals have protested a violation of good practices, a modification sometimes occurs. It is almost axiomatic that this has been the result of pressures from society instead of from a stirring of conscience. It is at this point that religious ethics speaks both to producer and consumer, seller and buyer, professional and client. The complexities of a technological society do not diminish the need. They require new adaptation in ethics.

The realization that no single formula is adequate to resolve the moral and ethical dilemmas created by the business activities of this generation constitutes a distinct gain. One of the dilemmas created for honest men has been the assumption that in the realm of religion there was a formula which, were it only to be known, could be applied. Failing to discover this, men have been disillusioned and disaffected from any attempt to discern the contribution of religious faith to business ethical dilemmas. The issues in business ethics require a grounding in the economic and social needs of society, but also an awareness of the depths of human involvement in the total range of life's resources such as the Christian gospel provides. The dimensions of man's relationship with God include a scope of human experience infinitely more extensive than those apparently inherent in normal business experience. For the Christian it is when these are brought to bear on the business decision that new ethical resources become apparent.

RESOURCES FOR BUSINESS ETHICS

"Even an ethical businessman of 1900 might be deemed unethical by today's norms," says Theodore L. Thau. "Conversely, an unethical businessman of today might well have been judged wholly normal in his conduct fifty or sixty years ago."[10] Earlier in this chapter it was recognized that just such changes have taken place. There followed some proposed explanations for those changes. It is axiomatic that changes in customs, mores, ethical practices and the like are effected only where demand for them has been great enough to warrant modification. If it is true, and we believe it is, that great improvements have taken place in the ethics of American business practices, one cannot but ask what the criteria are by which new patterns are established. When Secretary of Commerce Luther Hodges summoned a group of twenty-six businessmen, educators, clergymen, and publishers to form the Business Ethics Advisory Council, it was apparently assumed by the Secretary of Commerce and President Kennedy, who backed this venture, that the time was ripe for clarifying the objectives of business and reviewing the ethical criteria applicable in the second half of the twentieth century.

Many professions and business organizations have codes by which they and the public may evaluate their performance and which give bases for judgment of any proposed movements, experiments, projects, etc. When the moving picture producers were under fire for questionable practices and substandard productions regarded as offensive to the public moral standards, a code was established and an administrator, generally well regarded, was selected to administer the code. This practice has become common where an industry is sensitive to its reputation. Codes spell out explicitly what the industry regards as commendable. For the most part they constitute a "floor" of ethical practice. Since they rest on voluntary acceptance, the ones to whom they apply may be casual about their acceptance, as the public has come to experience. It is probably easier for a corporation dispensing a tangible product to hold itself and to be held accountable than for those identified with the entertainment industry, where art forms are less capable of appraisal and judgment. The Crown Zellerbach Corporation code may illustrate a statement of one industry's standard.[11]*

* 1. To regularly produce from our forest resources the highest quality lumber, cellulose, and chemical products at the lowest possible cost —and, while doing so, to maintain our plants in the highest degree of efficiency and safety.

2. To regularly sell such products to the most people at fair prices and with reasonable profits.

3. To regularly provide jobs at fair wages to as many people as we can gainfully employ.

4. To regularly pay a fair return to our shareholders on their invest-

The Business Ethics Advisory Council, concerning itself with the total gamut of business ethics in the United States, expresses itself in less specific but more inclusive terms. "We therefore now propose that current efforts be expanded and intensified and that new efforts now be undertaken by the American business community to hasten its attainment of those high ethical standards that derive from our heritage and traditions. We urge all enterprises, business groups and associations to accept responsibility—each for itself and in its own most appropriate way—to develop methods and programs for encouraging and sustaining these efforts on a continuous basis. We believe in this goal, we accept it, and we encourage all to pursue its attainment."[12]

More inclusive than codes of individual firms or corporations, though perhaps less idealistic than the hopes expressed in the Business Ethics Advisory Council proposal just quoted, is the blanket standard, undefined and unspecific but nevertheless intensely realistic, "The American Business Creed" which Francis Sutton and his colleagues have explicated in the volume by that name.[13] The authors contend that business ideology has no formal document or official line by which it lives. But that does not mean that it is not governed by standards and concepts which are just as vivid as those written into the Marxist doctrine for Communists. "Briefly, our thesis is that the content of the business ideology can best be explained in terms of the *strains* to which men in the business role are almost inevitably subject. Businessmen adhere to their particular kind of ideology because of the emotional conflicts, the anxieties, and the doubts engendered by the actions which their roles as businessmen compel them to take, and by the conflicting demands of other social roles which they must play, in family and community."[14] The Creed is explicit in the standards it expects of its adherents as they relate themselves to the life of their communities and in their personal conduct. All of this becomes apparent as one lives

---

ment in our business and to protect and safeguard such investment.
5. To always be a good citizen in the communities in which we operate.
6. To discharge our responsibilities to society by maintaining our business in a manner that will earn continual public trust and confidence.

and works in the milieu of American business. He may not have had a course in business ethics or conduct, but the standards about him and the norms observed by his peers tell him that there are criteria which stand over against any actual or proposed conduct on his part or that of his organization. The American Business Creed is a constantly evolving set of standards, raising its levels as the level of society itself rises. It has to be reckoned as one of the available resources for the establishment and the maintaining of ethical attitudes.

In the reports from the Occupational Ethics Groups and from Father Baumhart's study another resource comes to the fore with regularity and prominence. When an employee is confronted with an ethical decision, his guide for resolving that dilemma is probably his superior in the organization or the standards of the individuals who are the company's principal officers. The Baumhart formula is: "If you want to act ethically, find an ethical boss."[15]

In one Occupational Ethics Group men reported they had never been asked to do anything which the superior officers of the firm would not approve. No violation of conscience had ever been required. The quality of leadership in the firm determines the ethical standards all down the line.

Because a major consideration of the theological aspects of economics and business ethics has been included in the current volume, the implications of theology for ethics in business are treated here in only a limited fashion. In one of the Occupational Ethics Groups the members were told that the subject they were discussing had theological implications, and a member asked whether it wasn't in order to discuss those at that time. The reply from another member was: "Good Lord, no—things are bad enough without getting them mixed up with theology." Theology deals with the nature of man and his relation to God and the consequences to society because of that relationship. Religion brings into the consideration of business ethics a dimension which it cannot possess, namely, ultimate loyalties above those of one's community or one's business organization. It raises the question of one's final responsibility, whether it is to the company of which he is a part or whether to the well-being of other persons who are also fellow creatures of a common Father, of a God who is both Creator and Redeemer. The religious dimension greatly complicates business ethics because there is no absolute and final rightness in many decisions. They have to be made out of consideration for both the ongoing life of the institution and for society at large, whose concern is just as much that of God as is the more immediate set of loyalties in the company. To the Christian the ultimate standard of action is love, but rarely can one fulfill the full requirements of love in a business transaction. He must, therefore, act with the freedom with which he has been endowed and serve what, in the light of the circumstances at hand, most truly represents what he believes to be God's will and purpose for that situation.

The Role of the Church

How often is the cry heard, "Why doesn't the church do something about that?" Or perhaps even more frequently, "What business has the church got meddling in that situation?" There was a time (the Middle Ages) when neither of these questions was being asked, when no one, openly at least, questioned the propriety of the church's activities in any sphere and everyone took for granted that if anything was needed, the church would attend to it.

The explanation of the vast change from the day when the church was responsible for everything to the present day when its very relevance to social matters generally and to economics in particular is questioned, constitutes a fascinating study in culture, mores, political and scientific history, and the changing attitudes which have resulted in our present expectations of the church's role. Ernst Troeltsch, R. H. Tawney, and many others have described the process by which the power of the church declined in relation to economic processes, and there are many who bemoan this lessening of hegemony over the business and cultural life of society. We will not join in that dirge, not simply because it is "spilled milk" and there is no use crying about it, but because the separation is by no means all loss. One contemporary commentator states: "Today the marriage of the church and society is fast dissolving, brought on by the growing secularization of the West itself and by the challenge to western hegemony put by the peoples of Africa, Asia, and Latin America not only in political and economic affairs but in the realm of ideology."[1] Undoubtedly this is true, but it can hardly be contended that the marriage was of a sacramental nature to begin with, and it was certainly never by mutual consent. The parties had simply grown up together and had had insufficient opportunity to see what matrimony over the years might bring.

The simple fact is that neither the church nor the economic order has had the opportunity under modern conditions to explore their mutual contributions and their mutual dependence. There are many who would contend that there is no mutual dependence; they have full right to make as valid a case for their beliefs as possible. On the other hand, those who believe that the church has a function to perform in the contemporary world in relation to economic life likewise have a valid right to make a claim. It is the fundamental conviction of this writer and of most of the contributors to the Series on Ethics and Economics in Society that the church has something of utmost significance to contribute to economic thought. Likewise economics, serving as it does our industrial society, has much to contribute to religion and its potential for serving an industrial economy.

It is no accident that the subject discussed more than any other in theological circles in this generation is the nature and relevance of the church. Encyclopedias are required to do justice to the total gamut of that study. We will make our affirmations in terse and condensed form. The church derives its existence from the fact of the life, death, and resurrection of Jesus Christ. Those who have been influenced through the centuries by the events surrounding the central figure of the Christian faith have found themselves bound together both by a common devotion and by an institutional life. However great they may be, revolutionary events require historical forms to perpetuate them. So the church developed an institutional form in order to convey to its people and to interpret to those who were not a part of it the central fact of its faith. Down through the ages the church has remained a community bound together in large measure by a devotion to the God who is the God and Father of our Lord Jesus Christ. This community has been bound together in many institutional forms, but what is significant is that the church has had strength and continuity only where it had some institutional structure to undergird it.

As James Gustafson has expressed it, this institution has become a community of faith and a community of deed.[2] Neither is sufficient without the other. The supreme test of the church's faith has always been its giving itself to mankind as the continuing embodiment of its Lord, who was "the Man for others." It has been concerned for the welfare of people of all ages, but particularly of those who were least able to defend themselves—children, the aged, and the infirm. It has sought to alleviate injustice and injury because these were destructive of the human spirit and were in violation of God's will for man as seen in the life of our Lord.

In the minds of its most sensitive adherents the church was commissioned by its Lord to be a model of the new community which God desires among men. William Temple, who did much in his time to clarify the meaning of Christianity for the whole of society, contended that it was the purpose of the church to provide the earthly counterpart of the "City of God" which Augustine had portrayed.[3] It was not possible for man to achieve fully the City of God, but he could seek to bring the "City of Man" closer to that ideal.

As times and social environment changed, men who earnestly sought to fulfill their roles as part of the new community of Christ, a community without division, as the Apostle Paul vigorously insisted, were called to find ways in which their devotion to God as known in Christ could fulfill the obligation to create this City of Man. It was one thing to care for those who were in dire need in the years immediately after Jesus' departure from their midst; it was something else to translate that action into care for those who were the victims of economic and social systems whose power was too great and too remote to be reached and modified. While this has been a continuing dilemma for devoted Christians for two thousand years, it has increased since the Industrial Revolution. Those who have profited substantially by absence of interference from others who desired to create the City of Man after the pattern of the City of God, have resisted mightily attempts to modify their practices. Even some acts of private charity have been engaged in for this purpose. Such is man's propensity toward self-righteousness that he resists criticisms or modifications, however just their claims may be.

The Christian knows that the church in its institutionalized form and the world are indissolubly related. However impressive have been the attempts of a few to live apart from the world, their example does not contribute much to the life of our times, for their very existence has been largely dependent upon the willingness of others to live "sinfully" in the world and thus to free ascetics from its demands. Today we accept the fact that if the church is to be relevant to the life around us, it is out of a genuine desire to create the City of Man after the pattern for human life revealed in the Gospel and in the kingdom of Jesus Christ. When men have abandoned the ideal of living a life of justice and compassion for the welfare of others, the results have been chaotic and disintegrative to the human spirit. This we saw with terrifying force in the emergence of a brutal totalitarian regime under the Nazis in Germany and under the tactics of a Stalin in the Soviet Union. We saw it in the brutalities of the slave trade and in the exploitation of human life during the early stages of the Industrial Revolution.

It became apparent that the church was more than a soul-saving station. If each church itself was a colony of heaven, and if the total church was commissioned to become an instrument for achieving the ideal City of Man, it would require concerted action, voluntarily initiated and accepted. Oversight and control from a vast central source such as characterized the church of the Middle Ages could no longer be relied upon. Parenthetically it should be added that the break-up of that power did not begin with the Protestant Reformation; its roots anteceded 1517 by many years, but the Reformation was a protest against the continuing ineptitude and corruption of the church in its totalitarian form and its failure to support the values of human dignity which the new commercialism and the Renaissance with its new learning had inspired.

In England the state church, which understandably took its

pattern from the ecclesiastical body which preceded it, and the new "gathered" church composed of those inspired by familiarity with "the Book" and its description of the early church, both came to regard themselves as responsible for the quality of life around them. But an inevitable dualism arose. Those who were primarily concerned with individual salvation naturally came to expect it in whatever form of church existed. Those who regarded the church as a collective body responsible both for individual and communal life saw in the church an instrument for social reconstruction. The church has come to mean both of these things, sometimes emphasizing one to the exclusion of the other. In all periods there have been those who felt that the principal function of the church was to assure the eternal salvation of their souls. The English Reformation illustrated this dualism. It was no accident that in the Cromwellian Revolution the church was considered an instrument for implementing its ideals for political organization and public morals. Similarly, it was understandable that the church became the nerve center and inspiration for labor unions and cooperatives in England. The point is that the church has always had this dual role.

A look at the history of the church, however, reveals that its dual role has not been uniformly accepted, and the reasons are not far to seek. They lie in the differing understanding of the gospel's function, as interpreted by the two most influential figures in Protestantism, Martin Luther and John Calvin. (This difference was spelled out more fully in chapter one.) Luther's emphasis was primarily on the individual righteousness of the Christian deriving from God's gracious love for him. Presumably the Christian would do that which was good and just as the free response to God's love. Calvin was not so trustful that the free person would live righteously because of devotion to his Maker and Redeemer. Calvin's more explicit development of the positive function of law helped remind the faithful of their obligation to the total community of Christians and helped to prevent those who were not so committed from injuring others. While those in the Lutheran tradition contended that Christian social action should be expressed through the instrumentality of the state,

those of Calvinist persuasion conceived the church's social role
as that of a countervailing and coordinating force. Under the
latter institutional framework the church has seen its role as
helping to create the kind of society which would make it more
truly the ideal City of Man. It is understandable, therefore, that
the immigrants from England sought to establish on the new continent a new holy commonwealth, and their descendants—
physical and spiritual—have been much more interested in political and economic institutions than have been the immigrants who
came from lands influenced primarily by Martin Luther.

In addition to their differing views concerning the church's
relation to the state another factor which influenced the modern
complexion of the church was the differing importance attributed
to precise theological accord. The Lutheran concern for proper
doctrine hindered cooperation with other denominations in concerted social action, while the Calvinists' emphasis on the committed life, as distinguished from strict doctrinal correctness,
allowed them to engage more freely in such action. It is therefore
understandable that such organizations as the National Council
of Churches, the World Council of Churches, and the local
church federations have almost uniformly been the result of
original instigation on the part of individuals and groups whose
roots were in the Calvinistic tradition. It is equally significant that
today the leadership for many of these organizations is now
coming in increasing volume from the denominations which
had their origins in continental Europe.

The denominations originally formed on European soil have,
as has every other part of Christendom, been shaken to their
roots by the diabolical emergence of Nazism. As the Evanston
Report of the World Council meetings states in discussing the
European churches: "It has been shown in many studies how,
as a result of this period of discovery for the churches, 'some
of the narcotic effects of their silent alliance with the world
were at last shaken off. The realities of the situation became clear.
The churches found out that they had to fight or die. . . .' "[4]

But Europe was not alone in the "narcotic effects" of the
alliance with the world. The life of the churches and the life of

the world are for many church members indistinguishable. Church membership has not been based primarily on devotion to the gospel or commitment to its Lord. To a very large extent, church membership has been the product of the same type of sales program which business utilizes. It is hardly to be wondered, then, that the churches have not taken seriously their mandate to view the world in the light of a Christian view of man and society. Thus when church members "in good standing" raise the question "What business of the church is it to meddle in these economic matters?" it represents a complete unfamiliarity with the whole history and purpose of the Christian faith in its personal and communal forms.

This challenging of the church, in protest against its assuming responsibility for social life in general and economic life in particular, has had a beneficial chastening effect. The terrible catastrophe afflicting the German people came in part as a result of unfamiliarity with this basically indestructable relationship between faith and all forms of personal and social life. Awareness of this profound relationship has forced the German people and those of every other nation with Christian people to a rediscovery of their own roots. It has led to a large-scale pursuit of theological and biblical study.

The emergence of the World Council of Churches is testimony to the realized need for a rediscovery of our spiritual roots. The development of the ecumenical movement is a by-product of that discovery, but perhaps even more is it responsible for fostering that study. In the Oxford Conference on "The Life and Work of the Church" in 1937 and the Edinburg Conference on "Faith and Order" in the same year, with the dark clouds of totalitarianism rising over the world, it became apparent that the divisions in Christendom were cutting its vital nerve and rendering it less effective than it might be in a world where other values than the sacredness of human life were becoming dominant. Churches which became accustomed to aloofness from the forces that shape society realized when facing a common enemy that they had weakened themselves by insisting on their own little private bailiwicks and prejudices under the guise of the sacredness of their institutional forms. One of the miracles of modern times is the speed with which the churches united in the realization of their common sources and common purpose, when they faced realistically the disintegrative and destructive forces undermining the all-important work to which the churches were historically committed.

Now the circle is completed. It is the industrialization process and its economy which made possible the massing of great forces of evil as well as of good. The primary emphasis on power and the utilization of all the new-found sources of power have placed the industrial and economic institutions in the role of first importance. The key to their success is efficiency. Fascist nations became the tools of persons who had discovered that efficiency and the control of central power were to provide the only possibility, so they thought, for their expansion and domination over others. To all of this the church was and is now called on to present an alternative to sheer "efficiency" and power, based on its convictions about the nature of man and his purpose in living. This is the inheritance of the church and its mandate for appraising all systems and institutions.

So it is not meddling when the church enters into the discussion of economics or any other forms of human endeavor. In fact, if it did not participate in such activities and judgments, it would default on its commission. Because it has defaulted from time to time, the world is poorer. On the other hand, when its people have assumed magnificently the responsibility of bringing the light of the Christian gospel to bear on human activities and institutions, the world is greatly enriched. This does not mean that the church is qualified to speak for God. There is no absolute and final form which embodies the church—it can but say that in the light of its fullest comprehension and analysis of what God requires of man this is the best judgment available at the time. Obedience to the gospel and its Lord is the only source of its authority, and every decision must be held under that mandate. So with humility but with firmness the church must make its judgments relative to economic matters as in every other aspect of human life.

SPECIFIC FUNCTIONS FOR THE CHURCH

The principal function of the church can be expressed in many ways. Cunliffe-Jones states it very aptly. The task of the church, he says, "is to make plain for man's thinking the intimate relation between the fact of God and the personal life of man in himself and in community."[5] For the Christian the reality of God and the personal life of man can never be divorced. Out of his devotion to God, a test of which is also the measure of man's love for his neighbor, stem all of the beneficent forms, agencies, and institutions which man contrives. The church, then, is the community of those who readily ask that their devotion be tested by their love for God and neighbor. It is constantly on the alert for ways to enrich the community of neighbors, and by the same token it is on the alert for anything which injures the life of man in community.

The life of man in community is not his total life, but nearly everything he does is in part a product of community. His very existence is due to the union of others, and we know full well what warping and disintegration follow from the failures of society to accept man's basic needs for wholesome life in community. Hospitals, jails, and corrective institutions of all sorts owe their populations more to the deprivations and distortions of community life than to physical disabilities. And we know that many of the latter are also the product of injury in the limitless areas of human intercourse.

The church's concern for physical and mental welfare has centuries of experience behind it. Jesus' parable of the good Samaritan has inspired untold millions to care for the needs of others. Those communions and denominations with Lutheran backgrounds have, as was the pattern of the Roman Catholic Church which preceded their existence, a special concern for those afflicted by illness or too young or too old to provide for themselves. This story is eloquently and sensitively told in a volume prepared for the First National Conference on "The Churches and Social Welfare."[6] Alleviating the ill effects of industrial society, however, was not enough; it became apparent that much could be done to fore-stall the accidents and calamities which injured lives. Out of such a concern began to emerge movements and organizations designed to inspire, influence, and restrict the kind of society at whose core was a concern for the very nature of man himself. Here was a reaffirmation of one of Augustine's concerns expressed more than a thousand years earlier, namely, human rights should have precedence over property rights. Economics in its limited sense is primarily concerned with things—goods—in other words, wealth and its distribution. But unless the circumstances attending the acquisition of wealth and the distribution of goods are beneficial to society at large, they can be corrosive and destructive. It is for this reason that the church has contended with increasing vigor that the only economic practices it can approve are those which truly promote the general welfare and which are totally responsible in their administration and operation. From time to time, churches have erroneously identified themselves with particular economic systems. Disillusionment has followed the too-sanguine endorsement of political or economic systems, for none of them is to be trusted as a vehicle for expressing the basic needs of human life. Instead, the function of the church is to deal with "ends, in the sense of long-range goals, standards and principles in the light of which every concrete situation and every proposal for improving it must be tested."[7] At the same time the church realistically recognizes that ends and means cannot be separated. It is equally concerned with the manner in which the ends are attained.

The church itself is not a political or an economic instrument, even though it may carry weight in regard to political and economic issues and give encouragement to the institutions which are the vehicles of both. It is the role of the church to sense the needs of man whatever his place or affiliation, and where possible to initiate or encourage the giving of the cup of water or the loaf of bread wherever there is need. In comparatively recent years we have seen a vast amount of alleviation of suffering conducted in the name of the church and given in the spirit of Him who admonished man to minister to human need. However this is not the church's principal function. By ministering in this way it performs a function which in many instances can be better conducted by other agencies; for the church is not called—nor does it have the machinery—to serve the complete welfare need in a society which is otherwise equipped to perform such functions with greater efficiency. To the everlasting credit of the churches it must be said, however, that where efficiency and service needed to be combined, the human and mechanical facilities were often co-ordinated to that end and human suffering was alleviated.

An industrial society must inevitably place a high premium on its efficiency in production. Productivity has become the most sought for and honored criterion of industrial life. Surely this is good for the most part, but productivity itself is not the total end or objective of man's life; it is of very great importance that the things which he produces be useful and beneficial. If they are destructive, they must be restricted; if there are unmet needs for which production has not yet been sufficient, these must be lifted up. Here is another basic function the church must perform. It evaluates the whole productive process, including the efficiency ideal, and insists that a failure to serve these ends is a failure in efficiency. It is at this point that tension has arisen between those who have held such high purposes for the life of the church and those who believed that productivity in itself is a sufficient criterion. "It is good for the economy" has become a criterion. On this basis even gambling has been justified. The church can give no commendation to the gambling activities, however magnificently they may appear to benefit the public agencies. What adds nothing to the health of society at large must be renounced by the fellowship of those whose purpose is to foster a quality of life that is consistent with God's creation of man.

John C. Bennett effectively makes this point when he states: ". . . No degree of justice in the organization of economic life can compensate for failure to be efficiently productive, for on this depends the capacity to provide adequately the food, the clothing, the shelter, and other goods which are required by the community. Those who represent Christian theology and ethics are tempted to underestimate the significance of this test of effectiveness in their concern to apply ethical tests, just as economists have often shown an opposite kind of one-sideness and have declared the independence of economics from ethics."[8]

IMPLEMENTING THE CHURCH'S FUNCTIONS IN ECONOMIC LIFE

For reasons which are rooted in the historical development or its ethical concerns, the church in recent times has paid more attention to economic life than to political action. Possibly because the consequences of economic life were revealed in industrial activities and the communities which reflected them, the ills were more apparent and seemed more readily dealt with. Long before international affairs attracted the attention of the sensitive and far-ranging minds of some Christians, there had been developed organizations to modify the harshness of the industrial order. Such organizations as the Church Association for the Advancement of the Interests of Labor, the Society of Christian Socialists, Walter Rauschenbusch's Fellowship of the Kingdom, and more recently Christian Action were formed to espouse, among other things, economic justice. One by one the objectives of these organizations have become embodied in political forms sustained and regulated by government activities or have become the concerns of larger secular bodies. Significantly many of the movements initiated by the church have become embedded in the total life of our society.

Following World War I increasing attention was paid to international affairs, world peace, and race. The pseudo prosperity of the 1920s culminating in the 1929 crash reduced concern for economic problems. The Great Depression evoked interest in schemes designed to reconstruct our economic system, with many conscientious individuals looking wonderingly at the Soviet Union to see whether its program held substantial bases for hope. Increasingly it became apparent that the Marxist-Leninist-Stalinist "solution" overlooked or rejected some of the most elemental considerations which must be taken account of in any realistic approach to economics, and its attractiveness waned. Meanwhile, the "enterprise" economy evolved some correctives, and gains were made in economic welfare. A series of major innovations became established in American life.

If this is so, one asks, what then is there left to do, since the National Labor Relations Act, the Social Security Act on behalf of all levels and ages, child labor legislation and minimum wage legislation, Workmen's Compensation and many others, now provide safeguards which were not available during the lifetime of many people now living? The answer to this question is presumably to be seen in the continuous discovery of new areas of need by interdenominational church bodies, in some instances, by church agencies and of course by secular and governmental agencies. A list of the activities of the Department of Church and Economic Life of the National Council of Churches would be highly revealing, but too long to be included in these pages. Simply for illustration mention may be made of the Conferences or Consultations held on Peacetime Uses for Nuclear Energy, Agricultural Policy, the Ministry of the Churches to Labor and Management, the Christian Conscience and an Economy of Abundance, the Churches and Persistent Pockets of Poverty, the Economic Practices of the Churches, Ethical Implications of Rapid Economic Change in the U.S.A., and many others.

Illustrating a role the church may play in a situation obviously needing ethical judgment and clarification was the investigation of the steel strike in 1918. The cooperative efforts of leaders in many denominations were brought to bear on some tragic conditions. Happily major recommendations of the churchmen were adopted, and their efforts are credited with ultimately influencing the elimination of the twelve-hour day and the recognition of the right to organize for purposes of collective bargaining.

Forty years later, at the time of another bitter and extended strike, a special committee under authorization by the National Council of Churches dealt with the critical issues which closed mills and put five hundred thousand people out of work. The specific issues were different, but the fundamental problems were related: the use of power by big industrial organizations and its impingement on human freedom. Both labor and management were censured for their irresponsible use of power. The committee held that false claims and propaganda by both parties were designed to deceive the general public. The representatives of the churches then pointed to such profound and unresolved issues as a fair wage, a just price, adequate profits, and the definition of "public welfare" as questions inescapably related to Christian values. All of this was posited on "the basic conviction that Christians must be responsible for the quality of the social order in which they live."[9]

The Ethics and Economic Life Series which this volume concludes represents another major emphasis of the Department of Church and Economic Life. It embodies the attempt to cope realistically with the issues of economics in a Christian context.

Increasingly the churches in their cooperative endeavors have been finding readiness and even enthusiasm for cooperation on the part of so-called "secular forces," whether in government, in the universities, or in the multiplicity of private agencies operating for socially constructive ends. Often their immediate objectives are identical, though there may be fundamental differences in the philosophical or theological background of those engaged in these reconstructive activities.

The massive attempt currently being undertaken by government to overcome poverty was anticipated by several years on the part of cooperative church bodies which held a consultation among leaders of many denominations to discern possible lines of approach to the elimination of poverty in this seemingly affluent nation. Similarly, as national forces began to converge on the problem of school dropouts, the churches, through the National Council of Churches and working in cooperation with governmental and private agencies, sought to find means whereby the churches might give vigorous support to the movement, urging young people to prepare themselves in school for the kinds of earning opportunities our economy will be providing in the years ahead.

Not limited to the problems of economics, but designed to further the work of the church as it meets needs in many areas of life, has been the impressive increase in research functions, both within the individual denominations and in cooperation. The research program of the churches is turning to the unmet needs of human beings in many forms of individual and communal life.

The expressions of the life of the church as briefly portrayed above are, however, actually only a small part of the total action of the church as it seeks to minister to human needs in an industrial society. The spectacle of substantial portions of the church capitulating to the nationalistic interests of the nations in Europe— and, we must confess, to a less sensational degree but perhaps nonetheless also in the English-speaking world as well—has produced the realization that some of the forms of the church we have known may be inadequate. As Franklin H. Littell has so aptly portrayed, out of the ashes of this tragedy has come the realization that new forms of church life and new ways of expressing the Christian faith are required.[10] Small groups of searching Christians have sought means of relating their faith to the economic problems of their day. In these smaller groups, often assembled because of common vocational or professional interests, there has emerged the concern for the meaning of work in industrial society. With development of the Evangelical Academies in central Europe, and of Iona in Scotland under Sir George McCleod, and many other such experiments, it has become apparent that the church is not limited to its traditional forms of parish life in order to perform its role. In some of these new forms of parish life the real life issues are more readily dealt with. Those issues may center about the ethical dilemmas of the industrial society in whose midst the "parish" exists.

Reluctant though we be to relinquish so time-honored an institution as the parish church, there are evidences from all sides that the church should not be confined to any single form and that its very existence depends upon imaginative ways of relating the gospel to the needs of all men wherever they may be. "The picture of the local church," says Martin Marty, "is so powerful, it tends to exhaust the definition of the church."[11] We understand Marty's meaning when we realize how restricted have been our imaginations at the point of discovering new ways of bringing the witness of the church to bear on our common life. Such a useful little book as *Your Church in Your Community* by Huber Klemme is representative of many other volumes of this sort now coming to the fore that describe the ways in which parish churches, or perhaps more accurately, small groups within parish churches, have sought to make the witness of the church known in uncommon ways.[12]

Apparently the answer to the church's effective witness in an industrial society lies both in the forms of collective action cited above and in the action of small and committed groups whose members have sensed a need and have sought to minister to it. In the process they have called the attention of the larger church to similar concerns and needs. One such demonstration is the East Harlem Parish in New York and its spreading counterparts in many industrial cities. The most recent outgrowth of such interest is the formation, in process at the time of this writing, of the Urban Training Center in Chicago, whose purpose is to prepare church leadership for the unresolved needs of urban society. Likewise, out of unmet needs in town and country life there has been created and put into operation in Merom, Indiana, the Ecumenical Center of Renewal and Planning on behalf of town and country churches.

It has always been true that "new occasions teach new duties." Our times are experiencing a wealth of new illustrations relating the church to economic life in industrial society. None may contend that it is the only true expression of the church. The final test is its faithfulness to the healing ministry of Christ, that no injury be done "to the least of these" and that all men may be free to attain the measure of the full stature which they were intended to attain.

16

Spiritual Foundations

The first chapter of this book presented a brief historical survey of the relation between religion and economic life. That survey concluded with a characterization of the Social Gospel, America's most distinctive and imaginative contribution to religious thought. It was this nation's first comprehensive attempt to bring the resources of religion to bear on some of the issues related to industrialism.

In Europe prior to the twentieth century Roman Catholicism, with its ties to the feudal order, its leaders in government and economic life committed to more authoritarian structures, was losing its working people. It had not accommodated itself to the new industrial scene. Pope Leo XIII's encyclical *Rerum novarum* sought to remedy this situation. Likewise, Protestantism in Europe, with much of its ecclesiastical life still resembling the Roman Catholic patterns it had sought to rectify, found itself unable to cope with the major reorganization of thought and institutional life accompanying industrial changes. England, as noted earlier, with its roots deeper in democratic processes, witnessed the emergence of small clusters of persons determined to bring the humanizing and ameliorating influences of the Christian religion to bear on their social and economic problems.

American Religion and Economic Justice

A new continent, holding new expectations and unrestricted by ecclesiastical forms and theologies of the Old World, developed unconsciously but persistently a fresh approach to political as well as religious life. For many in the new land the new freedom for individuals had a religious rootage even though the official documents of the nation avoided specific mention thereof. Instead of seeking to develop a "Christian socialism" they accepted religious values as inherent in the common life and as standing in judgment of it. No single theological framework implemented this conviction. It was simply assumed by many to be built into the American way of life. The Social Gospel provided both the analytical tools and the ideal norms with which to confront some of the unchallenged assumptions of American life. It must be added that any realistic confrontation of the contemporary ethical problems will have to build on the pioneering of this religious emphasis. Utilizing the rapidly emerging social sciences as instruments for analyzing both individual and social life, it could delineate the evils and point to the good. The natural sciences too, newly spurred by Darwin, were quickly appropriated. All new learning, in so far as it was gained in a genuine search for truth, was a potential contributor. And by no means least in importance was the new emphasis on a study of the social and economic conditions lying behind the biblical record, based on belief that they might throw light on the knowledge derived from the study. In this atmosphere large and influential groups of both economists and sociologists joined in the efforts to remedy the ills which were evident in the industrial economy. With these resources, knowledge, and expertness a substantial number of men and women, both lay and professional, sought to bring religious convictions to bear on conditions within the emerging industrial society. Richly informed by familiarity with the life and teachings of Jesus—the Sermon on the Mount, in particular—they were moved by a profound conviction that there could be created a social order more nearly resembling what Jesus portrayed than the existing one. That determination has not disappeared, but some of the same disciplines used in the study of our own society and in the study of the biblical record have revealed that there were deeper forms of resistance to be overcome than might have been inferred at an earlier time.

Ethically responsible behavior rests on two foundations. One is factual and analytical, the other is spiritual. The factual and analytical foundation is the understanding of what the consequences of action, whether taken individually or through groups, will be for all persons affected by them. The spiritual foundation is the pattern of attitudes and values held by persons, which determines how they will act in view of the anticipated consequences of their action. Neither foundation alone will achieve ethical behavior. A sadistic person may fully understand the harmful consequences of his cruelty but may revel in them. A person who is completely pure in heart may cause equally harmful consequences by uninformed or ill-informed acts. Good intentions are necessary but not sufficient to assure ethically responsible action.

The individual person is not only responsible for his own actions but must share responsibility for those taken by groups of which he is a member. As industrial society has grown in complexity, the acts of the individual have had a wider and wider span of consequences, and the importance of the actions taken by groups has greatly increased. The factual and analytical foundations have accordingly become more difficult for anyone to gain empirically through personal experience and observation. Despite these difficulties we know more about the consequences of individual and group behavior than ever before, thanks to the development of the natural sciences, and particularly of the social sciences, and their application in careful and objective studies. Such studies are most likely to be relevant and fruitful for ethical behavior if they are carried on by persons who are concerned with ethical problems. The highly productive work of the Department of the Church and Economic Life of the National Council of Churches is evidence for this conclusion.

In addition to the growing complexity of industrial society is the fact of rapid social and economic change. In many economic relationships the consequences of personal or group actions, including the actions of government, that we concluded were true a generation ago cannot be counted on as being true today. Moreover new kinds of problems and new relationships are continuously coming into existence, or at least into importance. Hopeful progress has been made in building into the life of Western society moral standards derived from Hebrew-Christian ethical ideals. Our laws reflect this progress. For example, child labor in industry is for the most part eliminated, and social security and aid to dependent children have been provided by law for the aged, widows, and the fatherless. Safeguards in industry have been made mandatory by legislation, by the demands of labor and by the humanitarian concern of employers. The list is long and impressive, and each of these protective instruments has come about as a result of needs emerging in a particular time and place.

But now more new problems have emerged, and the solutions of earlier periods are not adequate to meet them. All of this change and complexity poses puzzling dilemmas for persons in economic life today. If the author may draw upon his experience with a number of business and industrial groups, it has been apparent that their members feel that the major brutalities of industrial and economic life have been refined and are no longer to be feared. At the same time there is almost complete agreement that religion in general and the church in particular are offering little help with the kind of dilemmas confronting industry in this generation. Those dilemmas have to do with such ethical questions as the necessity for increasing productivity in order that the economy may continue to expand, the contribution of labor organizations to the economy and the potential danger inherent in their power, the power concentration in industry itself, the role of salesmanship and advertising, collusion in bidding, and many others. The ethical formulas of another day offer little reliable guidance for such problems as these. Nevertheless there is widespread longing for just such reliable guidance. This does not insure that the guidance would be accepted even if it were available, but there is a deep surmise that there are norms for guidance somewhere and that the church with its roots in the Christian faith ought to be able to provide competent counsel.

It should be obvious that because of complexity and change in economic life the longing for definite answers, for a handbook available for quick consultation, or for a formula or formulas that can be readily applied, is not going to be satisfied. The approaches that are actually feasible have already been indicated. They are on the one hand the application of scientific study to determine the social consequences of actions, and on the other hand the strengthening and purifying of the ethical posture or stance of the individual as he faces up to those consequences. Here we see joined together in determining ethical behavior both science and religion, science supplying the knowledge of the consequences of our actions and religion supplying the pattern of values by which we decide our actions in the light of those consequences. Much of the discussion in the preceding chapters has been devoted to laying the foundations for analyses of the consequences of individual and group action. It will be the purpose of the present chapter to examine in summary form the major aspects of the spiritual foundations of ethical behavior in economic life.

Since this study is intended to present a Christian approach to ethical problems, emphasis will of course be placed on what is relevant in Christian teaching. Such emphasis is in no way intended to suggest that other religions, as well as persons who profess no religion, do not recognize ethical problems, or that many great truths about man's relations to his fellow man and his position in the universe have not been revealed by religious faith generally. In particular it is not intended to discount the implications and contributions of Hebrew thought and belief to the ethics of industrial society. The Jewish religion, grounded in the Torah with its commandments, prophets, and teachers, confronts the same ethical issues. Many common values and objectives would characterize the solutions to economic problems as sought by thoughtful Jews and Christians. Though the Christian has the same historical roots in the Old Testament, he has a special problem in the confusion of interpretations which have centered around the person of Jesus Christ. It is because of this confusion that there have been sharp differences among Christians as to the way their faith relates to economics. The Jew faces less ambiguity in the authoritative requirement, at least, of his faith. This is one reason we have attempted to deal primarily with the implications of the Christian faith. At the same time we realize that there would be a high degree of harmony among faithful adherents of both inheritors of the Hebrew-Christian religious foundations as they arrive at similar or identical solutions.

After two millenniums it might be thought that the institutional life of the church would be a safe guide for our ethical attitudes. The church as the custodian and exemplar of the Christian ethic should supposedly present such a clear example of high-minded business practices and attitudes toward economic life in general that businessmen would find in it a criterion for many of their own business practices. In fact, however, church leadership and membership often reflect the status drives and jockeying for position which are taken for granted as a part of the business world. Business practices of the churches have not differed so noticeably from business practices at large that they can stand as reminders of a standard of economic conduct higher than those which prevail around them. A study of business practices in the church reports: "A major finding of the study is that to a disturbing extent the churches and their various agencies take less seriously their corporate responsibilities than their official pronouncements on social and economic problems give the community a right to expect."[1] In its practices the church may have offered comfort and absence of criticism for those who are not overly sensitive to the application of Christian ethical ideals.

ECONOMIC RELEVANCE OF THEOLOGICAL PRESUPPOSITIONS

For the Christian the person of Jesus Christ throws light on the meaning of human existence in society, including the very large part which is economic life. Because of His death and resurrection men have been made aware that God entered into human existence in an unprecedented and incomparable fashion. The narrative of Jesus' life as told in the Gospels has moved countless millions to faith and compassion. God's revelation of himself in human history, giving evidence of his great compassion for his world, is for those who accept the Christian faith the most revolutionary event of all time. But to comprehend its significance requires a measure of depth for which the mind seeking easy answers is not prepared. The self-giving of God in Christ is for Christians the ultimate criterion of social existence, and the most durable element in human society is self-giving love.

Although economic life as we know it has never been fully conducted on this basis, every economy stands under the ultimate criterion of self-giving love as we find it in the total experience of Jesus as the Christ. The person who really accepts the criterion of Christian social life as the expression of self-giving love toward his neighbor cannot but conduct his social relationships in a manner different from that of one who believes that the purpose of life is to live only for himself and those closest to him. A society moved by the latter motivation can scarcely understand the divine purposes for man and the world; it has been immunized against the true meaning of existence. The first need, then, of the Christian community is a broader understanding of Jesus, not merely as a model for conduct and an ethical teacher but as the Incarnation of the eternal God. "The Word was made flesh."

Also basic to our attitudes in economic behavior is the acceptance of God as the ground and the source of all life and also the source of its redemption. This acceptance is difficult to achieve because it involves an intellectual and spiritual depth of probing and discovery for which the mind is seldom equipped and against which it has been insulated by most of the life around it. Today men tend to be no longer afraid of what the church can do to them by way of consigning them to punishment. They accept the view that life's rewards and punishments are in the here and now. Earlier generations, raised on a doctrine of punishment after death and a God who keeps some kind of a score, may have lived better lives out of a fear of consequences after this life. However with expanding education has come a lessening of concern over punishment in the hereafter. Such consequences were assumed to have been initiated by a God who acted as a personal judge and to whom the individual was personally responsible. This kind of God many men today feel they can well do without. The problem is that for many no adequate theological conviction, no profound sense of obligation has been substituted.

So long as God was "out there," there was no sense of immediate obligation or likelihood of retribution, and man felt himself free. The conventionally religious person may conduct himself in no significantly different way from the person who finds himself with no theological framework. For him there is a gulf between man and such a God. This gulf permits the kind of inconsistency which rationalizes racial conflict and justifies discrimination. The economic life of contemporary man will not be seriously or effectively modified through religious beliefs which posit a God who is primarily "out there" and is not deeply involved in man's relations with his fellow men—an "absentee God," to borrow a crude expression.

Some of the most truly constructive actions being taken in our time make no reference whatever to any theological foundations. By its very definition that which fosters the goodness of life and cooperates with the created universe as it has been given to us is in harmony with the Creator and Redeemer of life. Why, then, cannot all actions be entrusted to the common-sense ethical purpose of individuals and thus not be modified or complicated by theological formulas? An answer lies in the observation over the centuries that men become more responsible and more consistent in their responsibility once they have realized that their own lives and the life of all society are held together in a common bond of creation and of redemption. As they have comprehended the depth of their obligation to this source and have expressed their gratitude in lives of love and compassion, a meaning and cohesiveness appear which they had not recognized before.

It would be most extraordinary if traditional religious phrases, heard from infancy and often quoted by rote, did not lose some of their initial meaning. To offset such experience philosophers and theologians have sought to devise new and fresh terms from time to time to encompass the great and moving ideas which have engaged the thinking of all generations. In large measure the historic phrases have been found adequate and not readily replaceable.

No single word has been found more capable of bearing the original meaning than the word "creation," and no single phrase has been found more serviceable in expressing God's continued responsibility for the object of creation than the Psalmist's words: "The earth is the Lord's." For the person of Hebrew-Christian heritage, on this simple phrase hinges all forms of relationship between man and man and between man and the earth which is his home. In their search for reality men throughout history have again and again arrived at the same conclusion, that the real world is a creation of God and that the only possible assurance of a consistent and meaningful existence within it is found in living as a "tenant of the Almighty." It is presumably something of this response which Dietrich Bonhoeffer is expressing when he says: "I never experienced the reality of God without the reality of the world or the reality of the world without the reality of God."[2]

Many persons have paid little attention to the implications that follow from this revolutionary proposition that the earth is not man's but God's. Whether it is the brevity of man's life that urges him to secure for himself and his family the most that is possible in so short a time, or whether man's incapacity for grasping the nature of the created order has rendered him unresponsive to so far-reaching and profound a meaning, we of course cannot know. It remains very obvious, however, that a large part of mankind has not accepted seriously God's prior "ownership" and responsibility for the world. Instead of accepting the assumptions of biblical and theological thought "the secularist" feels that his patterns of thinking are more dependable, especially since he doubts the validity of restraints which come from religious sources. The panoply of forces attempting to provide man with his existential needs cry out that the biblical interpretation of the world complicates matters and inhibits many of the practices and desires which have been fostered by man's own man-made worldliness. So the secular world provides, he assumes, the only acceptable framework. But, comments Gayraud S. Wilmore, what we call secularity "is only the moralistic and ideological consensus of the American middle class or of those who aspire to that class, carefully prodded and patronized by businessmen and politicians, and made slightly aromatic by the illusive perfume of Christianity."[3]

Another of those phrases so frequently quoted that their meanings may have been reduced to only antiquarian value is: "None of us lives to himself, and none of us dies to himself. If we live, we live to the Lord, and if we die, we die to the Lord; so then whether we live or whether we die, we are the Lord's" (Rom. 14 : 7-8).

Affirmations and explanations are conditioned by time and carry meanings for one generation which are not the same for another. To many contemporary persons that affirmation of the Apostle Paul contains little meaning. Those phrases convey insight only if one accepts the assumption that the earth is God's kingdom. Expressing the same conviction in another phrase, Paul admonishes ". . . whatever you do, do all to the glory of God" (I Cor. 10 : 31). The reasoning is the same—that all that man is and has is held as a gift from God, and his total life has meaning only to the extent that he lives it as an expression of gratitude for that gift.

In a mass society moving with inexorable force toward further urbanization it becomes increasingly difficult to comprehend or accept the significance of individual lives. In the Hebrew-Christian foundations the Hebrew people were important as a nation because they gave evidence of collective devotion to their God, but it was the individual who in his devotion, compounded at the national level, bore the responsibility for the only quality of life which could survive. The importance of the individual, in Western society at least, can be attributed in large part to these biblical roots elevating the importance of the person because of his importance to God. As suggested earlier, much of the protective and welfare legislation of industrial society owes its origin to the deep-grounded religious foundations concerning the worth of the individual.

We have now come to a point in the industrialization of society where neglect of the individual can no longer be permitted. A spurious individualism, we can now recognize, is endangering society as a whole. The consequences of neglect are embarrassing to those more fortunate; more to the point, they threaten the entire social fabric. In the reputedly affluent American society the "pockets of poverty" become a hazard to the plateaus of prosperity because of neglect of community. It is insufficient that we have compassion for a few selected persons whose welfare holds special interest. All persons are of equal worth to God. Person-to-person measures of charity are commendable, but only constructive measures through collective action can be adequate. Individualism here takes the form of responsible action in concert with others of like mind and spirit. This is responsible individualism.

DOCTRINES AND THEIR APPLICATION

Out of awareness of his own origins and the source of his sustenance, of the mutual dependence of man upon man and upon the earth which sustains him, emerged the doctrine of stewardship, the most meaningful explanation of man's relationship to the life about him. He is not owner, he is not its creator or source. He is, however, responsible for what has been given to him.

It is understandable that man should look upon life around him, particularly the artifacts, systems, and institutions which men have created, and assume that these things are his, at least to the extent that he has had any part in them. He has been led to believe that in some vague way he is a "steward" of them. Here is another of those words which come easily to the lips when we attempt to portray the nature of responsibility for the life of the world. Stewardship has become too readily identified with the "every member canvass," connoting the giving of money. This is a serious belittling of its true scope and meaning. A faithful steward makes the best adjustment possible under the circumstances. Nor are the areas of decision related only to money. They may involve personnel—a school board decision on transportation, the preservation of land for recreation, or the choice of a political candidate. A faithful (and wise) steward goes into action on the trouble fronts, working for the best possible solution—and not being disillusioned if he and his cause do not win total victory.

In an economy which has traditionally placed a high premium on individual initiative, the importance of genuine stewardship has been delimited. This has been especially apparent in the stewardship of our natural resources. Too frequently they have been treated as personal possessions, subject only to the dictates of their "owner." Belatedly a nation—or a world—facing shortages of food, fiber, recreation space, and even room for family and community life, finds itself injured by the failure of men individually or collectively to acknowledge their stewardship. Too late it is recognized that they had defaulted on a trust involving resources they did not create.

The Christian doctrine of man includes, among many other things, the belief that he is responsible to the God who is his Creator and Redeemer and is responsible to his fellowmen who are held in a similar relationship. Because of this responsibility he stands under the judgment it imposes upon him. It is a personal judgment even though he may share it collectively along with others. Men have always preferred to avoid any judgment placed upon themselves by their fellow men, but even more have they resented the assumption that they stand under judgment for the way in which they have fulfilled their stewardship.* The responsible Christian must know that no one can avoid judgment upon himself either as an individual or in his collective relationships. This is true not only because of what one actually does. Failure to act when action is required can be even more self-corrupting than some negative actions. Literally, then, under no circumstances is a man able to enjoy the smugness of self-gratification. Reinhold Niebuhr has commented: "It is well to know that God judges all men and that in His sight no man is justified. But we are men and not God. We must make historic choices."[5] It is for those choices that the Christian seeks a wisdom grounded elsewhere than in his ever-present self-interest. Only a consistent awareness that his own life is bound by ties of gratitude to the Source of his being protects him from more impermanent and more partial answers. Man cannot understand his relationship to his Creator and Redeemer unless he holds in love the rest of mankind. ". . . For he who does not love his brother whom he has seen, cannot love God whom he has not seen" (I John 4 : 20).

We like to entertain the belief that our decisions are our own and that our beliefs have been arrived at through the exercise of sound thought and judgment. Calm analysis of the facts reveals this to be erroneous. Group or national interests have dictated

---

* In a study conducted by the author and a colleague, an attempt was made to ascertain the extent to which individuals acknowledge any judgment upon them for their actions in our society and its economy. An almost negligible number indicated that their understanding of God included a judgmental relationship. This was true regardless of denomination.[4]

mass opinion, and individuals have either accepted them unthinkingly or have rationalized their judgment. Mass convictions have rarely if ever been the result of careful thought. In modern mass society this condition may be more prevalent than previously for the obvious reason that the instruments for influencing opinion can reach so much larger audiences with the same ideas. It could be argued that with rising levels of education and more people having access to the means for making decisions the likelihood of more balanced judgment would follow. Such apparently is not the case.

In an economy increasingly dominated by ever larger units and the availability of resources to influence opinions and judgments of increasing numbers the question of individual and mass decision takes on greater significance. Large economic units are in position to bring pressure to bear on employees, communities served, and auditors or viewers of their message. Their objectives may or may not be meritorious. The same is true for causes and movements of all descriptions. The instruments for influencing judgment can be utilized for good as well as for evil. Of primary importance is the fact that decisions and judgments in our economy are likely to be influenced by forces determined on, or skilled in, securing their own desired ends. Within this framework the conscientious religious person has to operate.

In the last analysis, however, all decisions are personal, though they may be influenced by mass acceptance or action. It is through personal decision alone that love finds expression either in person-to-person relationships or where larger groups of one's fellow men are involved. Acting responsibly and out of gratitude for the life given him it is the individual who expresses in love what is called for by the circumstances in which he finds himself. Out of his love and gratitude to God he brings to the situations of his life a similar quality. This is no sentimental outburst or whimsical self-gratification. It is the most powerful element in existence—it is the adhesive which makes for the fullest humanity possible. In its simplest form it demands justice in human relationships. There can be no love without justice. The responsible person, then, knows that his return of God's love for him in all forms of human relationship is tested at the primary level in its fulfillment of elementary justice. Paul Tillich has commented: "It is regrettable that Christianity has often concealed its unwillingness to do justice or to fight for it by setting off love against justice and performing the works of love in the sense of 'charity' instead of battling for the removal of social injustice."[6] Love, then, which incorporates justice is the most distinctive element in all Christian ethics. Every economic system and every personal justification or rationalization must meet the test of this all-engulfing quality. It is the ultimate criterion by which all of man's actions are judged by God.

Sensitive and responsible persons know full well that they cannot carry fully to completion most, let alone all, of their noble objectives impelled by love and responsibility to God. No matter what vocation a person may follow, he is continually pressed into making partial and unsatisfactory decisions. Undoubtedly there are kinds of work which try one's soul more severely than others. The expectation that only perfection will be accepted has driven many individuals to find their fulfillment in isolation outside the range of ordinary human life. This is no solution for most people. All men are sinners, but to the extent that they are sinners and seeking forgiveness for their sinfulness, it is readily and freely given, and it is this which makes it possible for conscientious and responsible individuals to go on.

Briefly in the first chapter reference was made to the emergence of the Christian doctrine of vocation. A genuine difference in the appropriation of this doctrine was expressed by the respective followers of Luther and Calvin. A century ago greater differences could be discerned between the types of work chosen by them. The fact that the followers of Calvin believed their role was to serve God through their work inspired many to ask whether the work itself was truly a form of worship and glorification of God. The Lutheran adherent asked whether he might serve God in his work, with less concern as to whether the work itself contributed to this service. Today it seems that such differences are largely erased. The Christian doctrine of vocation has come into fresh prominence with the insistent pressure from many sources to discern whether one's work or prospects for work contribute meaningfully to the life of man. The certainty of personal summons may not be as great as we are led to believe some "calls" were in earlier times, but surely the meeting of a genuine human need is no less convincing as an indication of call.

Out of frustration over inability to make ideal and perfect choices some people, in disillusionment, may have ceased trying. It requires spiritual maturity to accept the fact that the faults of the economic order can be overcome only relatively, since in so large measure even benevolent human actions must leave some phases of life unaffected or even harmed. The test of one's integrity as a Christian, or of whatever religious persuasion, is the sincerity of intent to serve one's fellow man and to utilize all available resources toward that end. He seeks the good in so far as his understanding and resources permit. To him the admonition "Thou shalt love the Lord thy God with all thy heart and soul and mind, and thy neighbor as thyself" becomes not a counsel of perfection or one which is designed to leave man in disillusionment. It is not a counsel of perfection in the ways and works of man. It does provide a standard by which to appraise one's own integrity whether in person-to-person relationships, in family, in the community at large, or in economic relationships.

The Economy and Community

There is something fallacious in a discussion of the spiritual foundations of the Chirstian faith which separates individual concerns from the welfare of the community. If such a treatment has been apparent in this discussion, it is due solely to organizational requirements and the need for clarification in the meaning of terms. Certainly there is no such division in the Christian faith itself, as has been stated in several ways above. The Gospels make no such artificial division. The Old Testament and especially the prophets presume a cohesiveness of man and society. The early church and every valid demonstration of religious life down through the centuries have assumed that man and his community, his brother, or his neighbor are inseparable. Each man may have to do his own dying, as Martin Luther insisted, but while he is alive, he is an integral part of the whole human fabric.

Little is to be gained by discussing the various meanings attached

to the word "community," that is, whether it is primarily a theological or a sociological term. Events of recent years graphically
and frequently with chilling force point to the interdependence of
all mankind. So we use the term "community" here in the sense
of connoting the interrelatedness and interdependence of human
beings.

In the light of such a consideration of the term "community,"
we are compelled to ask in what way the forms and institutions
men have devised are consonant with the most fundamental understandings of human society. Against such ultimate and fundamental considerations the varying economic systems that men have
contrived must be evaluated. It is apparent that no system of
"pure" individualism or of collectivism (in the sense in which that
word is most commonly used—to refer to communism or socialism) can beget the unqualified support as being "Christian."

Hopefully the Christian has matured in his theological and
economic thinking to the point where labels are not determinative.
Of primary importance is the question of the quality of life which
is possible under whatever type of economy is chosen. For Western
nations three criteria have stood above others. They are freedom,
justice, and order. Does the economic system adopted permit a
degree of freedom which assures the maximum of opportunity to
all, with the fullest consideration of the rights of each individual
in relation to others? Is each person or group assured recourse to a
rule of law by which favoritism is denied and justice is attainable?
And is provision made for a maximum of continuity and harmony
in the carrying on of the activities needed for the preservation of
society?

None of these conditions is peculiarly Christian, yet they are
qualities that a mature Christian desires to see actualized. These
standards are a common denominator of society's ethical ideals.
A Christian is committed to constant pursuit of them. For that
reason he evaluates economic conditions, programs, and proposals
in the light of these three criteria. They are the minimal requirements for community, for only under them can the individual
have opportunity to be wholly an individual.

Because these are minimal conditions for society in general and its economy in particular, the Christian will support in the economy that which gives promise of providing them. This would include all measures which enhance human dignty. Long before public support was attained for aid to children and the aged, for slum elimination and maintenance of income for those afflicted in a variety of ways, for the right to organize and bargain collectively, for using our resources to relieve misery and build wholesome life in other lands, and for many other economic activities, members of churches and synagogues were engaging in activities of this kind and persuading others to do likewise. With much of this now embodied in our national policy the consistent Christian will direct his attention to the central economic issues of our own times, recognizing their spiritual import.

All men are equally the object of God's love despite the fact that they are not equally endowed either physically or mentally. Divisions which have been created because of inequalities in native capacities have always been used as rationalization for taking advantage of others. By this process community has been fractured and men have been alienated both from themselves and from the source of their being. The chief end of man is, as is stated in so manifold a fashion through the whole biblical record, the love of God and neighbor. It is the very simplest form of expressing the fact of human community. In the framework of that simply expressed but incomprehensibly magnificent conception the economic life of man is experienced. Jesus as the Christ, revealing the nature of God to man, confronts man with the basis for realization that all men are one in God.

Our immediate period in history is witnessing the tragic consequences of a flagrant denial of this profound truth in the form of racial tensions. Centuries of refusal to acknowledge the community of man as God's irreducible minimum has warped the minds and robbed the well-being of countless millions. Slowly some of those who perceive the magnitude of the losses to man's economic life are attempting to bridge the gap which poison has corroded. Is it not ironical that one of the most influential forces in restoring community is the awareness of economic loss? Understandably estimates vary and are at best inaccurate, but the loss to the economy due to racial discrimination could approximate 10 billion dollars annually. This is not mere money-consciousness. It is another indication that essentially economic life can itself be healthy only when it serves the total needs of the human community.

The human community is thus seen for what it truly is—a spiritual matter whose essence is portrayed in those affirmations —perhaps over-familiar—concerning the ultimate ownership of the earth and the interrelationship of man, his Creator, and his fellow man. This message comes to persons both in their solitude and as members of communities, as they realize at the same time that no person lives only in solitude or only in the midst of others. Under both circumstances, whether alone or actively engaging in the communal life about him, a man is experiencing a part of his relationship to God. From this fact he can never fully escape. When he attempts to do so, it results in peril to himself and to the society around him.

In the preceding sections of this book there have been briefly delineated some—not all, by any means—of the critical areas related to industrial society. No one conversant with the issues and with the "human factor" could have illusions as to the immediate resolution of those issues. Christians have just reason to ask, however, whether the purposes underlying present practices give promise of furthering the well-being of society. In this book we have tried to take into account the fact that few if any decisions can incorporate the full range of what is good. There remains the timeless question concerning man's awareness that his decisions and actions stand under the judgment of Eternal Wisdom.

There is rich substance for the conviction, in the face of the evidence of faith and the situation of our times, that man's role in his brief and perplexing life is to serve the Lord of creation who is also the God and Father of our Lord Jesus Christ. For all who accept this truth all economic and political systems will be ultimately judged by it.

Reflections on Ethics
and Economics

BY F. ERNEST JOHNSON

When planning this concluding volume of the series on Ethics and Economic Life the Study Committee of the Department and Dr. Obenhaus invited me to write a section dealing with some of the major fundamental and continually recurring issues that have arisen during our protracted inquiry. It was thought that, as Study Consultant to the project from 1953 on, I might contribute something to an understanding of its nature and significance. It has been a task that I relished; inevitably what I am offering is a rather highly personalized account.

At first glance the various topics discussed may seem to the reader to have been arbitrarily chosen, and presented without due regard to sequence. This would be a mistaken inference. To be sure, the breadth and depth of the subject itself have made necessary a degree of selectivity and may also have caused some abruptness in transition from one section to another. However, the selection of topics was deliberate and purposeful, and the sequence was designed.

The reader may be disposed to ask at the outset why so much attention is given to ethics *in general*—that is, to issues that are no more relevant to economics than to other areas of human interest and action. For example, the nature of moral decisions, the relation of moral "principles" to objective analysis of the situations in which the issues arise, the age-old problem of "means and ends," the distinction between compromise as moral *surrender* and compromise as moral *strategy*—why have these, and some other issues dealt with in these pages, been considered to require attention in a short essay on ethics in the sphere of economics?

This question goes to the heart of the matter. Underlying the entire discussion is a concern for the restoration in economic theory and practice, of a centuries' old belief that economics is not an autonomous, self-contained discipline, built upon a "business-is-business" philosophy, but a sphere of life in which ethics is a major factor. Hence the stress on the interplay of these disciplines, and upon the necessity of achieving and maintaining a moral consensus in the conduct, at all levels, of economic affairs. And, it must be added, the discussion that follows seeks to show that the present all-pervading anxiety over "rapid social change" cannot be allayed without a deepening of the conviction that social stability and social justice are two sides of one shield.

Since economic life is a conditioning factor in all phases of our culture and, conversely, since the community as a whole is the ultimate arbiter of economic disputes, everyone of us is among those "for whom the bell tolls."

"Ethics" and "Morals"

Let us now clear the air as to the meaning of the words "ethical" and "moral." Some scholars make a rather sharp distinction between ethics and morals—using the former word to characterize a philosophic and religious discipline and the latter to denote what its etymology suggests, namely, a set of behavior patterns, socially inherited, and imbedded in the "mores." This may explain why so many writers in our time have made a virtue of nonconformity and acquired something akin to contempt for the "conventional wisdom" that prevails in contemporary life. I have even been challenged by a graduate student in a class in educational philosophy, who contended that the words "moral" and "morality" connote a spurious ethics!

The distinctions just referred to are not without significance, but I am disposed to regard the words ethics and morals—one of Greek and the other of Latin derivation—as having virtually equivalent meanings in the context of this discussion.[1] Yet the word moral, through common usage, has come to connote an approved pattern of individual behavior which, while not unrelated to virtue, may leave much to be desired. This fact should be kept in mind as a corrective of the current mind-set against "conformity." Riesman's contention for "inner direction" of personality is no doubt sound in the intended context, but like all such generalizations it needs a sprinkling of Aristotelian wisdom: "nothing too much." For it hardly needs saying that the tendency to conform is the foundation of all communication, social activity, and group effort. Moreover, the "inner" self in large measure reflects the social environment. The phenomenon of leadership—that most important though elusive concept in the lexicon of democracy—demonstrates a type of rational, non-compulsive conformity.

Probing further, we discover that many scholars—notably those known as "positivist" in philosophy—are disposed to regard right and wrong as mental "constructs," having no ultimate significance. According to that view the statement "This is right" is to all intents equivalent to "I like it." Here we have a virtual identification of "ought to be" and "is," where the moral judgment has no more than descriptive significance. Now the descriptive phase of ethics—seeking to discover and interpret human behavior in value terms and to find the "springs" of moral impulse and action—is of great importance. But descriptive ethics is important for the very reason that it is an aid to normative ethics —the discipline concerned with analysis of behavior in terms of right and wrong, good and evil.

I hope it will be apparent that by "normative" I do not mean "authoritatively prescriptive," in the sense of seeking to bring all people to acceptance of a common mode of thought and behavior. Individual differences, which psychologists and anthropologists have taught us to take very seriously, stand in the way of any such endeavor. However people of serious mind and generous impulse are concerned with building "community." Such a concern indicates a large measure of like-mindedness, what we may call the "universal human"—essential postulate of any scheme of social order. It seems safe to say that there will always be enough in the way of individual differences to keep humanity interesting if there is enough shared conviction and purpose to keep the human adventure alive!

The perspective of such a study as we have been engaged in is, of course, sharply at variance with the positivist contention. We regard "ought" and "is" as distinct categories.[2] As descriptive, ethics may be properly called a science—a study of objective facts concerning human behavior in relation to values. As normative, it prescribes what its formulators believe to be "right"— that is, what "ought" to be done, and what is "good" as opposed to "evil." What is right is, by definition, also good, from the standpoint of the decision maker; but his value judgment may be in error as judged by his family, his community, or his church. In the last analysis he is obligated to obey his conscience in spite of adverse judgment from any source. This I understand to be in accord with Catholic and Jewish as well as Protestant teaching. But in the field of social ethics, where our inquiry lies, the individual himself is obligated to take serious account of the moral consensus of the community to which he belongs. He may then ally himself with the common judgment or oppose it by word or act. As will later appear, the matter of "moral consensus" is basic, in this writer's view, to all thinking about social ethics within a growing pluralist culture.

"Principle" and "Situation"

Here, however, a further problem arises—one with which some of our theologians have been wrestling in recent years. How should a person in the exercise of his freedom make up his mind on an issue of right and wrong about which people of high repute differ sharply? Where can he find guidance when confronted with a "forced option"—when either public duty or moral self-respect or both may compel decision? It is quite natural to all of us to reach out for explicit and trustworthy directions—partly because of a genuine yearning to "know and do the right," but partly because of a sense of insecurity. William James, one of America's truly great philosophers, spoke of the type of insecure person who wants to get a firm grasp of something that is "true, no matter what"! But truth and right are not matters for simple prescription. They do not exist "out of all relationship" but as accompaniments of intensive spiritual discipline, dedicated moral striving and—not least—intensive application of critical intelligence. They are profoundly personal.

Some Protestant theologians are now engaged in controversy over what are called the "principles" approach and the "contextual" (or "situational") approach to the making of ethical decisions. This problem is of the essence in social ethics and is at the root of much ethical turmoil in economic life; but I think it has been unhappily confused. The two "approaches" are not antithetical. On the contrary, close inspection will show them, I believe, to be inseparable authentic parts of a complete act of ethical decision.

It is a deceptively simple matter to apply what are called "general principles" to particular situations without analyzing the latter to discover the foreseeable consequences of a given course of action. This is not authentic ethical method. Rather it is an attempt to embody the "universal" in the "particular," whereas universal imperatives, such as the Decalogue embodies, can never be wholly contained in a particular case. Fitting a given principle to a particular situation may make sense with respect to "Thou shalt not covet," but doing likewise with respect to "Thou shalt not kill" has given rise to sharp controversy throughout the religious world. "Love thy neighbor as thyself"—a counsel of perfection, to be sure—is no doubt applicable to social situations generally, but it furnishes insufficient guidance in terms of practice. It gives no blueprint of what neighborly relations should be. The ethical demands in specific economic relationships present perhaps the most thorny questions of all. The "good life" cannot be determined by the number of ethical principles one has accepted for guidance, without reference to the quality of one's aims and the depth and breadth of the wisdom and courage that inform his decisions.

RESPONSIBILITY FOR CONSEQUENCES

At the heart of the matter is the relevance of probable consequences of alternative decisions on moral issues. Recently I heard one of the most eminent Protestant leaders in Europe say that the challenge to resolute action in a moral crisis is altogether independent of anticipated consequences; that one abdicates morally when he allows such considerations to influence his decision. The statement had reference to the challenge of Hitler's genocidal program to the Christian conscience. There is, of course, an authentic ring in such a statement. It recalls the declaration that faith is not "believing against the evidence, but living in scorn of consequences." If what was meant is that one should not decide a moral issue on the basis of consequences to himself, the churchman's statement readily commands assent. But the matter of foreseen consequences in their entirety is inevitably a datum for ethical judgment. As a matter of fact, great weight is given to anticipated consequences in all institutional policy and planning—religious and secular alike. How could it be otherwise?

Contemporary political conflict over "right-to-work" laws and the "right to strike," especially on the part of public employees, has intensified the "rights" issue in this country. A serious aspect of the unending controversy over the rights of labor and those of management is the fact that absolutist claims by either side can be made with deceptive plausibility. Employers tend to regard the demand for "union security" through the union shop as patently a violation of the right not to belong to a union. Labor leaders look upon "right-to-work" laws as an infringement of the right of a union member to work alongside his fellow unionists.

There could be no better illustration of the ethical confusion that results from seizing upon a single "principle" and giving to it a sort of "eminent domain" which takes precedence over all other factors in the working situation. Indeed, solutions in this kind of controversy can seldom be arrived at by "yes" or "no" decisions. As a contemporary writer has said, there is too much "gray" area—neither black nor white—to admit of such a facile judgment.

This matter is so important as to warrant more specific illustration. Take the prevalent attitude of union labor toward "crossing a picket line." It is a valid attitude for union labor and for the public in general—provided the cause that gave rise to the strike is a valid one. It can be argued that where the grievance against which the union concerned is protesting is a real one, and if there is reason to believe that the union strategy is well conceived—if these considerations have been met, then the public may be under ethical obligation to give the strikers moral support and perhaps to join them in making the strike effective. But there are some strikes that lack moral and economic justification, and it may happen that conscientious citizens will feel obligated to throw their influence on the other side and ignore the pickets.

Something should be said—and done—about absolute prohibition of labor strikes, which many people would like to see enacted into law. This is "extremism." Henry Ford II should have had an "Oscar" for his recent statement on the subject as reported in the press: "There seems to be a widespread assumption that government and public opinion will no longer tolerate strikes in major industries and therefore that a real strike in the automotive industry is out of the question this year. I am convinced that responsible bargaining is most unlikely if the very possibility of a strike is ruled out from the beginning. . . . The best and probably the only effective way to prevent [one party's] over-reaching is to preserve the possibility that a strike may occur." Elementary, as Sherlock Holmes might say.

As for prohibition of strikes by public employes, the state of New York has its Condon-Wadlin Act, which has been virtually a dead letter from the beginning. There is much to be said for its purpose, but it should be clear by now that unless the workers are convinced that ample compensation in pay or in some other form is given them for surrender of a "right" that other workers enjoy, the problem has not been solved. It is essential to a working principle of ethics or equity that it shall not violate the common man's conception of "fair play"—a common denominator of all successful social engineering.

By the same token labor's traditional, unconditional rejection of compulsory arbitration is an example of making an excellent working rule into an absolute principle—in spite of the obvious fact that in cases of nationwide involvement this could lead to industrial paralysis and national catastrophe. To repeat, nothing is more hazardous than the attempt to make a universal principle yield an authentic specific directive for ethical action, without regard for presumptive consequences in a particular situation.

To be sure, I have known a devout and renowned Christian leader to declare that God will never allow a person who trusts in him to be confronted by a situation so morally ambiguous that some absolute principle cannot be invoked to resolve it. This is surely a lamentable illusion. God summons the intellect as well as the conscience. How vastly more placid this life would be if its ambiguities could be so simply resolved! But would we still be men?

MEANS AND ENDS

The age-old problem of "means and ends" confronts us here. "The end justifies the means" is not a mere worldly maxim, as is often assumed. Strictly speaking, nothing but the end can validate the means. After all, what does "means" mean? Whatever is designated as "means" is a path leading to some end. The means can, of course, be so evil in itself as to "corrupt the end." But a means can be qualitatively validated only by reference to an end. "Doing evil that good may come" is really a self-contradictory formula: if predominantly good results flow from a deliberate deviation from an accepted moral code, a reappraisal of the code is in order. This is one way in which ethical progress comes about.

The controversy in the soft coal industry in the 1920s which resulted in a stoppage of work and other similar controversies have amply illustrated the confusion that may arise when an ethically ambiguous situation confronts a person, a group, or an organization with a forced option. We all probably have been involved in such situations. The mandate that usually emerges is "choose the lesser of two evils." But does not this miss the point?

The person involved is not so much "choosing" the one as avoiding the other. Perhaps the reason why many very conscientious people reject the "lesser evil" principle is that to "choose evil" is prima facie an unsanctifiable act. What is of paramount importance is to escape the unacceptable alternative of doing nothing. It seems to me that our moralists sometimes induce in inquiring minds a sort of emotional paralysis.

To put the whole matter in extreme form for emphasis, what guilt can possibly attach to the physician who closes his ears to a pitiful emergency call because he is hastening to another emergency case where the patient hovers between life and death? The very formulation of such a question seems childish. Yet if we insist on making the words "evil" and "sin" interchangeable, do we not thrust ourselves into a logical—and ethical—impasse? Life itself drives us to the recognition that ethical decisions are relative —or better perhaps, relational—in a prevailingly gray world where black-and-white contrasts are seldom encountered. But to affirm this does not negate principles, even absolutes. My duty to put forth my best effort to be of some use in the world admits of no diminution; it is absolute. "We have an absolute duty to do our relative best." Just as infinity is an indispensable concept in mathematics, so the unattainable ultimate is indispensable in ethics. Man's reach must "exceed his grasp." And concern with the ultimate is a distinguishing mark of religion at its highest level.

What Is a Principle?

To say all this is, of course, to invite the question, what precisely is a principle? In the view I am presenting and in the context of the above discussion a principle is a generalized statement of a moral value that we hold to be ultimate. Incidentally, a useful distinction with respect to the use of the word "value" was made by a noted educator some years ago: there are technical, economic values that are thought of as things one can enrich himself with by possessing—things one can have; but values that are thought of as improving what one will be, are in the moral category. This is a useful distinction. A principle derives its force from the value consensus behind it. But it stands in contrast to a rule, which is specific and explicit in what it enjoins.

To illustrate, a well-known company in the clothing industry many years ago experienced no little embarrassment over a clause in its union contract which stipulated the right of the employer to introduce labor-saving machinery. Although the union accepted it in principle, trouble arose when the company disclosed its intention to bring into the plant a machine that would eliminate a whole department! The union spokesmen, when the company cited the permissive clause in the contract, said, "Sure, we agreed to introduction of machinery, but we never meant anything like that!" The "impartial chairman" held up the company's proposal on the ground that it was likely to put too great a strain on the agreement. He knew that the letter of the contract was less important than keeping the structure of labor relations intact. A sound principle was involved, but it could not be translated into a specific, uniform rule of action without reckoning with conditioning factors in the situation that affected the requirements of equity.

A grievous industrial conflict in the soft coal industry into which I was once drawn made a lasting impression on my mind because the labor union, which had the stronger case in contractual—abstractly moral—terms, was on the weak side in economic terms. The industry was in the doldrums. The existing agreement was quite out of line with market conditions, but the union officials were disposed to focus attention on the one fact that the operators had gone back on the agreement to maintain the specified wage scale. That is to say, the mines were opened after many miners had begged for work on the company's terms, and the strike was broken. I spent hours one day discussing the matter with a union official, who began by unconditionally condemning the company for a palpably immoral act. But after an hour or so he said, "It seems that the more we talk about this, the more ethics moves into the background, while economics comes into the foreground." The real point, as I saw it, was that consideration of the context changed the nature of the ethical issue itself.

The lesson I drew from all this was that no working agreement that is out of line with economic realities—like an international treaty that is out of line with political realities—will prove viable. Hence it rests on a shaky moral foundation. Keeping one's word is indeed an indispensable condition of integrity and moral prestige. But if the conditions of fulfillment are lacking, the element of obligation calls for reassessment.

It is important to note, on the other hand, that those who seem to have become preoccupied with "situational ethics" to the point of relative unconcern with principles are also unrealistic. Principles, I have said, are generalized statements of moral values, which means that when appropriated by an individual, they have a dispositional effect that determines what kind of person he is. They become a wellspring from which he draws sustenance. The late John Dewey, America's foremost exponent of the pragmatic philosophy—in which the truth of a proposition is defined by the consequences of its acceptance for action—once wrote an impressive passage (which I suspect many of his students and followers have not read) that strikes me as embodying an important insight. I quote it here:

We are sure that the *attitude* of personal kindliness, of sincerity and fairness, will make our judgment of the effects of a proposed action on the good of others infinitely more likely to be correct than will those of hate, hypocrisy, and self-seeking. A man who trusted simply to details of external consequences might readily convince himself that the removal of a certain person by murder would contribute to general happiness. One cannot imagine an honest person convincing himself that a disposition of disregard for human life would have beneficial consequences. It is true, on one hand, that the ultimate standard for judgment of acts is their objective consequences; the outcome constitutes the meaning of an act. But it is equally true that the warrant for correctness of judgment and for power of judgment to operate as an influence in conduct lies in the intrinsic make-up of character; it would be safer to trust a man of a kind and honest disposition without much ability in calculation than it would a man having great power of foresight of the future who was malicious and insincere.[3]

Here we have the two aspects of the moral life shown in relation to each other: (1) concern for the consequences of one's decisions, which impels him to a searching analysis of the situation calling for a moral judgment; and (2) a character structure, a basic disposition, a discipline of the spirit, that will "weight" one's moral decisions on the side of the best in his cultural tradition—in other words, on the side of principle. Exclusive dependence on the foreseen consequences of a decision opens the door to expediency and "rationalizing." And since there are always contingencies involved in a forecast of consequences, the "probable error," as the statisticians say, in this process is more formidable. But what person of mature mind does not realize that there is an ineluctable element of tragedy in human life? Martin Luther's agonized cry when he made his momentous decision is a classic example of the birth pangs of a moral judgment that will have unpredictable consequences: "Here I stand. I cannot do otherwise. God help me. Amen."

Crucial moral decisions are made under pressures from without and from within. When subsequent events validate them, they become a part of our cultural heritage, of our wealth in terms of moral principle.

ETHICS OF COMPROMISE

What has just been said bears directly on the much-debated issue of compromise—a matter that surely needs clarification. The ambiguity is the result, I suppose, of our making one word do the work of two, for compromise has two distinct meanings. Compromising a principle is, of course, a moral fault, indicating cowardice or hypocrisy. On the other hand, compromising disputed claims in business, industry, or politics may be a valid and wise choice of "half a loaf" as an alternative to "no bread." This is implied in the familiar saying that "politics is the art of the possible." Compromise in this sense underlies the enlightened and growing practice of arbitration in the business world.

But difficulty arises when it is said that a compromise of this second kind is morally justifiable, and even "the will of God," and it is then added that nevertheless it is sinful. This seems to be carrying authentic paradox into outright contradiction! If a well-motivated decision leads to results that are, and were foreseen to be, in part bad but nevertheless the best that could be obtained, the person making this compromise has a deep moral need to feel that he is not fractionally right, but unexceptionably right—in this particular instance. The situations that life confronts us with are ambiguous enough, at best, and the inner impulsion to possess what the Latin poet Virgil called a *mens conscia recti* (a clear conscience) is, I must contend, unassailable. A morally right decision is certified as such not merely by the quantitative results to which it actually leads but by the intention it embodies and the plus value that it represents. One must bear responsibility for the consequences of his acts; this is a requirement of justice. But to be limited in foresight is often an inescapable human predicament. Paul Tillich has dealt with this point in an impressive paragraph:

We may ask . . . whether a moral decision can stand under an unconditional imperative if the decision is a moral risk—the "risk" implying that it might prove to be the wrong decision. The answer to this question is that the unconditional character does not refer to the content, but to the form of the moral decision. Whichever side of a moral alternative might be chosen, however great the risk in a bold decision may be, if it be a *moral* decision it is dependent only on the pure "ought to be" of the moral imperative. And should anyone be in doubt as to which of several possible acts conforms to the moral imperative, he should be reminded that each of them might be justified in a particular situation, but that whatever he chooses must be done with the consciousness of standing under an unconditional imperative.[4]

A striking brief statement on compromise is found in John Morley's essay bearing that title. He holds that the issue "obviously turns upon the placing of the boundary that divides wise suspense in forming opinions, wise reserve in expressing them, and wise tardiness in trying to realise them, from unavowed disingenuousness and self-illusion, from voluntary dissimulation, and from indolence and pusillanimity." *Multum in parvo!*

I said earlier that the "principle" and "contextual" aspects of decision making are inseparable parts of a complete ethical act. The ethics of compromise shows the reciprocal relationship strikingly. The art of political compromise can avoid the abyss of hypocrisy and shallow expediency only by keeping the ethical principles involved continually in mind. Only so will the boundaries of legitimate, objective compromise remain clear.

But what I have just written leaves out of account something that classical Christian theology holds essential, namely, the sinfulness of human nature at its best—in theological language, original sin. This term is puzzling to laymen. (A nationally known churchman and business executive who participated actively in the study that we are now bringing to conclusion once said to me, "I have read and reread Niebuhr's *The Nature and Destiny of Man*, but I don't believe in original sin!") What is the meaning of the biblical account of the human predicament "original righteousness," the "fall," and the consequent unfitness to dwell in the garden of God? Realistic theologians have utilized the category of myth to designate materials that have come down to us in narrative form but whose meaning is manifestly symbolic rather than historical. But no amount of critical analysis or interpretation of scripture can dissolve away the moral facts of experience on which man's need of salvation is predicated. These facts of experience have taught man that in the process of evolution he has changed from an unmoral being to a being equipped with a conscience and prone to make wrong decisions. That in our day this is thought of as a "rise" rather than a "fall" is beside the point.

It is therefore quite true that the conscious rectitude which a person is entitled to feel and needs to feel, with respect to a particular moral decision, would be vitiated by complacency and pride that obliterate the consciousness that the human condition is one of standing under the judgment of God. This, it seems to me, may be taken as a fitting commentary on the Scriptural confession, "We are unprofitable servants; we have done only what was our duty to do." That paradoxical cry embodies both a vast humility and the spiritual satisfaction of having rendered obedience.

I am contending for a resolution of this paradox, not by looking upon an ethically imperative compromise as infected with sin—which seems to me an egregious error and a counsel of moral despair—but rather by continual awareness that sincere acts of moral decision, though "reckoned unto us for righteousness," do not cancel out smugness and pride, to which Christian saints through the centuries have felt themselves prone. Nor does rendering a decision that is a morally necessary coming-to-terms with ugly realities lighten the burden of responsibility for doing something toward destroying the evil that frustrates the nobler strivings of which human beings are capable.

Is There a "Christian Social Ethics"?

In the course of this study we have heard from time to time the troubled inquiry, "What is distinctively Christian in what you are writing?" It is a serious and important challenge, which must be dealt with. My own answer is that we are dealing with public problems confronting a pluralist society and attempting to give some guidance to Christians with respect to issues whose resolution requires cooperation on the part of citizens belonging to different faiths or professing no religious faith; and that we are aiming at a moral consensus that is authentically but not exclusively Christian. An undertaking of this sort is inevitably concerned with "contextual" analysis of ethical problems whose impact is virtually the same on all citizens who have equivalent moral sensitiveness, regardless of religious affiliation. Not only so, but the body of moral "principles" generally recognized among us is basically a Judaeo-Christian heritage.

There is a Christian social ethics in the sense that Christians witness to the lordship of Christ and seek in the Christian *koinonia* (spiritual fellowship) distinctive ways of "practicing the presence of God." But in a pluralist society in which a biblical, Judaeo-Christian tradition is recognized, an effective moral consensus is essential for conceiving and implementing ethical ends. In such a society the moral consensus so seriously needed cannot be built on a foundation that is the exclusive possession of one faith group.

Nevertheless the question raised in the above caption is important. In his *Ethics in a Christian Context* Paul L. Lehmann, of

Union Theological Seminary, presents a systematic exposition of
koinonia ethics, that is, the ethics that grows out of the experience
of fellowship and work in a Christian community.[5] This *koinonia*
ethics contrasts sharply with traditional ethics, which is in the
philosophical tradition. In general, ethics is taught as a philosophic discipline. Every student of ethics must have been impressed by the fact that the various "schools" of ethics deal
with much the same subject matter. The *koinonia* ethics is constructed on a different pattern. It is contextual in the sense indicated above, and existential in its approach to ethical issues. Its
focus is on the concrete Christian community. This is to the good:
"Nothing is real until it becomes local." But it is also true that
nothing of basic spiritual importance is "real" until it transcends
the local and the particular.

Years of fruitful cooperation between Christians and Jews in
this country have set a pattern for interfaith efforts in the field
of social ethics. We have long been impressed with the parallel
between the social teachings of the Old Testament prophets and
the teachings of Jesus. For many years leaders of the several faiths
worked together in the pattern set for Protestants in the "Social
Ideals of the Churches," or equivalent declarations.

I have tried to make clear that the contextual or situational
approach to a working ethics has characterized this study; otherwise we would have been content with cataloguing the "principles"! Indeed, I would call the adherence to contextual method
a "first principle" of such inquiry. I have always emphasized it
in my efforts to teach ethics. There is a polarity between universal
and particular, between "principle" and context. And I venture
to suggest that when terms are fully defined, the area of conflict
among students of ethics is much reduced. Consider the following
passage in Lehmann's book:

A contextual ethic deals with behavior basically in *indicative* rather
than in imperative terms. This does not mean that there are no
ethical demands. It means that such ethical demands as are authentic
acquire meaning and authority from specific ethical relationships,
and the latter constitute the context out of which these demands
emerge and which shapes the demands. This is why the definitive

question with which Christian ethics has to do has been formulated, not as "what *ought* I . . . ," but rather as "what *am* I, as a believer in Jesus Christ and as a member of his church, to do?"[6]

This, it seems to me, means that the "ethical demands"—which constitute our "principles"—"acquire meaning and authority" only as their relevance to specific situations is established. Only so can the question "What am I . . . to do?" be answered. It seems to me also that the "imperative" is not wanting in this ethical framework but is implied in the urgent inquiry "What ought I . . . ?" The indicative—the "what" of that question— emerges as a result of an inner compulsion to respond to the challenge of an actual situation. John C. Bennett's discussion of this subject has impressed me so much that I am prompted to quote rather extensively from it.[7]

The trend toward contextual ethics has many sources. One is the recognition by students of Christian Ethics of the complexity of the factors that enter into our concrete decisions. All of us agree that there is no direct line from Christian ideals to these concrete decisions, that they involve many technical judgments concerning which there is no distinctively Christian guidance, that there are judgments of strategy in relation to the use of power which belong to a different world from that of abstract Christian principles, that many of our choices are difficult, indeed agonizing, choices between evils, no one of which fits ideal prescriptions. The "existentialist" mood of the times casts discredit on universal ethical judgments. Many of our most influential theologians have sharply challenged any Christian ethic that is based upon principles.

Here it is appropriate to notice the "existentialist" element in contextualism. The late H. R. Niebuhr made a revealing statement in his *Christ and Culture*. Of the decisions Christians have to make "in the midst of cultural history" he said:

They are existential as well as relative decisions; that is to say, they are decisions that cannot be reached by speculative inquiry, but must be made in freedom by a responsible subject acting in the present moment on the basis of what is true for him. Kierkegaard, to whom belongs the honor of having underscored and ministered to this existential nature of the irreducible self more than any other modern thinker, can be something of a guide to us in our effort to understand how, in facing our enduring problem, we must and can arrive at our answer, rather than at *the* Christian answer.[8]

Returning to Bennett's comments, we find an illuminating passage:

Sometimes the contextual emphasis is presented in such a way that it seems to provide a religious short-cut to wisdom about the situation because of the language that is used. We are exhorted to respond to what God is doing in the situation. . . . To determine what God is doing in the situation is no easier than it is to decide what we should do, though exhortations of this kind often seem to assume that what God is doing is an obvious matter.

Bennett makes this specific comment on the *koinonia* ethic:

There is a special problem in connection with "koinonia ethics." When Christians make decisions about matters of public policy, they must usually think and act with non-Christians and so there must be some common moral convictions which guide them. These convictions may be derived from revelation ultimately in a society which is strongly influenced by Christianity but even so they can still be defended by considerations which have a broader base than the Christian revelation. There is operating here at least an equivalent of the idea of "natural law," if that phrase seems to represent too rigid a pattern to be useful.

I think an especially valuable contribution to this entire discussion is Bennett's emphasis on "what Christians bring to the situation." Even though an interfaith group, including perhaps some secular humanists, may find their substantive contributions to the analysis of the situation calling for decision quite similar, there are sure to be significant elements in the discussion which grow out of the several religious and ethical traditions. To bring these out is a major purpose of "dialogue."

It interests me in this connection that H. R. Niebuhr in his book *The Meaning of Revelation* says that revelation should be understood as confessional, that is, as having particular relevance to distinctive elements in the prevailing tradition.

It seems strange that a distinction well established in the Scholastic theology has not been capitalized in Protestant theology.

Two Greek words (found in an English dictionary) distinguish the two phases of moral decision making. *Synteresis* (conscience, in the general sense of recognizing moral obligation) corresponds to "principle," as I have used it in this discussion. *Syneidesis* is the denotative term, expressing a particular judgment as to what the moral imperative demands in terms of action in a particular situation. The second of those moral categories is the realm of casuistry, in the valid and useful sense of that term.

I don't expect these classical terms to find their way into Protestant theological discourse, but what they stand for would be helpful in Protestant thinking.

THE QUEST OF CERTAINTY

The preceding discussion almost inevitably raises the question of moral certainty as prelude to decision. A troublesome question arises between morality and religion on the one hand and science on the other, concerning the ultimate test of "truth." The late Edmund W. Sinnott of Yale, a noted scientist, forcefully and impressively defended the claim of religion to be regarded as a source of truth, parallel with that of science. He said that "most of our attitudes and reactions are not the result of reason, of taking logical thought about them, but spring directly into consciousness through the natural qualities of our minds, molded by conditioning and experience. . . . These deep, instinctive feelings, coming directly from living stuff itself, just as the still more primitive physiological reactions do, and without the mediation of conscious mind, may be our closest contact with reality. This is the province of the human spirit."[9]

Nevertheless, is there not a harmful confusion in identifying truth, in the sense of correspondence with factual reality—which science undertakes to establish—with the kind of validity and worth which the religious seer or moral philosopher feels he has established in his own way? I was struck by a remark made to me by an eminent and scholarly Jewish rabbi: "You Christians think differently from us on theological matters. You think *propositionally.*" His point was sharpened by what another learned rabbi said to me: "Any statement in the form 'God is . . .' is untrue; we can't make factual, existential statements about deity." Such statements suggest the existentialist slogan *Wahrheit ist Begegnung* (Truth is Encounter).

They also call to mind that the original name for the Apostles' Creed was the Old Roman Symbol and that in the theological curriculum the study of creeds was once known as "symbolics."

In a recent book John Herman Randall, Jr., one of our foremost American philosophers, discusses the scope and limits of "knowledge" and "knowing." He concludes: "It is well to keep 'truth' for the knowledge that is science, with all its complex procedures and criteria for verifying propositions that can be stated in words."[10] He discerns, however, in the scientists' own current vocabulary a tendency to employ such terms as "warranted assertibility" instead of "scientific truth" where the latter would imply finality of empirical inquiry and intellectual grasp. And he adds: "Perhaps, after all, we have at last come the full circle. Perhaps it is now the visions of the unified possibilities of the world—of the Divine, of the 'order of splendor'—that we are once more permitted to call 'true.'"

This is a rugged road for mental travel, but we may find on it guideposts to what Felix Adler called "the knowledge and practice and love of the right." Also it somehow calls to my mind that simple, nontheological, now centuries-old Christian classic, Brother Lawrence's "Practice of the Presence of God."

Economic Change—Cultural Lag

Since our protracted study was begun, this country has become greatly concerned over "rapid social change." The intensity of this concern was inevitable because of the profound influence that the "technological revolution" has already had on our culture. To say this is not to embrace a philosophy of economic determinism but only to recognize the obvious effects of economic patterns and levels of life upon an industrial society.

But there is an aspect of this subject that I think has not had sufficient attention. It has to do with the concept "cultural lag," which claimed the attention of sociologists a few decades ago. In other words, it has to do not with the over-all facts of social change but with an ominous differential between the rates of change in different parts of our culture. I will try to show that this fact is of great importance for the ethical progress of the nation. As elaborated by an eminent American sociologist this phrase expressed the characteristic difference between the rates of growth in the "material culture" and the "adaptive culture."[11] For example, the factory system came into being long before workmen's compensation for injuries was established and before industry recognized the evils of child labor. Automobiles and airplanes filled highways and skyways with almost incredible rapidity while society groped for methods and measures that would bring the new monsters under rational human control. Today automation confronts us with the same problem in a new dimension: can social invention—the development of new services and new ways of employing time in creative fashion—keep pace with our galloping technology in pursuit of the goal of full employment? In other words, can the adaptive phase of our culture be made to keep abreast of the material, mechanical phase?

No one is able to answer this question unless he is ready to assume an improbable lowering of living standards. My concern here is less with the answer than with the nature of the problem. It seems clear to me that the main reason why society is so tardy in adapting itself socially and politically to the brisk march of technology is that the financial rewards afforded by material progress are so great in comparison with those of activities in the nonprofit area, particularly in what is commonly designated the "public sector" of the economy. A conspicuous example today is the plight of public education. It should be obvious that the need for school plants, equipment, and personnel increases as the tempo of social change is stepped up and the functions of citizenship become more complicated and at the same time more vital. Incidentally, if this country should actually find ways to recruit, train, and maintain a body of teachers adequate for the nation's needs, a very considerable part of its unemployment problem in this area of automation would be solved.

PROFIT SYSTEM AND PROFIT MOTIVE

Much ink has been spilled in controversy over the profit motive, as if it were necessary to make a virtue of it in order to defend the profit system. Such discussion misses the point. Indeed, there is a rather surprising correspondence between what some of our realistic theologians have written about the sinfulness of man and what defenders of the classical economics have had to say about the necessity of the profit incentive because of the self-interest inherent in human nature. One can be as critical of the motive of private profit as any economic radical, yet defend the profit system as the only demonstrated way to accumulate and conserve the social surplus. Not only so, but one may consistently contend for a rigorous discipline of the profit motive as essential to the continued workability of the profit system. The making of profit is essential to the survival of economic enterprise, regardless of whether it accrues to individual owners, is shared with employees, is "plowed back" into plant and equipment as capital, or—one may add—used to compensate management for what the income tax has taken out of their salaries! In any case, there is good reason to think that whatever may have been true in the past, the "maximization of profit" as an end in itself is far from being an exclusive concern on the part of business and industrial management. The late John Maurice Clark, one of the most far-seeing and ethically sensitive among American economists in this century, had this to say on the point:

Corporate business must still consider profits, and it has an obligation to do as well by its equity investors as it reasonably can. But when economic theorists describe business as "maximizing profits," they are indulging in an impossible and unrealistic degree of precision. The farther a firm's policies extend into the future, the less certain can it be just what policy will precisely "maximize profits." The company is more likely to be consciously concerned with reasonably assured survival as a paramount aim, and beyond this, to formulate its governing policies in terms of some such concept as "sound business," usually contributory to healthy growth. . . .

Where there is this margin of uncertainty as to precisely what policy would "maximize profits," there is room for management to give the benefit of the doubt to policies that represent good economic citizenship. And it seems that an increasing number of managements are giving increasing weight to this kind of consideration.[12]

The reason for the well-known opposition of the early church to the taking of interest seems to have been the strong belief that only effort can earn—that money is "sterile" as far as creating wealth is concerned. Profit in the strict sense was unknown in those early days, it came into being along with the "entrepreneur." He was the person who organized the establishment; he was the enterpriser. Theoretically he went into the capital market for the needed money and into the labor market for workers, rented the required land, erected plant, equipped it, and began to manufacture or to buy and sell goods. Against the proceeds he charged wages for labor and management including his own, "ground rent" on the land, and interest on invested capital. The balance, if any, was his profit.

Today the distinction between interest and dividends has been blurred, but the essence of the matter has not changed. That is to say, profit is the excess of earnings over all fixed or legal charges. This is why critics of the profit system call profit "something for nothing," that is, for no physical or mental labor, since all work at every level is rewarded in the wage category. As already said, the question of legitimacy of profit would seem to be one of the over-all utility of private profit as a means of conserving the "social surplus." In the matter of motive I see no essential ethical difference between profit and earned income—if we assume that the profit justifies itself in the respect just indicated. One can be exploitative in the use of money that comes to him in salary or wages as well as in his use of a dividend check. When the late Stanley Baldwin presented the British government with one-half of his wealth, hoping many other wealthy citizens would follow suit, he was illustrating the fact that one can dedicate his profit as well as his earned income. The hoped for result seems never to have come.

"CONSUMER SOVEREIGNTY"

Much has been written about the "sovereign" role of the consumer in the operation of the market. While management, labor, and government exercise "countervailing power," consumers are in general not in position to use economic power to equivalent advantage. Leland Gordon, an authority on this subject, has written:

The concept of consumer sovereignty has persisted 180 years. Among businessmen it is still popular. Defenders of the *status quo* pay it faithful lip service. Operating within the social and economic institutional framework of the United States, the traditional function of the consumer has been to guide production. Responding to his wishes, producers produce only those goods and services consumers want, according to this concept. The consumer expresses his wishes by casting dollar votes. Everytime he spends money in the market place, or fails to spend, he "votes." Producers fit their actions to his wishes. By ordering only what he wants, by rejecting inferior quality and insufficient quantity, and by paying only a fair price, the consumer determines what shall be produced, what shall not be produced, and at the same time eliminates the unscrupulous producer.

A serious defect in the concept of dollar voting lies in the fact that income is unevenly distributed. Consumers with many dollars can cast many votes, while those with few dollars have correspondingly few votes. Like corporation stockholders, consumers vote according to the number of dollar "shares" they have in the economy. Obviously such a system of voting gives some consumers more influence.[13]

Toward a Moral Consensus

This discussion is not designed to be a defense or a rejection of any "system." Its main purpose is to direct attention to a cultural situation in America—a situation in which it is very difficult to find a "moral consensus" concerning national goals. In brief, I mean the seeming predominance in our culture of divisive over integrative forces. To be sure, most of us would doubtless agree that our economic system contrasts favorably with the crude mercantilism which it displaced. Also we are probably agreed that what we were taught to call "laissez-faire" economics has been greatly modified. Altered patterns of economic power in America under the impact first of the Great Depression and then of World War II have gone far to make the term "welfare state" a recognized descriptive phrase instead of "fighting words."

In spite of all this there goes on among us what may perhaps be called an economic "cold war" between some of the greatest of our corporations and the federal government—both its executive and judicial branches. And the sharpest encounters are over violations of a fundamental tenet of the classical economics: "free competition." "Big Labor" now and then enters the same arena in defiance of government and in spite of public protests. Indeed, a significant aspect of this situation is the nonexistence of definitive public opinion because there is no such entity as the "general public" in relation to particular issues and events. Rather there are variant *ad hoc* "publics" which take form in response to fortuitous and unpredictable developments.

There is nothing really novel about this. It stems from the fragmentizing of the culture politically and religiously with the transition from the medieval to the modern era. The most significant feature of that transition is, I think, the acquisition by the economy of an autonomous status—in sharp contrast to the medieval system which preceded it. "Business is business" sloganizes this modern philosophy.

It will, I think, clarify and fortify this discussion to present here two illuminating descriptive accounts of the bearing of ethics and religion on economic life at the close of the medieval period. The first is by Ernst Troeltsch, in his monumental two-volume work *The Social Teachings of the Christian Churches*. Concerning the ethics of the age in its economic aspect, Troeltsch says:

> The whole spirit of this way of thinking on economic matters may be summed up thus: property and gain are based upon the personal performance of work; goods are exchanged only when necessary, and then only according to the principles of a just price, which does not give an undue advantage to anyone; (this 'just price' is best regulated by the Government), consumption is regulated (a) in accordance with the principle of moderation, which only permits the natural purpose of the maintenance of existence to be fulfilled, and (b) which makes room for a generosity which takes the needs of others into account; at the same time great differences in social position and in fortune, and therefore in the exercise of liberality, are fully recognized.[14]

The second passage is from the pen of the late R. H. Tawney in his well-known book *Religion and the Rise of Capitalism*.

The criticism which dismisses the concern of Churches with economic relations and social organization as a modern innovation finds little support in past history. What requires explanation is not the view that these matters are part of the province of religion, but the view that they are not. When the age of the Reformation begins, economics is still a branch of ethics, and ethics of theology; all human activities are treated as falling within a single scheme, whose character is determined by the spiritual destiny of mankind; the appeal of theorists is to natural law, not to utility; the legitimacy of economic transactions is tried by reference, less to the movements of the market, than to moral standards derived from the traditional teaching of the Christian Church; the Church itself is regarded as a society wielding theoretical, and sometimes practical, authority in social affairs. The secularization of political thought, which was to be the work of the next two centuries, had profound reactions on social speculation, and by the Restoration the whole perspective, at least in England, has been revolutionized. Religion has been converted from the keystone which holds together the social edifice into one department within it, and the idea of a rule of right is replaced by economic expediency as the arbiter of policy and the criterion of conduct.[15]

The disposition, of course, to glorify the Middle Ages because of this "mediaeval synthesis" of all aspects of life, built upon a common faith, reflects a superficial view of that era, but the historical significance of the latter, as Tawney depicts it, is beyond question. The task with which it confronts us is not that of turning back the clock but of building out of an ample heritage a value structure that will bear the weight of a vast and complex civilization—the "Great Society," as it is being called.

To repeat, we are in a period of rapid economic change, due in the first instance to developments in technology. It sets the pace, so to speak, because it makes possible two coveted achievements: a great increase in productivity and an indeterminate but very substantial reduction in labor costs. This will mean a quantitative, not a qualitative, change in the economic scene, but sheer magnitude may make the difference between the "developmental" and the "revolutionary." Our history indicates that "cultural lag" will widen the gap between lucrative productivity and the social adjustments which that entails. This may be expected to increase the moral ambivalence and confusion on the economic scene, and what I have called the predominance of the divisive over the integrative forces in our national life. To prevent this, it seems to me, is the problem of problems in our time for "general" education on all cultural levels.

"Natural Law"

Walter Lippmann has written cogently on this theme in his book *The Public Philosophy*,[16] by which term he means the "natural law." Now, the "natural law" concept does not, of course, refer to the field of the natural sciences but to the moral law conceived of as given by an all-wise Creator. It was current among American intellectuals in the Revolutionary era, as witness the use of the phrase "the laws of Nature and of Nature's God." Philosophically it is a deistic rather than a theistic formula. Since the time of Jefferson, however, natural law has come to be a familiar term in theological writings.

In spite of what he calls the "semantic confusion" to which this term gives rise and the general neglect of the idea of a "public philosophy," Lippmann defends it emphatically. "If," he writes, "the discussion of public philosophy has been, so to speak, tabled in the liberal democracies, can we assume that, though it is not being discussed, there is a public philosophy? Is there a body of positive principles and precepts which a good citizen cannot deny or ignore? I am writing this book in the conviction that there is. It is a conviction which I have acquired gradually, not so much from a theoretical education, but rather from the practical experience of seeing how hard it is for our generation to make democracy work." He says further: "Except on the premises of this philosophy, it is impossible to reach intelligible and workable conceptions of popular election, majority rule, representative assemblies, free speech, loyalty, property, corporations and voluntary associations. The founders of these institutions, which the recently enfranchised democracies have inherited, were all of them adherents of some one of the various schools of natural law."

Mr. Lippmann sees a progressive alienation of the citizenry from the public philosophy, on which their own institutions were founded. He is not calling for a return to the Middle Ages, but he asks the startling, "poignant" question whether modern men can recover contact with the lost traditions, and if so, how. If I understand him, he is in search of a way to insure the ascendancy of the integrative forces in our culture.

Protestants have had much difficulty with the "natural law" concept as Roman Catholic writers have freely used it, because they believe that it encourages an artificial, stereotyped casuistry and freezes patterns of moral behavior for which authority is claimed. It will be evident to the reader that in terms of the preceding discussion Lippmann, who is highly esteemed as a social and political analyst, is arguing for the indispensability of principle in relation to situational context.

"Legitimate Power"

Let me put alongside the Lippmann analysis some statements by Peter Drucker, one of the most perceptive contemporary students of our industrial society. In this book *The Future of Industrial Man*[17] he examines the nature and locus of power in our society and distinguishes two types, "legitimate" and "illegitimate." His definitions are intriguing and, I think, bear significantly on the argument I am trying to sketch. "Legitimate power," he writes, "stems from the same *basic belief of society regarding man's nature and fulfillment* on which the individual's social status and function rest. Indeed, legitimate power can be defined as rulership which finds its justification in *the basic ethos of the society*" (my italics). In contrast, "illegitimate power is a power which does not derive its claim from the basic beliefs of the society. Accordingly, there is no possibility to decide whether the ruler wielding the power is exercising it in conformity with the purpose of power or not; for there is no social purpose." By its very nature it is irresponsible, since "there is no criterion of responsibility, no socially accepted final authority for its justification."

But alongside this somber picture we may place a more encouraging prospect. Ernst Troeltsch has said of Thomism, "the great fundamental form of Catholic social philosophy," that "alongside of the ordinary secular institutions an idea has arisen, an idea which will certainly never be allowed to die out, a universal, ethical, and religious idea, the idea, namely, of personality united with God, and of human society united with God, and this idea is struggling to create a society which will accord with its point of view, and it must aspire to carry out those ideas into the life of the whole, far beyond the circle of the particular religious community."[18]

Here we have a prefiguring of the vision which the Social Gospel movement long afterward undertook to fix in men's minds. Also the words "a universal, ethical, and religious idea . . . of a human society united with God" express the goal toward which this essay is pointed.

ETHICS OF DEMOCRACY

Reference was made by Walter Lippmann to the problem of "making democracy work." Even the basic concepts embodied in that word—equality, liberty, universal suffrage, popular sovereignty, and so on—call insistently for scrutiny and definition today. Equality is admittedly not a matter of fact in any general sense, yet we cannot escape it as ethical mandate. Liberty—the word is politically oriented—is thought of as absence of restraint, and as such it is a bedrock concept, for it stands between the person and the political state. In ethical terms it means freeing individual persons for voluntary dedication to self-chosen ends. Freedom means obedience, as Saint Paul insisted—obedience not to a tribunal but to a divine imperative that engages conscience. When a person is consciously committed to the "more excellent way," he feels free. Liberty has to be defined and assured by government. Freedom is won in voluntary commitment.

> Our fathers, chained in prisons dark,
> Were still in heart and conscience free.

We have stressed the different rates of change between the "material" culture and the "adaptive" culture and the further widening of the gap which automation may be expected to bring about. It is not a bright picture, if one takes seriously what I have tried to set forth—with the aid of wisdom borrowed from others —concerning the imperative need of a moral consensus among the American people. The lack of such a consensus needs no proof.

Let us take a close look at what we may call the democratic situation. The word "democracy" seems not to be in as high repute among us—except at celebrations—as we assume in dialectic. I was shocked on the occasion of a college dinner to hear the head of the institution, a prominent educational leader, declare in a formal address that he had discontinued use of the word "democracy." He thought it had lost meaning. Even more impressive to me was the fact that he "got away with it." I never heard a criticism from a member of his audience of educators.

The relatively low status of the democratic idea is, of course, due in part to a certain vagueness that envelops it and in part to an unhappy connotation of ineptitude and even corruption that is often found in a formally democratic political regime. The latter seems to have been the chief reason for Plato's skepticism concerning democratic rule. The late Harold Laski was fond of saying that he knew no political argument for democracy that he could not refute in ten minutes—and then adding that he knew no alternative to it that would last five!

It is significant that in Lincoln's Gettysburg Address he declared that this nation was *"dedicated to the proposition* that all men are created equal." He did not base that declaration on accomplished fact. To him it was a proposition to be validated in the course of the nation's history. The outlook for political democracy was dim in 1863. But "dedicated to a proposition" is a formidable cluster of words. The substance of the proposition, taken literally, is palpably untrue: there is no sense in which the equality of all men can be called a fact. Inequality lends itself more readily to factual statement. When we say that all persons are equal, we often add "before the law" or "in the eyes of God." This is not very helpful, since we cannot see with the eyes of God and positive "law" often fails to implement democratic principle.

A teacher of mine—later a colleague—once said, "Democracy means an opportunity for every person to be all that is in him to be, and recognition of every person for all that he is." I think most of us would settle for that as a statement of the ethical meaning of democracy as a way of life, but functional problems remain. I have found a measure of satisfaction in this form of the statement: I am ethically bound to accept an obligation to do all in my power to see that all persons have equal opportunity to become all they have the potential to become. This affirms, not a "fact," but an ethical imperative.

Many years ago I was impressed by a statement about men and government by an outstanding sociologist. He was quite ready to grant that the mass of citizens were incapable of making decisions on many policies and measures on which lawmaking bodies must act. But, said he, the people can do the necessary thing—they are wise enough to select leaders who can represent their interests in government.

That sounded good to me. Incidentally, it was very like what Walter Lippmann said years ago in *The Phantom Public*. But as years passed, the names of certain notorious "leaders" who enjoyed appalling political longevity became household words of opprobrium. It was a sobering spectacle. We seem to have demonstrated in our national history that the rank and file of our people are not politically minded. They are better as humans than as citizens. When a national campaign is approaching, large numbers of people never think of studying issues; many of them are quite unprepared to vote either on issues or on candidates; many do not go to the polls at all; and many who do vote are actuated by superficial motives—perhaps having been shamed into doing so by "bring-out-the-vote" crusades. It does not seem to occur to the zealous citizens who persist in such efforts that voting in order to get it off one's conscience or in response to an appeal to "vote, no matter how, but vote" is not an exercise in good citizenship but an assault upon it. Unhappy thought though it is, I strongly suspect that the results of some of our elections would be more useful if men and women who are not prepared to vote intelligently stayed at home. There is no duty to vote, period; there is duty to be informed, to arrive at convictions, and then to vote.

With every year that passes economics and politics become

more closely bound together. Not only so, but a major goal—a vastly improved nationwide program of general education—will not be reached except through very extensive cooperation by the federal government and the states. Thus the problem becomes a political one. Indeed, practically every issue discussed in this book has a national political outreach. I cannot put too strongly the need for a cultural "leap forward" that will measurably overcome cultural lag and will contribute heavily toward making the integrative forces in the nation predominant over the divisive forces. To the probable rejoinder that cultural leaps are not easily made and that they usually "come high," one can say only that the time is past when America can regard herself as a pocket of safety in a world that is in revolution. We are in an economic and cultural crisis—the kind that will not just "go away."

In spite of all this we should be reassured by the fact that "rapid social change," which is the highest common denominator of present concern and discussion, is after all not the most pervasive social fact. Continuity bulks larger than change. Our language, our institutions, our susceptibilities, and our conscious elemental needs do not change rapidly. Nostalgia we may feel, and frustration we may suffer, but the way ahead is open.

Moreover, change is not only inevitable: it is salutary in a way we seldom allow ourselves to think about. A revolutionary period in history is not a time of altogether essential novelty; revolutionary stirrings spring from a sense of having lost something. The rising demand for civil rights is in reality a harking back to the vision—however imperfect—of the founding fathers. A discerning look backward gives us a direction forward.

DEMOCRACY AND HUMAN NATURE

There seems to be an unfortunate confusion in our thinking about the implications of the rise of modern democracy concerning human nature. As a secular phenomenon it certainly has emphasized the essential goodness, the indeterminate "perfectibility" of mankind. This does not mean that "progress" is automatic, though it cannot be denied that much of the literature of democracy has conveyed that idea. Indeed, it has been said that in the eighteenth century man became convinced that "by taking thought he could add a cubit to his stature," and in the nineteenth century he was convinced that "a cubit would be added whether he took thought or not"! Certainly there is a broad streak of "Enlightenment" optimism in secular democratic "ideology."

In the realm of classical theology, however, the emphasis is in sharp contrast to the "melioristic" view of man. Casserley has expressed this well: "The great difference between the interpretations of democracy provided by secular humanists and the interpretation of democracy put forward by the Christian theologian is this: the secular humanist tends to understand and defend democracy in terms of a romantic belief in human perfectibility, whereas the Christian theologian prefers to understand and defend democracy in terms of one of his basic Biblical conceptions, the doctrine of original sin." And again: "It is because men are everywhere corruptible and always corrupted that no single man or group of men can be trusted with too much power, indeed with any power at all that is not in some way balanced and checked by the power of other men."[19]

Reinhold Niebuhr, in a widely quoted aphorism, has brought these ideas into polar relationship: "Man's capacity for justice makes democracy possible; man's inclination to injustice makes democracy necessary." There is a world of difference between "necessary" and "automatic." But if the "liberal" emphasis on the improvability of human nature points to a "built-in" tendency, so do the immortal words of Augustine: "Thou hast formed us for Thyself, and our hearts are restless till they rest in Thee."

ETHICS AND THE LAW

Commonly heard is the saying "You can't make people good by law." This is so broadly and significantly true as to obscure the very important limits of its application! Behavior most certainly has been improved by law, for everybody knows that food and drug laws can greatly reduce addiction and can protect the community, in large measure, from dangerous poisons. Traffic laws are a necessity and in large measure effectual in checking murderous recklessness on the highways. Not only so, but a statutory requirement or prohibition—in the nature of a building code, for example—may be the initial stimulus to the growth of social responsibility.

I believe there has been some criticism overseas of the "American faith in law as an educational instrument." We have had abundant proof that such a faith may be, so to say, "more than the traffic will bear." Yet our history has demonstrated that the American people can assimilate political experience pointing to higher and more consistent moral living, though the amount of lawbreaking and evasion is shameful. We can learn by failures as well as through successes, though the immediate results of majority rule are often disappointing. Democracy has "growing pains," but it does grow. It is typically in some sense experimental and exploratory, never quite sure of itself.

A troublesome issue arises as a result of this experimental character of legislation, combined with our doctrine and practice of "judicial review." This is the power and assumed duty of the federal courts to pass on the constitutionality of an act of Congress, or of one of the states, which has been plausibly challenged on constitutional grounds. Since it is substantially accepted that "the Constitution is what the judges say it is," it follows that a statute that remains in doubt while the case that raised the issue is pending may enjoy many months, or even years, of spurious validity. It is not strange that interested parties should withhold compliance in the interim, yet it must put an ethical strain on individuals or corporations to find themselves in defiance of the lawmaking body, thus appropriating an advantage in ways that may presently be found criminal.

All this is said not by way of disparaging "judicial review," as many have done. A nation like ours, which embodies a federal system and has a written constitution, could scarcely maintain political and economic equilibrium without provision for judicial review, culminating if necessary in decision by a tribunal of last resort. Indeed, the recent revival of attacks on our Supreme Court reflects, it seems to me, an ominous regression to provincialism that could become a grievous hindrance to national unity.

The particular point I wish to make here is that what we may call an ethical gap exists between the enactment of a law affecting business procedures, possibly in a vital way, and the final judicial determination as to its constitutionality. A negative decision means that the "law" is not and never was really a law at all, and government has no sanction to invoke for its enforcement. It would seem that in the case of a law that has wide legislative approval and a substantial popular sanction, all parties concerned have a prima-facie duty to comply rather than to enjoy the possible fruits of immunity during a succession of court procedures that may continue for years. "Assumed to be innocent until proved guilty" is held by all of us to be a basic principle of justice in criminal law. May it be that "valid until authoritatively pronounced invalid" would be a wholesome standard for business, industry, and labor when confronted by legal requirements which are regarded as unfair? Is not pressure for judicial review consistent with observance during the time required for that process? It should go without saying that genuinely conscientious withholding of obedience to a law, such as the military draft, is a quite different issue, which our government has recognized.

No theoretical fixing of a boundary to legislative action in relation to moral conduct, individual or corporate, can stand up against popular indignation at gross defiance of the public will and the public interest. The first responsibility of government is to govern—to maintain order and the conditions of wholesome living. The widely publicized violations of law by persons of high standing in the business and industrial world has doubtless seriously affected our national unity and impaired America's influence abroad.

I know of no more striking statement of business practices at their worst than the following, by Chancellor Louis Finkelstein of the Jewish Theological Seminary of America, published a few years ago in *Fortune*:[20]

The most casual observer is aware of the transgressions that go on daily in the American business community. He hears of tax returns that are outright perjury; he hears of purchasing agents who are taking bribes from suppliers, of businessmen offering bribes for false testimony or for police protection of some dubious enterprise. He reads of industries attempting to suborn state legislators for favorable legislation. He reads of businessmen bestowing favors on government officials to win special privileges. Even in my ivory tower on Morningside Heights, I have been urged by businessmen to accept a gift for the Theological Seminary in return for admitting a student—and have been threatened by withdrawal of contributions to the school if I failed to do so.

We hear of businessmen using wire taps to obtain information about their competitors, of management acting in collusion with racketeers, of men using prostitution to promote the sale of their goods. We hear of businessmen violating the most elementary requirements of city building codes and profiting from rat-infested tenements.

It would be less than fair to let that stand without quoting Rabbi Finkelstein's further comment:

> Business leaders who generously advised me in the preparation of this article said, "The majority of the American business community are not evil men, and want to do right. Let us say we admit the indictment and accept our responsibility—what can we do?"

ETHICS OF COLLECTIVE BARGAINING

Let us look now at a major problem of democracy that is organized labor's most distinctive function and prime concern—collective bargaining. Many of us are sympathetic with the criticism that "bargaining" has an unfortunate flavor of hostile encounter—which has often been an accurate designation of what goes on at the bargaining table. I must say first, however, that it is better to be realistic about this institution than to perpetuate the fiction that "the interests of labor and capital are identical." That statement is perhaps no more fictional than the declaration in the Clayton Antitrust Act, on behalf of the unions, that "labor is not a commodity." Everybody knows that what makes bargaining possible in labor-management relations is the fact that both sides have a financial stake in the contract negotiations. Union labor considers wages as the price put upon its work. It should be said, of course, that what presumably was really meant by the slogan written into the Clayton Antitrust Act is that the laborer himself is not to be treated as a commodity. That, of course, should go without saying.

While the 1964 contract negotiations in the automobile industry were in progress, the *New York Times* in a leading editorial (Mar. 28, p. 18) said:

> The initial wage proposals offered by the automobile industry's big three and their immediate rejection by the United Automobile Workers follow a traditional and dreary ritual. Both management and the union possess responsible and imaginative talent that is equipped to exercise creative leadership on the economic and technological problems confronting industry, but they are put into the back seat at contract time. . . .
>
> The bargaining-as-usual attitude displayed by both sides reflects a dodging of the real issue. It is clear that business is far better than usual, with an excellent chance that consumer demand will remain strong for an unprecedented fourth year in a row. It also is clear that a simple dividing up of the cake of increasing productivity between shareholders and workers is contrary to the public interest. With its huge profits, the big three could absorb a substantial rise without any increase in prices.

The bedrock trouble here seems to be that this incomparably huge industrial society, the United States of America, has no adequate constitutional government for its industry. We are rightly, as a nation, opposed to the "omnicompetent state" and devoted to free initiative, in principle, but we have no constitutional provision for balancing economic power—no stable policy for preventing recurrent crises resulting from economic strife. An Industrial Councils plan has been advocated by the Roman Catholic Church—a tripartite organization of economic power representing management, labor, and government. It should have more attention.

The burden of all this is that the "common interest" of labor and management is in the maintenance of a profitable and socially wholesome enterprise. One of my most honored professors of philosophy, the late Felix Adler, used to call this shared purpose the "overarching end." He made it the key to a functional reciprocality, applicable to the areas of conflict in human life.

AND WHAT OF THE CHURCH?

We have passed through what is commonly called the "social gospel" era when pulpits and ecclesiastical assemblies often spoke in radical terms on controversial issues, deriving inspiration from some outstanding leaders, chief among whom in the early days was Walter Rauschenbusch. I recall with some wonderment that his books were prominent in reading lists for young ministers during my own "novitiate," though he was a "Christian Socialist" who would probably have encountered vigorous opposition a generation later. It might be instructive to inquire into the reasons for the change in the religious climate during recent decades. Why have our Protestant churches seemed to be moving to the "right" while the Nation has been moving politically to the "left"? The latter observation refers, of course, not to ideology but to the growth of the public sector of the economy, the development of a powerful labor movement, the growth of a sense of managerial responsibility in business and industry, the firm establishment of social security, the civil rights "revolution," and other characteristics of what used to be disapprovingly called the "welfare state."

I think the "social gospel" movement swept over the churches —I should say, *some* of them, for many were apparently little affected by it—as the religious counterpart of a wave of social and political liberalism and, like the latter, subsided, but not until it had left its mark. The social gospel did not vanish when it ceased to be an impressive "movement" any more than the sea vanishes with an ebbing of the tide. To be sure, there was an element of "utopianism" in the literature it produced. But changes in thought and mood seem to come that way, and Utopia has its uses.

Whatever other causes may have been operating to alter the posture of the churches with respect to socioeconomic issues, I think the rapid growth of church membership is one. This has been a major religious phenomenon. More and more the religious population tends to approximate, at the cultural level, the temper and mood of the secular community. In physical science "force" is defined as "mass times acceleration." It is not strange that this should be true—with exceptions—of the churches, that acceleration—drive for needed social change—diminishes as size increases. Historically, it has been only in the smaller religious bodies that religion sharply challenged the community as a whole on any issue, except perhaps Prohibition. It is true, however, that when leaders of great representative religious bodies "take the field" on behalf of minority groups and unpopular liberating movements, the impact is impressive. This has been a striking feature of the civil rights crusade.

A point to emphasize here is that the church—the inclusive church—has two functions, related but distinct. As "the community on its knees," having "some of everybody" in its membership, the church can properly rejoice in seeing "the weakest saint upon his knees." It has its doors open and its altar accessible to all who want to "practice the presence of God." A church that is inclusive, as to race and class, can therefore say to its community, "Whosoever will, may come." But the soul of the church should be a disciplined fellowship, recognizable as an embodiment of the Christian redemptive enterprise always and everywhere.

The great historian Ernst Troeltsch has called the first of these the church-type and the second the sect-type. In a significant passage in his great work already referred to he says:

Very often in the so-called "sects" it is precisely the essential elements of the Gospel which are fully expressed; they themselves always appeal to the Gospel and to Primitive Christianity, and accuse the Church of having fallen away from its ideal; these impulses are always those which have been either suppressed or undeveloped in the official churches, of course for good and characteristic reasons, which again are not taken into account by the passionate party polemics of the sects. There can, however, be no doubt about the actual fact: the sects, with their greater independence of the world, and their continual emphasis upon the original ideals of Christianity, often represent in a very direct and characteristic way the essential fundamental ideas of Christianity; to a very great extent they are a most important factor in the study of the development of the sociological consequences of Christian thought.[21]

Again he writes:

The Church is that type of organization which is overwhelmingly conservative, which to a certain extent accepts the secular order, and dominates the masses; in principle, therefore, it is universal, i.e., it desires to cover the whole life of humanity. The sects, on the other hand, are comparatively small groups; they aspire after personal inward perfection, and they aim at a direct personal fellowship between the members of each group.[22]

It seems quite apparent that the "church-type" is normative for the vast majority of the church-going population. But what is ideally called for is incorporation of the sect within the church. The inclusive "whosoever will" church should foster within itself the growth of self-limiting, self-disciplining fellowships for the pursuit of excellence within their religious tradition. In such groups would be found, as Vida Scudder put it, the "leaven" which causes the "loaf"—the church as a whole—to "rise." The church is loaf, she said, not leaven!

We must never forget that the church is, in the first instance, a religious more than an ethical organization. That is to say, people come to the church to worship, to find comfort, and to have their faith strengthened. Before admission to membership they are examined in one or another manner as to their faith, but seldom as to their works! Ecclesiastical discipline is rarely resorted to in Protestantism, and never, as far as I know, because of practices that violated the "Social Ideals of the Churches." I have known a group of ministers to discuss perplexedly this lack of a membership discipline, but nothing that seemed practicable was formulated. Our churches, for the most part, have theological creeds but few guides to behavior in the field of social ethics. Ethical sensitiveness at the higher levels is not a common denominator of our church congregations. "Straight is the gate and narrow is the way. . . ."

With respect to the decline in issuance of vigorous radical pronouncements on controversial social issues, I think it is on the whole a good omen. We are now having fewer and better social pronouncements. The trouble with many of those earlier resolutions was that they appeared to represent the views of the communion, synod, conference, or other ecclesiastical unit, while as a matter of fact they were minority utterances. This is not to say that they were unbiblical or in any other sense invalid but that they were too often not the voice of the church.

No one should write in this fashion without giving attention to the constructive aspects of the situation he is dealing with. As just intimated, my criticism is not of pronouncements per se; it concerns what or whom they are supposed to represent. In the period when pronouncements were numerous, ardent reform groups were often eager to "put more teeth into it than we did last time" when framing a statement on the social order. And if the assembly—denominational or interchurch—really wanted to pass it after ample debate, the action was valid. But too often, I fear, the study and discussion that should have come first came afterward, and with disillusioning force.

What has just been said does not of course mean that a church body which is small is *ipso facto* liberal with respect to social and political issues. The sect-type religious body, in our time, more characteristically expresses its nonconformity in religious or cultural terms, or in both. The point is that to be consistently and effectually "against the world" a religious body must have a membership consisting predominantly of persons who are ready to challenge the prevailing way of life in some significant respect. Christianity itself began as a sect and behaved as a sect during its early history. When it began to grow, taking into its fellowship persons who lived at peace with the secular world, Christianity became less and less able to challenge the prevailing culture. And it has been well said that the "natural history of a sect is to become a church."

A large church body has been known to take a virtually absolutist stand against war, only to recede from the pacifist position under pressure from its own constituency. The great influence of the Protestant churches in the movement culminating in national Prohibition was preceded by generations of teaching and discipline aimed at "total abstinence." This judgment is, of course, quite independent of any appraisals of the regime thus inaugurated, as a matter of social policy.

If the principle I am trying to state can be put into concise, epigrammatic form, it would be something like this: a church body can successfully challenge the community, at the local or national level, only when it has developed an internal discipline corresponding to its external testimony. Moreover, I do not mean to imply that no utterance on controversial subjects should be made until the members of the "judicatory" body have expressly authorized it. Elected or appointed representatives of constituent groups are not chosen merely to reflect present opinions of the constituency. A thoroughly responsible person, chosen as a representative of a constituency, knows that not just his voice but his brain and his conscience have been laid under tribute to a cause. "Concern" groups should be encouraged to "speak out," but always for themselves—not for the church. Some of our larger communions and the National Council of Churches have been setting a pattern for pronouncements, studies, and problem analyses that meets the issue of representativeness through a process of unhurried, patient study and—especially—of consultation with the most knowledgeable people available and with the parties who have a stake in the outcome.

A similar problem arises, or should arise, with respect to the pulpit. A few years ago many pulpits rang with bold pronouncements about the social order. They bespoke courage, and I suppose that in the main the fighting stance of the preachers was justified and their utterances were biblically wellfounded. But the pulpit is not the church, and some of those utterances would have been more appropriate in the parish lecture hall, where laymen can and should talk back if they are moved to do so. In that case, of course, they should speak as Christian laymen and laywomen, not as representatives of secular interest groups. I am here writing of the denominational bodies whose membership is qualitatively very nearly coextensive with the community. Granted, our pews are in no small part occupied by people whose acquaintance with scripture is not impressive and whose opinions on the social-ethical issues of our time were not molded under sacred auspices! But if they are bona fide members of the church, they are entitled to a voice. I shall not forget a long conversation with a brilliant young minister, typical of the prophetic school at its best. He told me with evident satisfaction of a remonstrance from some of his official members occasioned by a forthright social sermon. "I said to them," he told me, " 'Brethren, nobody goes with me into the pulpit, not even my wife. Only God goes with me into the pulpit'." Courageous, yes, but very presumptuous.

Does this limit the prophetic office? Not the real prophetic office. Prophecy is not a lone-star performance. The prophetic voice belongs to a person who is in such intimate relationship with the people he serves that he knows the word that will awaken an authentic response. Prophecy, someone has said, is "reminding people of what they have forgotten—on purpose." The hearer in the pew may at first be resentful and indignant, but sooner or later he is likely to say, "The preacher was right." God speaks to the people, we say, through the preacher. It is equally true that God speaks to the preacher through the people.

Another factor in the situation under discussion is the change in the Protestant theological climate during recent decades. The impact of the "realistic" theology—with its stress on human fallibility and the illusory character of Utopias—has been pronounced. Its corrective influence on superficial ethical optimism should be acknowledged by all of us. At the same time it seems probable that excessive emphasis on human self-regard and profit-motivation which has often characterized the literature of employing interests has in some measure found support in the writings of the theological realists, with their stern emphasis on original sin!

It cannot be too strongly emphasized that the "social gospel," now almost always referred to in the past tense, has continued to be a vital force. The purpose of the movement was from the beginning to apply the Christian gospel to the social structure itself, thus developing a climate in which Christian character can come to flower. As these lines are written, the revised Social Creed of the Methodist Church is being publicized. "We believe," it declares, "that it is our duty not only to bring Christ to the individual, but also to bring the increasingly technological society within which we live more nearly into conformity with the teachings of Christ." This is certainly what the Social Gospel set out to do.

Jewish religious leaders have participated in this social thrust, evidencing kinship in spirit and purpose between the Old Testament prophets and the writers of the New Testament Gospels. The Roman Catholic Church has long been working at this task, especially through its great encyclicals. The realistic theologians themselves, earlier referred to, are for the most part, I believe, committed to this effort. If the movement for social redemption was "dated," was that not, in part, because its main drive—to challenge the social order itself in the name of Christianity—had measurably succeeded? The transformation is, alas, still lagging. The name given the movement is perhaps unfortunate: there is only one gospel in Christianity. But the main contention of those who have sought to interpret the gospel socially is recognized, I believe, by most of our theologians of whatever school.

Just as the important function of myth in the religious sphere as a means of interpreting the past is recognized by theologians of various schools, it is reasonable to grant the validity of what may be thought of as inverted myth in depicting the indeterminate future. "These things shall be" is not predictive so much as imperative! "Thy Kingdom come on earth" is still a valid prayer.

One of the greatest weaknesses in the educational programs of our churches is the neglect of "occupational ethics." Religious vocation commonly means the ministry or some related form of professional religious activity. Quite as important and almost completely neglected is the task of organizing and conducting groups on an occupational basis for the purpose of studying the import of Christian teaching for a particular vocational group. Some useful pioneering has been done, but it is a pity that with thousands of adult classes in the churches so little has been done in the way of teaching what is being called "ethics on the job." Here is a field well suited to exploration, especially by councils of churches.

It seems strange that so limited use is made by the churches of our thoroughly radical doctrine of the stewardship of possessions. Tithing—dedicating a part of one's income "to the Lord"—is a useful device for stimulating giving, but it has little intrinsic relation to stewardship, which rests on the proposition that Christians own no private wealth but hold all their property in trust for almighty God. We all have known persons who approximate genuine Christian stewardship, but total stewardship of possessions is still a vague concept. It could bring economic life to the fore in a religious context, dominating the consideration of family budgets as well as the conduct of business. It would involve families in the solution of a major contemporary problem: how to reconcile an inherited ideal of frugality in spending with the now recognized economic necessity of increased consumption. High priority should be given to the ethics of consumption for a generation nurtured in an economy of scarcity and conditioned by a discipline of frugality.

In planning our long study we were strongly impressed that we should not omit the corporate practices of the church itself. I quote from the volume embodying the results of this phase of the inquiry: "A major finding of the study is that to a disturbing extent the churches and their various agencies take less seriously their corporate responsibilities than their official pronouncements on social and economic problems give the community a right to expect." Also the study revealed "a marked contrast between the way in which a denominational or an interdenominational assembly addresses itself to economic issues and the indifferent attitude —the lack of a sense of involvement—shown by individual churches with respect to such matters in the conduct of their business affairs."[23]

Indeed, it is hardly too much to say that most of the ethical blind spots and most of the questionable practices—barring criminal offenses—that are evident in secular business can be found somewhere and in some measure in the conduct of church affairs. Notable among these blemishes upon church corporate practices in the economic sphere are those having to do with the salaries of church employees; personnel and labor policies in large church organizations; discrimination in employment on the basis of sex, age, and color; use of objectionable methods of raising money; and investment of church funds.

Moreover, I fear there is a too little noted tendency for church policies and practices to share the defects that critics of contemporary society are continually pointing out as accompaniments of "bigness." It seems that the larger an organization becomes, the stronger is the tendency to give priority to its own corporate interests at the expense of individual needs and the claims of human dignity. Big church organizations, like their secular counterparts, often exhibit this fault. Now, I think it wrong to assume that bigness is *ipso facto* and inevitably a corrupter of values; but there can scarcely be any question that the qualities which are assumed to characterize the "organization man" continually threaten the ethical standards of religious organizations as well as those of a secular character. In both types size and corporate prestige may inflate organization loyalty beyond ethical limits.

Earlier, I referred to what has been called *"koinonia* ethics"— the ethos, so to speak, of the living, worshiping, working Christian community as a creative spiritual fellowship. Surely we can all agree that we shall not meet the crisis with which this age confronts us without a new "baptism of the Spirit" that will bring the existential church far closer to its historic ideal as the Body of Christ.

Notes

CHAPTER 1. ROOTS OF RELIGIOUS CONCERN FOR ECONOMIC LIFE

1. Charles L. Taylor, "Old Testament Foundations," in *Christianity and Property*, ed. Joseph F. Fletcher (Philadelphia: Westminster Press, 1947), p. 30.

2. Edward Hardy, Jr., "The Way of the Early Church," in *Christianity and Property*, p. 59.

3. A. T. Mollegen, "Historical Development of the Christian Testimony Concerning Economic Relations," in *Information Service* (New York: Federal Council of Churches of Christ in America), Jan. 11, 1947.

4. A. J. Carlyle, "The Theory of Property in Medieval Theology," in *Property*, 3rd edn. (London: Macmillan, 1915), p. 131.

5. Frederick H. Smyth, "The Middle Ages," in *Christianity and Property*, pp. 76–77.

6. A. J. Carlyle, *op. cit.*, p. 137.

7. Richard H. Tawney, *Religion and the Rise of Capitalism* (New York: Penguin Books, 1926), p. 30.

8. Ibid., p. 34.

9. John H. Randall, Jr., *The Making of a Modern Mind* (Boston & New York: Houghton & Mifflin Co., 1926), p. 114.

10. Paul Lehmann, "The Standpoint of the Reformation," in *Christianity and Property*, p. 122.

11. H. T. Kerr, Jr., *Compend of the Institutes* (Philadelphia: Presbyterian Board of Christian Education, 1939).

12. Paul Lehmann, op. cit., p. 114.

13. John H. Randall, Jr., op. cit., p. 274.

14. Charles Kingsley, *Letters and Memories of His Life*, p. 250.

15. Idem, *Kingsley Letters*, I, 248.

16. John M. Ludlow, "The New Idea," in *The Christian Socialist*, Vol. I, Nov. 2, 1850; quoted from Harry W. Laidler, *Social Economic Movements* (New York: Thomas Y. Crowell Co., 1946), p. 726.

17. Harry W. Laidler, *Social Economic Movements*, p. 730.

CHAPTER 2. INDUSTRIALISM AS OUR CULTURE

1. Mimeographed report of the seminar "Christian Responsibility in the Emerging World Situation: The Population Explosion, Industrialization, and

World Mission," the Federated Theological Faculty, University of Chicago, March, 1959. Quoted in Paul Abrecht, *The Church and Rapid Social Change,* (Garden City, N.Y.: Doubleday, 1961), p. 151.

2. Clark Kerr, John T. Dunlop, Frederick H. Harbison, and Charles A. Myers, *Industrialism and Industrial Man* (Cambridge, Mass.: Harvard Univ. Press, 1960), p. 28.

3. Ibid., p. 43.

4. Ibid., p. 89.

5. W. W. Rostow, *Stages of Economic Growth* (Cambridge, Eng.: Cambridge Univ. Press, 1964).

6. Peter Drucker, *Landmarks of Tomorrow* (New York: Harper & Row, 1957), pp. 42–43.

7. Kerr et al., op. cit., p. 47.

8. Gerhard Lenski, *The Religious Factor* (New York: Doubleday, 1961).

9. W. Widick Schroeder and Victor Obenhaus, *Religion in American Culture* (New York: Free Press of Glencoe, 1964).

10. *Business Week,* April 15, 1961, p. 162.

Chapter 3. Issues Challenging Industrialism

1. "Jobs for Youth," Report on a Consultation on the Church and Youth Employment sponsored by the Department of Church and Economic Life, with other units of the National Council of Churches of Christ in the U.S.A. (January, 1964).

2. Eli E. Cohen, "Jobs for Youth," p. 8.

3. "The Captive," Department of Church in Town and Country, Division of Home Missions, The National Council of Churches of Christ in the U.S.A.

4. Dr. Oscar Ornati, "Poverty in America," Report of National Policy Committee on Pockets of Poverty (Washington, D.C., 1964), p. 18.

5. Daniel P. Moynihan, in "Christ in the Technological Revolution," a Presentation to the General Board, National Council of Churches of Christ in the U.S.A., (February 27, 1964), p. 10.

6. Michael Harrington, *The Other America* (New York: Macmillan, 1962), p. 126.

7. "The Churches and Persistent Pockets of Poverty," a report of The National Council of Churches of Christ in the U.S.A. (1962), p. 11.

8. Ibid., p. 10.

9. Ibid., p. 11.

10. Ibid., p. 14.

11. Roy Blough, "Technology and Livelihood," in *Servants of the Eternal Christ,* source book for 1963 General Assembly, National Council of Churches of Christ in the U.S.A., p. 60.

12. William P. Bundy, *Goals for Americans,* the Report of the President's Commission on National Goals (New York: The American Assembly, Columbia Univ.), p. 369.

13. Gunnar Myrdal, *Beyond the Welfare State* (New Haven: Yale Univ. Press, 1960), p. 228.

14. Peter Drucker, *Landmarks of Tomorrow,* (New York: Harper & Bros., 1957), p. 187.

15. Kerr et al., *Industrialism and Industrial Man*, (Cambridge, Mass.: Harvard Univ. Press, 1960), p. 185.

CHAPTER 4. AUTOMATION—CYBERNATION

1. Automation issue of *Information Service* (New York: National Council of Churches of Christ in the U.S.A.), September 13, 1958, p. 3.
2. John Diebold, *Automation: Its Impact on Business and Labor* (Washington, D. C.: National Planning Association Pamphlet No. 106, May 1959).
3. Typical are: Yale Brozen, Univ. of Chicago, and W. Allen Wallis, President of Univ. of Rochester.
4. Seymour L. Wolfbein, "Automation and Manpower in the 1960s," in *The Ethical Aftermath of Automation*, ed. Francis X. Quinn, S.J. (Westminster, Md.: Newman Press, 1962), p. 29.
5. John Stuart Mill, *Essay on Liberty* (Harvard Classics).
6. James Bright, in *Automation*, ed. Walter Buckingham. (New York: Harper & Row, 1961).
7. Bruno Bettelheim, in *Automation*.
8. Paul Einzig, *The Economic Consequences of Automation* (New York: W. W. Norton & Co., 1957), p. 23.
9. Gustave Weigel, S.J., "Automation in the Life of a Catholic," in *The Ethical Aftermath of Automation*, p. 179.
10. Lester Velie, "Automation, Friend or Foe," in *Reader's Digest*, October, 1962 (repr.), p. 5.

CHAPTER 5. WELFARE AND OUR INDUSTRIAL ECONOMY

1. Harold L. Wilensky and Charles N. Lebeaux, *Industrial Society and Social Welfare* (New York: Russell Sage Foundation, 1958), p. 56.
2. Charles Frankel, "Obstacles to Action for Human Welfare," in *The Social Welfare Forum—1961* (New York: Columbia Univ. Press), pp. 274–275.
3. Wilensky and Lebeaux, op. cit., pp. 132–133.
4. Charles Frankel, op. cit., p. 274.
5. Thomas Gladwin, "The Anthropologist's View of Poverty," in *The Social Welfare Forum—1961*, p. 77.
6. Wilensky and Lebeaux, op. cit., p. 147.
7. Edgar May, "The Disjointed Trio: Poverty, Politics, and Power," in *The Social Welfare Forum—1963*, p. 52.
8. Roy Blough, *Servants of The Eternal Christ*, source book for 1963 General Assembly, National Council of Churches of Christ in the U.S.A., p. 68.
9. Theodore W. Schultz, *The Economic Value of Education* (New York: Columbia Univ. Press, 1963), p. 65.
10. UNESCO, *International Survey of Progress of Social Development* (New York: United Nations, Document E/CN5/301, 1955).
11. Gunnar Myrdal, *Beyond the Welfare State*, (New Haven: Yale Univ. Press, 1960), p. 179.

CHAPTER 6. U. S. AGRICULTURE IN DOMESTIC AND WORLD ECONOMY

1. Philip F. Aylesworth, *Keeping Abreast of Change in the Rural Community*, (U. S. Dept. of Agriculture, Federal Extension Service, Agricultural Information Bulletin No. 215, October 1959).

2. Quoted from "Food Costs—Farm Prices," a compilation of information related to agriculture by the Committee on Agriculture, House of Representatives, 88th Cong., July 1964.

3. D. Gale Johnson, "The Dimensions of the Farm Problem," in *Problems and Policies of American Agriculture* (Ames, Iowa: State Univ. Center for Agricultural Adjustment), pp. 47–48.

4. Kenneth E. Boulding, *Farm Goals in Conflict* (Ames: Iowa State Univ.), 1963.

5. Don F. Hadwiger, *Goals and Values in Agricultural Policy*, p. 233. Quoted from *Wisconsin Agriculturist* (Iowa State University, 1960).

6. Mervin G. Smith, quoted from a study paper on Agricultural Policy for the Department of Church and Economic Life, National Council of Churches of Christ, in the U.S.A. (1962).

7. Emerson W. Shideler, quoted in Boulding, *Farm Goals in Conflict*, p. 211.

8. Farm Bureau policy for 1963.

9. Gilbert Rohde, "Goals and Values Underlying Programs of Farmers Union," in *Farm Goals in Conflict*, p. 81.

10. Herschel D. Newsom, "Goals and Values Underlying Programs of the Grange," in *Farm Goals in Conflict*, pp. 87–88.

11. Oren Lee Staley, "The National Farmers Organization," in *Farm Goals in Conflict*, pp. 108–109.

12. Walter W. Wilcox, *Social Responsibility in Farm Leadership* (New York: Harper & Row, 1956), p. 32.

13. E. W. Hofstee, "European Perspectives of Agricultural Changes and Societal Adaptations," in *Farm Goals in Conflict*, pp. 204–205.

14. Earl O. Heady, "Feasible Criteria and Programs," in *Problems and Policies of American Agriculture*, pp. 206–207.

15. Robin M. Williams, Jr., "How to Judge Institutional Programs," in *Farm Goals in Conflict*, p. 182.

16. Quoted from "An Adaptive Program for Agriculture," a statement on national policy by the Research and Policy Committee of the Committee for Economic Development (1962).

17. Edward Higbee, in *Farms and Farmers in an Urban Age* (New York: Twentieth Century Fund, 1963), p. 143.

18. Byron Johnson, "Enlarging the Dimensions of the Food for Peace Program," address delivered at Food for Peace Conference, Denver, 1961.

19. Charles M. Hardin, "Economic Adjustment—An Instrument to Political Preservation," in *Problems and Policies in American Agriculture*, p. 163.

20. John D. Black, "Societal Obligations To and Of Agriculture," in *Problems and Policies of American Agriculture*, p. 79.

21. Byron Johnson, op. cit.

22. Ibid.

23. Willard W. Cochrane, "Beliefs and Values Underlying Agricultural Policies and Programs," in *Farm Goals in Conflict*, p. 57.

24. Robin M. Williams, Jr., op. cit., p. 7.

25. Theodore W. Schultz, "Welfare State and the Welfare People" University of Chicago Office of Agricultural Economics Research Paper No. 6406 (Feb. 5, 1964).

26. Walter W. Wilcox, "Policy Conflicts Relating to the Economic Organization of Agriculture," in Hadwiger, *Goals and Values in Agricultural Policy*, pp. 181–182.

27. Statement on Ethical Goals for Agricultural Policy, adopted by the General Board of the National Council of the Churches of Christ in the U.S.A. (June 4, 1958).

28. Resolution adopted December 9, 1960, p. 1.

CHAPTER 7. THE CONSUMER—POWER OR PUSHOVER

1. Leland Gordon, "The Role and Responsibility of the Consumer and How He Exercises It," study paper for the Fourth National Study Conference on the Church and Economic Life, National Council of Churches of Christ in the U.S.A. (Nov. 1962), p. 6.

2. Source of tobacco and liquor statistics: *Survey of Current Business*, U. S. Department of Commerce, Office of Business Economics; July 1964, Table 14, p. 16.

3. Margaret G. Reid, *American Income and Its Use* (New York: Harper & Row, 1954), pp. 164–165.

4. W. H. Ferry, *The Economy Under Law* (Santa Barbara, Calif.: Center for the Study of Democratic Institutions, 1960), p. 22.

5. Quoted from *Congressional Record*, April 1961, pp. 4170–4171.

6. Leland Gordon, *The Function of the Consumer*, (Westport, Conn.: Kazanjian Economics Foundation, 1957), p. 35.

CHAPTER 8. ORGANIZED LABOR'S ROLE

1. *The New York Times*, Sept. 17, 1922.

2. *AFL–CIO NEWS*, Aug. 8, 1964.

3. *The Adult Teacher*, Nov. 1960.

4. *Life*, Oct. 14, 1957.

5. Eric Sevareid, "The Other Side of the Coin," in *The Reporter*, Sept. 18, 1958.

6. Paul Jacobs, *Old Before Its Time—Collective Bargaining at Twenty-Eight* (Santa Barbara: Center for the Study of Democratic Institutions, 1963), p. 10.

7. Albert Rees, *Economics of Trade Unions* (Univ. of Chicago Press, 1962), pp. 44–45.

8. H. G. Lewis, *Unionism and Relative Wages in the United States* (Univ. of Chicago Press, 1963), p. 5.

9. Solomon Barkin, *The Decline of the Labor Movement* (Santa Barbara: Center for the Study of Democratic Institutions, 1961), p. 27.

10. John A. Fitch, *Social Responsibilities of Organized Labor* (New York: Harper & Row, 1957), p. 153.

11. Ibid., p. 154.

12. Gus Tyler, *A New Philosophy for Labor* (New York: Fund for the Republic, 1959), p. 11.

CHAPTER 9. DISARMAMENT AND THE ECONOMY

1. *Economic Impacts of Disarmament* (Washington, D. C.: U. S. Arms Control and Disarmament Agency, Jan., 1962), p. 3.

2. Emile Benoit, "Disarmament in the United States," in *Disarmament: Its Politics and Economics,* ed. Seymour Melman (Boston: American Academy of Arts and Sciences, 1962), pp. 139–140.

3. Ibid., p. 137.

4. *Economic Impacts of Disarmament,* p. 4.

5. Seymour Melman, "Economic Alternatives to Arms Prosperity," in *Annals* of the American Academy of Political and Social Science, Jan. 1964, p. 123.

6. Ibid., p. 122.

7. Allan L. Madian, "The Depletion of Education and the Conversion of University Defense Research," paper read at the Second Annual Conference of Scientists on Survival (New York: June 1963). Quoted in Melman, op. cit.

8. Fred J. Cook, "The Warfare State," in *Annals* of the American Academy of Political and Social Science, p. 105.

9. Figures from Air Transport Assn., Washington, D.C. and *Statistical Abstract of the U.S.,* 1964, p. 264.

10. Adolf Sturmthal, "Measures to Deal With Labor Displacement in Disarmament," in *Disarmament and the Economy* ed. Emile Benoit and Kenneth E. Boulding (New York: Harper & Row, 1963), p. 195.

11. Murray L. Weidenbaum, "Problems of Adjustment for Defense Industries," in *Disarmament and the Economy,* p. 67.

12. *Economic Impacts of Disarmament,* p. 9.

13. Irving L. Horowitz, "Non-Economic Factors in the Institutionalization of the Cold War," in *Annals* of the American Academy of Political and Social Science, p. 111.

14. *Economic Aspects of Disarmament,* p. 11.

15. Emile Benoit, op. cit., p. 146.

16. Irving L. Horowitz, op. cit., p. 117.

17. *Economic Aspects of Disarmament,* p. 12.

18. Emile Benoit, op. cit., pp. 144–145.

19. Seymour Melman, op. cit., p. 129.

20. Emile Benoit, in *Economic Aspects of Disarmament,* p. 14.

21. Benoit and Boulding, op. cit., pp. 9–10.

22. Marion Hoffenberg and W. W. Leontief, "The Economic Effects of Disarmament," in *Scientific American,* April 1961.

23. Richard K. Nelson, "Research and Development," in *Disarmament and the Economy,* p. 125.

24. Emile Benoit, in *Economic Aspects of Disarmament,* pp. 18–19.

25. Benoit and Boulding, op. cit., p. 296.

CHAPTER 10. INTERNATIONAL TRADE AND AID

1. Paul G. Hoffman, *World Without Want* (New York: Harper & Row, 1962), p. 118.

2. From the report on Topic 6, "The United States Economy and World Economy," in *General and Group Reports*, Fourth National Study Conference on Church and Economic Life, National Council of Churches of Christ in the U.S.A. (Nov. 1962), p. 41.

3. William Butler, "Trade and the Less Developed Areas," in *Foreign Affairs*, XLI (Oct. 1962–July 1963), 373–374.

4. Roy Blough, "International Developments Affecting Business," address at the 77th Annual Meeting of the American Institute of Certified Public Accountants, October 4, 1964, in Miami, Florida, pp. 10–11.

5. Egbert DeVries, Director, Institute of Social Studies, The Hague, Netherlands.

6. John W. Haight, Study paper on "The U. S. Economy and the World Economy" prep. for the Fourth National Study Conference on the Church and Economic Life (1962), p. 3.

7. Charles P. Taft, "The U. S. Economy and the World Economy," address at the Fourth National Study Conference on Church and Economic Life (1962).

8. From the report on Topic 6, Fourth National Study Conference (1962), p. 43.

9. Benjamin H. Javits and Leon H. Keyserling, *The World Development Corp.* (Washington D.C., 1959), p. 3.

10. Paul G. Hoffman, op. cit., p. 118.

11. "Focus on Foreign Aid," Foreign Policy Association, Vol. 5, No. 4, p. 14.

12. William Butler, op. cit., p. 383.

13. John Nuveen, "Foreign Aid Is Like An Elephant," in *The Christian Century*, Nov. 7, 1963.

14. "New Directions in U. S. Foreign Economic Policy," Headline Series, No. 133, p. 23.

15. "Understanding Foreign Aid," Headline Series, No. 160, July 1963, p. 50.

16. Quoted from Draft Reports of the Preparatory Study Commission on Patterns of Economic and Social Change, National Council of Churches of Christ in the U.S.A., p. 21.

17. Ibid., p. 21.

18. From the Report on Topic 6, Fourth National Study Conference (1962), p. 44.

CHAPTER 11. GOVERNMENT POWER IN THE ECONOMY

1. Gunnar Myrdal, *Beyond the Welfare State*, (New Haven: Yale Univ. Press, 1960), p. 82.

2. Ibid., pp. 82–83.

3. Adolph A. Berle, Jr., "Evolving Capitalism and Political Federalism," in *Federalism—Mature and Emergent* (New York: Doubleday, 1955), p. 79.

4. Adolph A. Berle, Jr., "Economic Power and the Free Society," in *The Fund for the Republic* (1957), p. 14.

5. Kenneth Boulding, *The Organizational Revolution* (New York: Harper & Bros., 1953), p. 35; a book in this series.

6. Dwight D. Eisenhower, "Spending Into Trouble," in *Saturday Evening Post*, May 18, 1963, pp. 15ff.

7. Roy Blough, *Servants of the Eternal Christ*, source book for 1963 General Assembly, National Council of Churches of Christ in the U.S.A., p. 66.

8. Ibid., p. 69.

9. W. H. Ferry, *The Corporation and the Economy* (Santa Barbara, Calif.: Center for the Study of Democratic Institutions, 1959), p. 14.

10. David Bazelon, "Non-Rule in America," in *Commentary*, XXXVI: 6 (Dec. 1963), 439.

11. Sidney Hook, "Welfare State—A Debate That Isn't," in *The New York Times Magazine*, Nov. 27, 1960.

Chapter 12. The New Meaning of Leisure and Work

1. J. L. Hurlburt, *The Story of Chautauqua* (New York: J. P. Putnam Son, 1921), p. 184. Quoted from "Leisure in America—Blessing or Curse?" In the *Annals* of the American Academy of Political and Social Science (April 1964), p. 47.

2. Robert Lee, *Religion and Leisure in America* (Nashville: Abingdon Press, 1964), pp. 28–29.

3. Marion Clawson, in "Leisure in America—Blessing or Curse?" p. 1.

4. Robert Lee, op. cit., p. 37.

5. James C. Charlesworth, "A Comprehensive Plan for the Wise Use of Leisure," in "Leisure in America—Blessing or Curse?" p. 32.

6. Paul Weiss, "A Philosophical Definition of Leisure," in "Leisure in America—Blessing or Curse?" p. 22.

7. Emil Brunner, *The Divine Imperative* (Philadelphia: Westminster Press, 1947), p. 384.

8. Robert S. Michaelson, "Work and Vocation in American Industrial Society," in *Work and Vocation*, ed. John Oliver Nelson (New York: Harper & Row, 1954), p. 119.

9. Paul S. Minear, "Work and Vocation in Scripture," in *Work and Vocation*, p. 39.

10. Ibid., p. 40.

11. Robert L. Calhoun, "Work and Vocation in Christian History," in *Work and Vocation*, p. 88.

12. Elton Mayo, *Social Problems of an Industrial Civilization* (Boston, Division of Research, Graduate School of Business, Harvard Univ. 1945).

13. Cameron P. Hall, *The Christian at His Daily Work* (Department of Church and Economic Life, National Council of Churches, 1951), p. 20.

Chapter 13. Status and Stratification in Industrial Life

1. H. H. Gerth and C. Wright Mills, "Class, Status, Party," in *From Max Weber—Essays in Sociology* (New York: Oxford Univ. Press, 1946).

2. Robin M. Williams, Jr., *American Society* (New York: Alfred A. Knopf, 1960), p. 96.

3. S. M. Lipset and R. Bendix, *Social Mobility in Industrial Society* (Berkeley: Univ. of California Press, 1959).

4. Ibid., p. 6.

5. Gerth and Mills, op. cit.

6. From National Opinion Research Center; reported in Opinion News, Vol. IX, Sept. 1, 1947.

CHAPTER 14. ETHICS AND BUSINESS

1. J. Irwin Miller, *The Corporation and the Union* (Santa Barbara, Calif.: Center for the Study of Democratic Institutions, 1962); from one of a series of interviews on the American character.

2. Cameron P. Hall, ed., *On the Job Ethics* (Department of Church & Economic Life, The National Council of the Churches of Christ in the U.S.A. 1963); a pioneering analysis by men engaged in six major occupations.

3. Bernard D. Nossiter, "The Troubled Conscience of American Business," in *Harper's Magazine*, Sept. 1963, p. 38.

4. Howard R. Bowen, *Social Responsibilities of the Businessman* (New York: Harper & Row, 1953), p. 135.

5. Raymond C. Baumhart, S.J., "How Ethical Are Businessmen?" in *Harvard Business Review*, July–Aug. 1961.

6. William H. Cohea, Jr., in *On The Job Ethics*.

7. Harold L. Johnson, "Alternative Views of Big Business," in the *Annals* of the American Academy of Political and Social Science, Sept. 1962, p. 8.

8. James C. Worthy, notes on "Business and the Good Society," privately circulated Oct. 12, 1963.

9. Kenneth Underwood, "The New Social Ethic in American Business," in *Christianity and Crisis*, March 5, 1962, p. 23.

10. Theodore L. Thau, "The Business Ethics Advisory Council," in the *Annals*, Sept. 1962.

11. Harold L. Johnson, noted in *The Christian As a Businessman* (New York: Association Press, 1964), p. 71.

12. Theodore L. Thau, op. cit., p. 138.

13. Francis X. Sutton, Seymour E. Harris, Carl Kaysen, and James Tobin, *The American Business Creed* (Cambridge, Mass.: Harvard Univ. Press, 1956).

14. Ibid., p. 11.

15. Raymond C. Baumhart, S.J., op. cit.

CHAPTER 15. THE ROLE OF THE CHURCH

1. Arthur E. Walmsley, ed., "The Mission of the Church in the New Era," in *The Church in a Society of Abundance* (New York: Seabury Press, 1963), p. 58.

2. James M. Gustafson, *Treasure in Earthen Vessels* (New York: Harper & Row, 1961), p. 86.

3. William Temple, *The Church Looks Forward* (New York: Macmillan & Co., 1944), p. 3.

4. "The Christian Hope and the Task of the Church," in *The Responsible Society in a World Perspective* (New York: Harper & Row, 1954), p. 28.

5. H. Cunliffe Jones, *Technology, Community and Church* (London: Independent Press, Ltd., 1961.), p. 149.

6. E. Theodore Bachmann, ed., *The Activating Concern*, in Series on Churches and Social Welfare, Vol. 1 (New York: National Council of Churches of Christ in the U.S.A.), 1955.

7. *The Economic Order*, official reports of the Oxford Conference (Chicago: Willett, Clark & Co.; copyright held by Harper & Row, 1937), p. 98.

8. John C. Bennett, "A Theological Conception of Goals for Economic Life," in *Goals of Economic Life*, ed. Dudley A. Ward (New York: Harper & Row, 1953), p. 399.

9. From *Some Ethical Implications of the 1959–60 Dispute in the Steel Industry*, Report of the Special Committee.

10. Franklin H. Littell, *The German Phoenix* (New York: Doubleday, 1960).

11. Martin E. Marty, *The New Shape of American Religion* (New York: Harper & Row, 1958), p. 123.

12. Huber Klemme, *Your Church in Your Community* (Philadelphia: Christian Education Press, 1957).

Chapter 16. Spiritual Foundations

1. F. Ernest Johnson and J. Emery Ackerman, *The Church as Employer, Money Raiser, and Investor* (New York: Harper & Row, 1959), p. 122.

2. Dietrich Bonhoeffer, *Ethics*, ed. Eberhard Bethge (New York: Macmillan Co., 1955), p. 62.

3. Gayraud S. Wilmore, *The Secular Relevance of the Church* (Philadelphia: The Westminster Press, 1962), p. 34.

4. W. Widick Schroeder and Victor Obenhaus, *Religion in American Culture* (New York: Free Press of Glencoe, 1964), p. 138.

5. Reinhold Niebuhr, "Leaves from the Notebook of a War-Bound American," in *The Christian Century*, LVI (Nov. 15, 1939), 1405–1406.

6. Paul Tillich, *Morality and Beyond* (New York: Harper & Row, 1963), p. 39.

Afterword. Reflections on Ethics and Economics

1. Dr. Paul Tillich, in his book *Morality and Beyond*, remarks: "In this study, I use the terms 'morality,' 'morals,' and 'moral' throughout most of the text. And sometimes the term 'ethical' appears. There would be no confusion if, as I now suggest, we defined ethics as the 'science of the moral.' But this is not a generally accepted definition, the chief reason being that the word 'moral,' through historical accidents, has received several distorting connotations" (New York: Harper & Row, 1963), p. 21.

2. "Distinct" here does not mean separate. I am in agreement at this point with James Gustafson that "oughtness" must be "rooted in some ground of 'isness' "; in *Faith and Ethics: The Theology of H. Richard Niebuhr*, ed. Paul Ramsay, (New York: Harper & Row, 1957), p. 120.

3. John Dewey and James Tufts, *Ethics*, rev. edn. (New York: Henry Holt and Co., 1932), p. 265.

4. Paul Tillich, op. cit., p. 231.

5. (New York: Harper & Row, 1963).

6. Ibid., p. 159.

7. In an unpublished ms.; used by permission.

8. (New York: Harper & Row, 1956), p. 241.

9. *Two Roads to Truth* (New York: Viking, 1953), p. 43.

10. *The Role of Knowledge in Western Religion* (Boston: Starr King, 1958), p. 133.

11. William F. Ogburn, *Social Change* (New York: Huebsh, 1922), p. 268 ff.

12. *Economic Institutions and Human Welfare* (New York: Alfred A. Knopf, 1957), p. 218.

13. In C. H. Sandage and Vernon Fryburger, *The Role of Advertising: A Book of Readings* (Homewood, Ill.: R. D. Irwin, 1960), p. 106.

14. I (New York: The Macmillan Co., 1931), p. 320.

15. (New York: Harcourt, Brace & Co., 1926), pp. 278–279.

16. (Boston: Atlantic-Little Brown & Co., 1955), pp. 101–102.

17. (New York: John Day, 1942).

18. Ernst Troeltsch, op. cit., p. 277.

19. Both passages from *The Bent World*, J. V. Langmead Casserley (New York: Oxford Univ. Press, 1955), pp. 85, 89.

20. "The Businessman's Moral Failure," Sept. 1958.

21. Op. cit., p. 334.

22. Ibid., p. 331.

23. F. Ernest Johnson and J. Emory Ackerman, *The Church as Employer, Money-Raiser, and Investor* (New York: Harper & Row, 1959), p. 122.

Index

Adler, Felix, 292, 309
Advertising, 108-109, 113, 234, 258
Africa, 52, 159, 166, 239
Agency for International Development, 165
"Agribusiness," 83, 87
Agricultural Trade Development and Assistance Act, 95
Agriculture, 22, 53, 86-87, 99
  and cooperatives, 89, 171-172
  employment in, 83, 85, 87-89
  and the family farm, 89, 91, 94
  and the farm problem, 83-85, 89 f.
  and foreign policy, 95, 161-162
  and government, 82, 84, 93, 96, 98, 171 f.
  income in, 84-85, 90-91
  migrant workers in, 46, 48, 87-88, 93
  part-time workers in, 87 f.
  solutions for, 89-95
  surpluses in, 70, 84-85, 92, 95-100
  "vertical integration" in, 88
Aircraft industry, 141, 178
Allis-Chalmers, 113 n.
Ambrose, 8
"American Business Creed," 236
American Capitalism, 184
American Dental Association, 115
American Dilemma, An, 53
American Farm Bureau Federation, 89 f.
American Federation of Labor, 117 f., 121, 126, 133, 135
American Home Economics Association, 115
American Medical Association, 115
American Telephone and Telegraph Company, 179-180, 229
Apostles' Creed, 292
Appalachia, 45 f.
Aquinas, Thomas, 10, 74
Aristotle, 189
Arms Control Disarmament Agency, 137, 142, 146 f., 149
Asia, 166, 239

Atomic Energy Commission, 140
  see also Nuclear energy
Augustine, 8 f., 74, 241, 248, 305
Australia, 162
Austria, 19
Automation, 56-67
  consequences of, 40, 45, 58-60, 64-67
  definitions of, 57-58
  grounds of concern with, 62-63
  and labor, 59, 62-63, 123, 126
  social costs of, 60-62, 198
  and unemployment, 45, 60-61, 62-63, 67, 148, 293

Baker, Bobby, 221
Baldwin, Stanley, 295
Barkin, Solomon, 132
Barnard, Chester I., 222, 225
Baumhart, Raymond C., 224, 237
Bazelon, David, 186
Beck, Dave, 123
Belgium, 19, 158, 166
Bendix, R., 216
Bennett, John C., 249, 289 f.
Benoit, Emile, 138, 146, 149
Bentham, Jeremy, 171
Berle, Adolf A., Jr., 178, 218, 223
Bethlehem Steel, 218
Bettelheim, Bruno, 63
Better Business Bureaus, 115
Beveridge Plan, 185
Bible, 21, 193, 200-202, 269
  New Testament, 5-9
  Old Testament, 1-5, 15
Birth rates, 33, 51-52
Bismarck, 78
Black, John D., 96, 98
Blue Cross and Blue Shield, 34
Blough, Roy, x, xiii, 49, 77, 155, 183
Bonhoeffer, Dietrich, 263
Boulding, Kenneth, 86, 148, 179
Bowen, Howard R., ix, 224
Bright, James, 63
British Commonwealth, 153, 157
Brown, William Adams, Jr., 169

Brunner, Emil, 196
Burma, 166
Business, 223-224
    ethical attitudes in, 228-234
    and government, 177-180, 230-233
    resources for ethics in, 234-238
    unethical practices in, 224-228
    unionism in, 121, 131 f.
Business Ethics Advisory Council, 235-236
Butler, William, 154, 164

Calvin, John, 12 ff., 22, 38, 203, 243-244, 268
Canada, 159, 162
Casserley, 305
Central America, 159
Chicago, 120, 212, 254
Child labor, 73, 251, 258, 293
China, 52, 155, 166
Christ and Culture, 289
Christian Action, 250
Christian Socialism, 18-20, 22, 24, 250, 256
Christian Socialist, The, 19
Christian Socialist League, 19
Christian Values and Economic Life, 169
Chrysostom, 8
Church, Samuel Harden, 117
Church, 23, 48, 203, 207, 260
    early, 7-9, 269, 295
    functions of, 247-250, 250-254, 311
    membership of, 245, 260, 310-311
    in Middle Ages, 9-11, 239, 242, 298
    role of, 239-254
    socioeconomic role of, 244 f., 247-248, 310-318
    and state, 8 ff., 244
Church and Economic Life, conference on, 101 n., 153, 160, 168
Church Association for the Advancement of the Interests of Labor, 250
Churches and Social Welfare, conference on, 247
Civil rights, 188, 304, 311
Civil War, 171, 174
Clark, John Maurice, 294
Class, 30, 32, 118, 202, 210 f., 212-213
Clawson, Marion, 190

Clayton Antitrust Act, 115, 232, 308 f.
Clement of Alexandria, 8
Cochrane, Willard W., 97
Cohea, William H., Jr., 224
Collective bargaining, 69, 126 f., 129, 133, 136, 251
    ethics of, 308-309
    farmers and, 85, 91
Colleges, land-grant, 84, 171
Common Market, Central American, 159
    European, 129, 153, 157 ff.
Communism, 28, 44, 51, 102, 132, 226, 230, 250
    and disarmament, 143, 144-145
    and foreign aid, 161, 163, 165 f.
Communist bloc, 153, 154-155, 166
Communist Manifesto, 19, 208
Community, 70, 134-135, 179, 204 f., 216, 233, 275, 288
    and church, 247, 253-254
    and the economy, 269-272
    and poverty, 48, 264
Compromise, 273, 284-287
Condon-Wadlin Act, 279
Consequences, concern for, 277-280, 283-284, 285
Constantine, 9
Consumer, 101-102, 295-296
    assumptions of, 104-109
    and economic system, 102-104
    influencing judgment of, 109-114
    resources for, 114-116
Consumer Affairs, Special Assistant for, 101, 114
Consumers Research, 116
Consumers Union, 116
Cook, Clair, 121
Cook, Fred J., 140
Cooperatives, 20, 89, 115-116, 243
Cornell Study, 47
Corporations, 105-106, 177 ff., 216, 227-228, 297
    responsibility of, 222-223, 226-227, 229-230
Council of Economic Advisors, 53
Cousins, Norman, 56
Cromwellian Revolution, 243
Crown Zellerbach Corporation, 235
Cuba, 155
Cultural lag, 292-293, 298

Cunliffe-Jones, H., 247
Cybernation, 57 f., 214
Cyprian, 8
Czechoslovakia, 166

Danhof, Clarence A., 207
Death rates, 51
de Chardin, Teilhard, 64-65
Defense, 43, 95, 102, 106, 128, 137 f., 184
  modication of, 146-150
  scope and consequences of, 139-142
de Lamennais, 18
Delaware, 140
Democracy, 127, 301-305
Democratic party, 231
Detroit, 37
De Vries, Egbert, 156
Dewey, John, 283
Diebold, John, 60
Dignity, human, 58, 65, 67, 152, 219 f., 271, 318
Disarmament, and the economy, 137-150
  resistance to, 142-145
Dropouts, 33, 42-43, 73-74, 252
Drucker, Peter, 34, 57, 300
Durkheim, Emile, 230

East Harlem Parish, 254
Economic Development, Committee for, 94
Economic Opportunity Act of 1964, 44
Economic Value of Education, The, 78
Economics of Trade Unions, 129
Ecumenical Center of Renewal and Planning, 254
Edinburgh Conference, 245
Education, 24, 50, 52-55, 78, 84, 214-215, 293
  and government, 29, 175, 304
  in the U.S.S.R., 52, 54
Efficiency, 86-87, 127, 246, 249
Egypt, 30, 52, 166
Einzig, Paul, 63
Eisenhower, Dwight D., 182
Electrical industry, 232
England, 17 ff., 31, 139, 209, 242 ff., 255, 298
Enlightenment, the, 75
Estes, Billy Sol, 113, 221

Ethics, 274, 280-281
  "Christian social," 287-291
  of collective bargaining, 308-309
  of compromise, 284-287
  of democracy, 301-304
  koinonia, 288, 290, 318
  and the law, 305-308
  situational, 283, 285, 289
Ethics in a Christian Context, 287
Europe, 92, 96, 129, 153, 162, 164, 174, 210, 244, 253, 255
European Atomic Energy Community, 157
European Coal and Steel Community, 157
European Economic Community. See Common Market
European Free Trade Association, 157 f.
Evangelical Academies, 253
Evanston Report, 244
Existentialism, 289, 292, 318

Faith, 39, 149-150, 197-198, 206
Family, 31-32, 34, 48, 72, 148-149
Far East, 159
Farm Goals in Conflict, 86
Farmers Union, 89, 91
Federal Council of the Churches of Christ in America, vii f., 23, 99
Federal Land Policy, 170
Federal Reserve Act, 181
Federal Trade Commission, 115, 232
Federalist Party, 169
Fellowship of the Kingdom, 250
Ferry, W. H., 185
Finkelstein, Louis, 307
Fiscal policies, 147, 181-183
Food and Agriculture Organization, 96, 100
Food and Drug Administration, 104, 115
Ford, Henry, II, 279
Foreign aid, 81, 159-168
  and communism, 161, 163, 165 f.
  and underdeveloped nations, 152, 159-161, 162, 164, 167-168
Fortune, 307
France, 19, 139, 158
Frankel, Charles, 71, 73
Free Trade Association, 159
Freedom from Hunger, 96, 100

Fromm, Erich, 63
Future of Industrial Man, The, 300

Galbraith, John Kenneth, 184
Garfield, James A., 189
General Agreement of Trades and Tariffs, 159
General Electric, 113 n., 221
General Motors, 140, 179, 218, 229
Germany, 19, 78, 158, 167, 217, 242, 245
Gladden, Washington, 21
Gladwin, Thomas, 74
Goals and Values in Agricultural Policy, 86
Goals of Economic Life, 207
Gompers, Samuel, 118
Gordon, Leland, 101, 103, 114, 296
Government, 27, 30, 55, 143, 146, 149, 151-152, 306
   and agriculture, 82, 84, 93, 96, 98, 171 f.
   and business, 177-180, 230-233, 297
   centralization of, 64, 147, 169, 172-173, 187
   and the consumer, 101-102, 115, 173
   and education, 29, 175, 304
   emerging-functions of, 183-187
   expansion of, 170-173
   and labor, 128-129, 136, 171 f., 184, 297
   and the national economy, 180-183
   and unemployment, 127, 144
   and welfare, 46, 69 f., 76-78, 173-177
Grange, 89, 91
Great Britain, 46, 129, 158, 185, 209, 215
Great Depression, 23, 44, 69, 78, 90, 105, 174, 180 f., 183, 250, 296
Greece, 166
Greeley, Horace, 170
Greenwood, Elma, xiii
Gregory XVI, Pope, 18
Gross National Product, 46, 139, 141
Gustafson, James, 241

Hall, Cameron P., ix, xiii, 204
Hamilton, Alexander, 169
Hanford, 140
Hardin, Charles M., 95

Hardy, Earl O., 92
Harrington, Michael, 46 f.
Hart, Senator Philip, 113
Haymarket Riot, 120
Health services, 34
Hebrew-Christian heritage, 1-5, 41, 65, 69, 75, 151, 257, 259, 262-263, 264, 287
Herron, George D., 21
Hight, John W., 158
Hodges, Luther, 231, 235
Hoffa, James, 123, 221
Hoffman, Paul G., 152, 162
Hofstee, E. W., 92
Homestead Act of 1862, 170
Homestead Strike, 120, 212
Hook, Sidney, 187
Hopkins, Harry, 78
Horowitz, Irving, 142
Humanitarianism, 40-41, 69, 75
Hume, David, 17, 171

Immigrants, 31, 70-71, 210, 244
In His Steps, 22
India, 30, 52, 167
Indiana, 254
Indians, American, 46, 77, 212
Individual, the, 47-48, 59-60, 69, 198, 205, 264-265, 267, 270
Industrial Councils, 309
Industrial Revolution, 17, 56, 198, 241 f.
Industrial Workers of the World, 118
Industrialism, adaptations for, 37-39, 71-76
   consequences of, 30-33, 38
   nature and requirements of, 25-30
   specialization of skills in, 35-37
   and welfare, 33-34
Insurance, 34, 133 f., 149
International Harvester, 229
International trade, 129, 151-155
   issues in, 155-159
Iona, 253
Iowa State University, 86, 99
Italy, 158

James, William, 276
Japan, 164
Jefferson, Thomas, 54, 82, 169, 172, 187, 299

Jesus Christ, 201 f., 207 ff., 247, 256
  to the Christian, 240, 259, 260-261
  economic implications of, 5-6, 271 f.,
    287 f.
Jews, 71, 288, 315-316
John, Saint, 8
John XXIII, Pope, 99
Johnson, Byron, 95
Johnson, D. Gale, 85
Johnson, F. Ernest, ix, xiii
Johnson, Harold L., 226
Johnson, Lyndon B., 43 f., 101, 114
Justice, 3, 255-260, 267-268, 270, 285
Juvenile delinquency, 73-74

Kagawa, Toyohiko, 20
Kefauver, Estes, 107
Kennedy, John F., 46, 53, 235
Kentucky, 127
Kerr, Clark, 29, 36
Keynes, J. M., 181
Kierkegaard, Søren, 289
Kingsley, Charles, 18
Klemme, Huber, 253
Knights of Labor, 118
Koinonia, 287 f., 290, 318
Korean War, 70, 95, 139, 141

Labor, organized, 22-23, 25 f., 35, 106,
    115, 117 ff., 199, 243, 258, 279-280
  and automation, 59, 62-63, 123, 126
  and class, 118, 125-126, 212
  and collective bargaining, 69, 127,
    136, 308-309
  and government, 128-129, 136, 171 f.,
    184, 297
  and management, 26, 75, 134, 278
  membership of, 120, 122-123, 126
  new problems of, 125-129
  new roles for, 129-136
  in politics, 128, 231
  strengths and weaknesses of, 120-125
  and welfare, 79-80, 122, 135
Land, 2, 4, 84, 170 f., 174
Landrum-Griffin Act, 120
Laski, Harold, 302
Latin America, 71, 96, 154, 159, 239
Lawrence, Brother, 292
Leadership, 36, 233, 260, 275
League for Industrial Democracy, 120
Lebeaux, Charles N., 72

Lee, Robert, 190
Lehmann, Paul L., 14, 287 f.
Leisure, 65, 199, 206, 219
  definition of, 189-191
  extent of, 191-193
  and work, 193-197
Lenski, Gerhard, 36
Leo XII, Pope, 18
Leo XIII, Pope, 119, 255
Lewis, H. G., 130
Life, 122
Lincoln, Abraham, 302
Lippmann, Walter, 299, 301, 303
Lipset, S. M., 216
Littell, Franklin H., 253
Living standards, 65-66, 74-75, 161-162,
    167-168, 293
Locke, John, 17, 74, 171
Loeschen, John, xiii
Long Island, 139
Los Angeles, 31, 139
Luddites, 127
Ludlow, John M., 18 f.
Luther, Martin, 12 ff., 16, 203, 243-244,
    268 f., 284
  and vocation, 13 f., 22, 38
Luxembourg, 158

McCarran-Walter Immigration Act,
    135
McClellan Committee, 121
McLeod, Sir George, 253
McNary-Haugenism, 98
Management, 59, 62-63, 79, 126-127,
    184
  and labor, 26, 75, 127, 134, 278
Managers, 35-36, 218, 226
Marshall Plan, 156, 166 f.
Marty, Martin, 253
Marx, Karl, 19, 27 f., 30, 40, 208
Mater et Magistra, 99
Maurice, Frederick Denison, 18 f.
May, Edgar, 77
Mayo, Elton, 204
Meaning of Revelation, The, 290
Melman, Seymour, 147
Memorial Day Massacre, 120, 212
Merom (Indiana), 254
Methodist Church, Social Creed of, 315
Michigan, University of, 141-144

Middle Ages, xi, 37, 40, 203, 208-209
   church in, 9-11, 221-222, 239, 242,
   297 f.
Middle East, 159, 165
Migrant workers, 46, 48, 87-88, 93
Mill, John Stuart, 62, 74
Miller, J. Irwin, 221
"Milorg," 148
Mining, 127, 212, 215, 280, 282
Missions, 24, 151-152
Mollegen, A. T., 9
Monasticism, 8-9, 11, 202
Morals, 274, 276, 280-281, 291-292,
   296-299
Morley, John, 285
Moscow, 108 n.
Moynihan, Daniel P., 45
Mutual Security Program, 163
Myrdal, Gunnar, 50, 53, 81, 164, 176,
   186

National Aeronautics and Space Ad-
   ministration, 140, 146
National Council of the Churches of
   Christ in the U.S.A., vii f., x, 23,
   99-100, 221, 244, 251, 257, 314
National Farmers Organization, 89, 91
National Labor Relations Act, 69, 251
National Planning Association, 185, 196
National Policy Committee on Pockets
   of Poverty, 45
National Recovery Administration, 112
National Religion and Labor Founda-
   tion, 120
Natural law, 299-300
Nature and Destiny of Man, The, 286
Nazism, 217, 242, 244, 278
Negroes, 46, 53, 71, 118, 212-213
Netherlands, 158
Nevada, 114
New Deal, 98
New England, 210
New Hampshire, 114
New York City, 108 n., 254
New York State, 77, 279
New York Times, 309
New Zealand, 162
Niebuhr, H. R., 289 f.
Niebuhr, Reinhold, 208 n., 266, 286,
   305
1984, 64

Nonwhites, 42 f., 45 f., 53, 212 f.
North Atlantic Treaty Organization, 158
North Dakota, 170
Nossiter, Bernard D., 223
Nuclear energy, 55, 135, 140-141, 146,
   178
Nuveen, John, 166

Oak Ridge, 140
Occupational Ethics Groups, 237
Ohio, 88
On The Job Ethics, 224, 232
Open society, 209 f., 215, 220
Organization Man, The, 216
Origen, 8
Ornati, Oscar, 48-49
Orwell, George, 64
Other America, The, 46
Outdoor Recreation Resources Review
   Commission, 196
Oxford Conference, 245

Packaging, 110-111, 113, 234
Paducah, 140
Panama Canal, 140
Park Forest, 216
Paul, Apostle, 7-8, 201 f., 241, 264, 301
Peabody, George I., 21
Pennsylvania, 87
Peterson, Esther, 101
Phantom Public, The, 303
Pius XI, Pope, 120
Plato, 208, 302
Poland, 166
Population, 33, 51-52, 70, 167
Populist Movement, 171
Portsmouth, 140
Poverty, 50 ff., 68, 131, 183, 252
   causes of, 48
   consequences of, 46-48
   and industrialism, 43-49
Power, 130, 188, 203, 207, 210, 218,
   246, 251
   "legitimate," 300-301
Power Without Property, 218
Presidential Commission on National
   Goals, 185
Pride, 2 ff., 208, 286
Principle, 277, 281-284, 285-286, 300
Problems and Policies of American Agri-
   culture, 86

Profit, 226-227, 294-295
Property, 9-10, 16, 28, 210 f., 218
  and the Bible, 2-9
Prophets, Hebrew, 2-4, 21, 269, 288
"Protestant ethic," the, 65, 172, 194
Protestantism, 12, 276 ff., 300
  and agriculture, 99-100
  and industrialism, 36, 255
  and labor, 119, 243
  present-day, 310, 312, 315
Public Philosophy, The, 299
Public Works Administration, 78, 181
Puerto Ricans, 213

Quadragesimo amo, 120

Racial problems, 134 f., 271-272
Railroads, 62-63, 125 n., 134, 170 f.
Randall, John Herman, Jr., 12, 292
Raskin, A. H., 57
Rauschenbusch, Walter, 21-22, 250, 310
Reader's Digest, 66
Reconstruction Finance Corporation, 175, 181
Rees, Albert, 129
Reformation, 11-18, 38, 201, 203, 242 f., 298
Refugee Relief Act, 135
Religion, xi, 1 ff.
  application of doctrines of, 265-269
  and business ethics, 234, 238
  and community, 269-272
  and economic justice, 255-260
  economic relevance of, 260-265
  and industrialism, 30, 32, 38, 64, 67
  and work, 194-195, 197-199
Religion and Labor Council, 120
Religion and the Rise of Capitalism, 297
Renaissance, 12, 17, 75, 242
Republic Aviation Corporation, 139
Republican party, 231
Rerum novarum, 119, 255
Research, 27, 84, 138, 140 f., 252
Research on Economic Adjustments to Disarmament, 141
Responsibility, 151 f., 224, 256-257, 266 ff., 277-280, 285
Revolutionary War, 174
Riesman, David, 275
Ritsch, Frances, xiv
Robinson-Patman Act, 232

Rockefeller Foundation, ix
Roman Catholicism, 36, 99, 119-120, 247, 255, 276, 300-301, 309, 316
Roosevelt, Franklin D., 44 f., 78, 181
Roosevelt, Theodore, 221
Rostow, W. W., 33

San Diego, 139
Saturday Review, 56
Savannah River, 140
Scandinavia, 157 f.
Schultz, Theodore W., 78, 98
Scotland, 209, 253
Scudder, Vida, 312
Sears-Roebuck, 229
Seattle, 139
Seaver, Charles H., x
Sevareid, Eric, 123
Sheldon, Charles M., 22
Sherman Antitrust Act, 115, 173, 232
Shideler, Emerson, 89
Sinnot, Edmund W., 291
Situational ethics, 277, 283, 285, 289, 300
Smith, Adam, 227
Smith, Mervin G., 88
Social Gospel, xi, 20-23, 24, 205, 255, 301, 310, 315
  and labor, 22-23, 119
Social security, 34, 181
Social Security Act of 1935, 69 f., 251
Social service, 23, 37, 76, 226-227
Social Teachings of the Christian Churches, The, 297
Society of Christian Socialists, 250
Stalin, Joseph, 242
Standard Oil, 218, 229
Status, 207 ff., 228, 260
  in contemporary society, 211-214
  forces reorganizing, 214-218
  signicance of, 218-220
Steel industry, 119, 191, 251
Stewardship, 2 ff., 15-17, 18, 265, 316
Strikes, 119, 121, 212, 251, 279, 282
Supreme Court, 82, 135, 218 f., 306
Surpluses, 32, 70, 102
Survey Research Center, 144
Sutton, Francis, 236
Sweden, 158
Swift & Company, 229

Taft, Charles P., 158
Taft-Hartley Act, 120, 126
Tariffs, 129, 153
Tawney, Richard H., 10, 12, 239, 297
Taylor, Charles L., 4-5
Temple, William, 241
Thau, Theodore L., 234
Tillich, Paul, 268, 285
Trade Expansion Act of 1962, 96, 159
Trading stamps, 111-112
Troeltsch, Ernst, 12, 239, 297, 300, 311
Twentieth Century Capitalist Revolution, The, 223
Tyler, Gus, 136

Underdeveloped nations, 50-52, 80-81, 167-168
  and Communism, 51, 80, 166
  and foreign aid, 152, 159-161, 162, 164, 167-168
  and international trade, 152, 153-154
Underwood, Kenneth, 233
Unemployment, 41-42, 132, 144
  and automation, 60-63, 67, 127, 148, 293
  insurance for, 133 f., 149
Union of Soviet Socialist Republics. 27, 44, 68, 108 n., 154 f., 242, 250
  education in, 52, 54
  and underdeveloped nations, 51, 80, 166
United Automobile Workers, 134, 309
United Kingdom, 46, 158, 162
United Mine Workers, 127
United Nations, 37-38, 96, 100, 168
United States Department of Agriculture, 84, 87
United States Department of Defense, 128, 139 ff.
United States Department of Health, Education, and Welfare, 46 n, 176
United States Department of Labor, 58, 192, 196
United States Steel Corporation, 229
Universities, 140 f., 223-224
Urban Training Center, 254
Urbanization, 26 f., 29, 71
Uruguay, 166
U Thant, 168

Venezuela, 154
Vocation, 13-15, 22, 38, 201-202, 268-269

War, 23, 313
War of 1812, 171, 174
Ward, A. Dudley, ix
Warren, Earl, 221
Wealth, 2-3, 6, 15, 40, 248
Weber, Max, 12, 36, 65, 194, 210, 217
Weigal, Gustav, 64
Weiss, Paul, 195
Welfare, 33-34
  evolution of, 68-71, 71-76
  and government, 76-78, 173-177
  and private agencies, 79-80, 122, 135
  and underdeveloped nations, 80-81
Welfare state, 68, 98, 174, 176, 186, 296, 310
Wesley, John, 17-18
West Virginia, 46
Western Electric, 204
Westinghouse, 113 n., 221
Whyte, William F., 216
Wichita, 139
Wilcox, Walter, 91, 98
Wilensky, Harold L., 72
Williams, Robin, 93, 98, 212
Wilmore, Gayraud, S., 263
Wisconsin, 87
Work, 65, 204-206, 253, 297
  Christian meaning of, 200-204
  current attitudes toward, 196-199
  and leisure, 193-196
  and religion, 194-195, 197-199
  as vocation, 14, 201-202
Workmen's Compensation, 251, 293
Works Progress Administration, 78, 175, 181
World Council of Churches, 244 f.
World Peace Authority, 146
World War I, 23, 70, 90, 98, 142, 191, 250
World War II, 105, 112, 139, 141 f., 156, 167, 296
  and agriculture, 70, 95
  and labor, 120, 126
World Without Want, 162
Worthy, James, 226

Your Church in Your Community, 253
Yugoslavia, 139